# TRAVELING
# WELL

d

# LING
# L

asive
ur
ad

form
sher.

c.
16

ica

en, M.D.

Data

MPANY

191

*To travelers all over the wor*

Published by Dodd, Mead & Company, I
79 Madison Avenue, New York, N.Y. 10(

Distributed in Canada by
McClelland and Stewart Limited, Toron

Manufactured in the United States of Am

Designed by Berta Lewis

First Edition

Library of Congress Cataloging in Publicatic

Harkonen, W. Scott.
 Traveling well.

 Bibliography: p.
 Includes index.
 1. Travel—Hygienic aspects.  I. Title.
RA783.5.H37   1984       613.6'8       84-1
ISBN 0-396-08394-3 (pbk.)

# CONTENTS

## SECTION I
## Preparing Well Before You Go

## SECTION II
# Getting There Well

## SECTION III
# Staying Well Abroad

## SECTION IV
# Health Problems During Travel

# ACKNOWLEDGMENTS

For their unremitting surveillance of health conditions throughout the world, the United States Department of Human Services, the World Health Organization, and the International Association for Medical Assistance to Travelers deserve special acknowledgment. For their support and assistance in the preparation of *Traveling Well*, I would like to thank Richard and Angela.

# Introduction

"Don't drink the water." That old admonition is all the health advice many travelers receive before leaving home, whether they are sailing south for a vacation, embarking on an expedition to some distant land, or flying on the Concorde to London. But that advice is often not enough, and far too many trips have been ruined by health problems that could have been avoided with a little advance planning.

Traveling well means traveling healthy. And, of the fifteen million Americans who travel abroad each year, most can expect to stay healthy. Few of us would leave home if we didn't. But, as itineraries have expanded in recent years, so have the number of health problems travelers encounter: Machiavellian vaccination requirements, exotic tropical diseases, the infamous *tourista* (diarrhea), as well as any of the common health problems that can happen at home.

And not everyone travels well. Each year millions of Americans become sick or injured overseas. Intestinal ailments affect almost half of all travelers to Mexico and other developing countries. Malaria is spreading and it is afflicting travelers at an alarming rate. An illness or an accident could happen to any of us. In fact, it is estimated that one out of five Americans develops health problems while traveling overseas. To be sure, many of these problems are minor, but some are not, and most can be prevented.

Prevention is the key to traveling well. By knowing what health risks you might encounter, you can prepare yourself to prevent them. Unfortunately, many travelers, myself included, have had to learn the health risks through personal experience. We have suffered through jet lag and spells of motion sickness, bouts of travelers' diarrhea, and encounters with exotic tropical diseases. When problems arose, we have often searched in vain for competent, English-speaking physicians. Or, because we forgot to check our health insurance before we left, we have faced enormous medical bills as patients in strange and foreign hospitals. We have returned home the worse for wear, knowing how to travel better the next time. This guide was written as a result of those hard-earned experiences. It will help you be better prepared before you leave, so that all of your travel experiences are healthy ones.

*Traveling Well* is for every traveler. Whether you are traveling for business, vacation, or adventure, traveling well is vital to the success of your journey. Whether you are traveling with a chronic medical condition or disability, during pregnancy, with children, or during your golden years, your health is the most important asset you will bring with you. The purpose of *Traveling Well* is not to burden you with concerns about your health; its purpose is to help you prepare to travel healthy. The better prepared you are before you leave, the less concerned you'll be about your health while you are away.

*Traveling Well* explains the pre-trip health preparations you'll need, including a visit to your doctor, health insurance, and vaccinations. To assure that getting there remains half of the fun, this guide explains how to reduce jet lag, curb motion sickness, and avoid the other problems encountered in getting from one place to another. And, most importantly, *Traveling Well* explains how to stay healthy abroad. It covers food and water safety, malaria and tropical disease prevention, protection from the elements, and how to prevent minor health problems from becoming major, and major problems from becoming disastrous. Remember, the most serious health risk for most travelers is leaving home unprepared. So, before you go, make certain that you are well prepared to travel well.

# TRAVELING
# WELL

# SECTION I

# Preparing Well Before You Go

# 1

# Health Preparations
# Before You Go

Traveling well begins at home. While thumbing through travel brochures and dreaming of exotic destinations, start considering the health preparations you'll need to stay healthy when you leave. The brochures, while quick to extol the beauty of the scenery, rarely mention the health hazards you might encounter. So it is up to you to find out. Once you are aware of what problems might occur, you can start getting ready to prevent them.

## BE PREPARED

What preparations will you need in order to travel well? That depends upon your current state of health, your itinerary, and how you plan to travel once you are abroad. If you are currently under treatment for a medical condition, for example, you will need more health preparation than a traveler who has never been sick a day in his life. All travelers, however, need some preparation before they leave.

Your itinerary will determine some of the health prep-

3

aration you need. Health risks vary from country to country and often within countries themselves; the preparation you need for a safe journey to Dar es Salaam differ from that needed for a vacation at Zell-am-See. Find out what health risks exist in the countries you plan to visit.

How you plan to travel—whether you'll be checking into resort hotels or checking out campsites off the beaten path—is just as important as where you'll travel. In general, travel into remote regions away from the usual tourist routes, especially in developing countries, requires more health preparation than travel to large cities and resort areas. By knowing where you are going, how you are going, and what to expect when you get there, you can be prepared to stay healthy when you arrive.

This section explains the health preparations you need before you go. It explains the general health preparations required for all travelers, such as medical and dental examinations, as well as the special preparations required for travelers with chronic medical conditions. Information is included that explains how to determine what health risks, such as malaria and travelers' diarrhea, exist in the countries you plan to visit and the additional preparations needed to prevent them. Finally, this section enables you to determine what vaccinations, if any, you will need for your next journey.

## DO YOU NEED A MEDICAL CHECKUP?

One of the most important ways to make sure that you stay healthy abroad is to leave home healthy. The time to discover health problems is before you leave—when you can do something about it—not after. You should get a pre-trip medical checkup if you

- have any history of medical problems.
- are currently taking any medications.
- are over forty years of age and have not had a physical examination during the past year.
- will be traveling for longer than four weeks.
- are pregnant or are likely to become pregnant while traveling.
- will be traveling to a developing region of the world where health risks, such as malaria and other tropical diseases, are present.
- will be traveling to any country that requires additional vaccinations.
- are concerned about the risk of travelers' diarrhea.

If you have recently had a medical checkup and know that you are in good health, a pre-trip visit to your doctor can still be helpful. Your doctor can advise you on how to prevent many of the health problems you might encounter.

## WHAT TO ASK YOUR DOCTOR

For a routine pre-trip medical checkup, schedule your appointment at least four weeks before you plan to leave. This will allow enough time for any tests, vaccinations, or return visits that are needed. When you see your doctor, you should

- ask for a general physical examination.
- ask your doctor to review your itinerary with you to be certain that your travel plans won't put a strain on your health. Extremes in heat or altitude, for example, can cause severe physical stress.

- ask your doctor to review your routine series of vaccinations to make sure that they are up to date.
- ask your doctor about any additional vaccinations that may be required and whether or not you should receive them.
- discuss with your doctor ways to prevent motion sickness if you are concerned about it.
- ask about the appropriate medication to prevent malaria if you will be exposed to it.
- discuss the steps you should take to prevent travelers' diarrhea if it might be a problem, and how to treat it if it occurs.
- review the contents of your medical kit with your doctor, if you are planning to carry one.
- ask for your physician's telephone number and carry it with you.

## IF YOU HAVE A MEDICAL CONDITION

If you are currently being treated for a medical condition, your attending physician is the person who can best advise you on the safety of your proposed trip. Schedule an appointment at least two months in advance of your planned departure. Discuss your itinerary with your physician, and ask how your medical condition could be affected by your trip. For certain medical conditions, some places will be healthier to visit than others.

Spend enough time with your doctor to thoroughly learn about your medical condition. Be sure you understand what medications you are taking and why. Find out what early warning signs to look out for that could mean your condition is worsening, and when you should seek medical help. Additional information about traveling with health problems is provided in chapter 16.

## A MEDICAL SUMMARY

If you have a medical condition, or if you are traveling with any medications, one of the most important documents you should carry with you is a written medical summary. Ask your doctor to provide you with a complete summary of your current medical condition. It should be written on your doctor's letterhead and should explain in detail any treatment you are currently undergoing. Copies of relevant laboratory and diagnostic tests should be included. This medical summary will be invaluable in the event that a serious medical problem arises overseas.

## HEALTH IDENTIFICATION

Travelers with health problems should carry some form of identification that lists their health problems and whom to call in the event of an emergency. Bracelets, neck tags, and wallet cards can all provide urgently needed information; bracelets and neck tags are preferable because they are more likely to be seen. In Japan, for instance, it would be unthinkable for someone to search your possessions for information, and it is unlikely that a wallet card would be found.

Med-Ident bracelets and neck tags are available in many drugstores. A medical condition such as "diabetes" or "allergic to penicillin" is stamped on them. Simple identification such as this will be sufficient when medical problems are not complicated.

Medic Alert Foundation International is an organization that provides a medical identification and information system for travelers with health conditions. In return for a small fee, Medic Alert will provide you with a metal tag that lists your medical condition, an identification number, and a phone number to be called in the event of an emergency. Within seconds of being called from anywhere in the world, Medic Alert operators can relay health information from your personal medical file. Additional information can be obtained by contacting

— Medic Alert Foundation International, Inc.
  P.O. Box 1009
  Turlock, CA 95380
  209-634-4917

## TRAVELING WITH MEDICINE

Medications are a frequent source of problems for travelers. Vials full of pills are often far too conspicuous under the scrutiny of customs agents, yet the very same items seem to disappear the moment that you need them the most. The following advice should help keep your travels with medicine trouble free.

- Carry with you several copies of a written statement from your physician listing all of your medicines and the reason you are taking each one of them. A copy of this statement may be withheld at customs.
- Keep all medicines in their original, labeled containers. Do not mix drugs together in one vial. This inevitably leads to confusion when trying to sort them out, not only for you, but for customs officials as well. And confusion at customs generally leads to suspicion and delay.
- Bring along enough medicine to last your entire trip. Purchasing medicine overseas is a potential source of trouble that can be easily avoided by making sure you bring an adequate supply with you.
- In case you stay longer than originally planned or lose your supply, bring along an extra set of prescriptions from your doctor that identifies the generic names of all your medicines. Trade names vary

markedly overseas and errors in translation may lead to accidental and dangerous drug substitutions.

- Carry your medicine with you at all times. For example, in flight your medicine should be carried in your hand luggage. That way, if you get off in Rome and your baggage goes on to Naples, you won't have the added hassle of being without your medicine. Even while sightseeing, it is wise to carry your medicine with you, or at least enough to last several days, just in case your belongings disappear while you are away from your hotel.

- Make sure you fully understand the proper dosage of any medicine, the length of time you should take it, and all of its possible side effects. Drug reactions are a frequent cause of illness among travelers. While you are overseas is the wrong time to expose yourself to unfamiliar drugs.

- Do not bring any narcotic or other habit-forming medicine with you unless it is absolutely necessary. Controlled drugs can cause problems—sometimes big problems—at customs. If it is necessary to travel with one of these medicines, make sure that the reason you are taking it is clearly and convincingly documented in your written medical history.

## HOW TO PREPARE A MEDICAL KIT

When you're away from home and minor medical problems arise, you often have no one but yourself to rely on. A well-stocked medical kit will enable you to manage most of the minor problems you might encounter.

Your medical kit needs to fit your own health requirements as well as the nature of your trip. The longer you will be away from home and the farther you will be from medical care, the more extensive your medical kit should be. In every case, you should review the contents of your medical kit with your physician. Following is a suggested list of contents.

| Items | Comment |
| --- | --- |
| Regular prescription medications | Carry a sufficient supply to last your entire trip |
| Extra written prescriptions | Should give the generic names of drugs |
| Written medical summary | Carry several copies |
| Aspirin or acetaminophen | For minor pain and fever |
| Antihistamine medication | An antihistamine such as Benadryl has multiple uses: decongestant for colds and allergies antimotion-sickness mild sleeping medication anti-itching medication |
| Decongestant nasal spray | To reduce nasal congestion during air flight |
| Motion sickness medications | See chapter 5 |
| Antimalarial medications | See chapter 9 |
| Antidiarrheal medications | See chapter 11 |
| Water purification kit —tablets or solutions —water-boiling coil | Available at drugstores—to make water safe for drinking |
| Antacids | For stomach upsets. Tablets are more convenient, but liquid is more effective. |
| Antibiotics | For travelers to remote areas; discuss with your physician |

| *Items* | *Comment* |
|---|---|
| Allergy kit | For travelers with known allergies to insect bites and stings |
| Mild laxative | Constipation is a common problem. |
| Sunscreen | See chapter 12 |
| Steroid Skin Cream | For certain skin irritations such as poison ivy, poison oak, etc. |
| Antibacterial ointment | For cuts, scrapes, and bites |
| Syrup of ipecac | Available in drugstores. Travelers with children may want to include this to treat accidental poisoning. Discuss its use with your physician. |

| *Recommended or "Must" Items* | *Don't Forget if Appropriate* |
|---|---|
| Thermometer | Contraceptives |
| Soap | Insect repellent |
| Adhesive tape | Mosquito netting |
| Gauze bandages | Extra pair of corrective glasses or lenses |
| Ace bandages | Copy of lens prescription |
| Band-Aids | Contact lens solution |
| Moleskin | |
| Knife | |
| Scissors | |
| Tweezers | |
| Flashlight | |
| Sunglasses | |

## DENTAL CHECKUP

Schedule a dental checkup before you leave, and allow enough time to have any necessary work performed. Discuss your travel plans with your dentist, and ask to have any potential dental problems taken care of now so they won't surprise you abroad. A toothache is something you want to avoid overseas, especially in a remote area where the quality of dentistry is reflected by a toothless smile.

## EYE CARE

If you wear eyeglasses or contact lenses, bring along at least one extra pair. In addition, include a copy of the prescription for your lenses in your medical kit. It will save time and expense if you have to get replacement lenses overseas. Contact wearers should pack an ample supply of a cleaning solution.

Travelers planning to stay overseas for six months or longer should have a full eye examination performed by an ophthalmologist before they leave. If you are already being treated for an eye condition, you should receive a checkup regardless of how long you will be away.

## HEALTH PREPARATIONS FOR YOUR ITINERARY

In addition to the health preparations described above, you will need to consider some specific aspects of your particular itinerary. What vaccinations will you need? What malaria and tropical disease risks will you encounter? How much water and food safety can you depend on? The following steps will help you determine what your needs are.

1. List the countries on your itinerary in the order that you plan to visit them.

2. Determine the vaccinations that you need.
   — Routine vaccinations should be up-to-date for all travelers.
   — Required vaccinations—cholera and yellow fever—are determined by International Health Regulations. The sequence of countries on your itinerary will determine which ones you need.
   — Additional vaccinations may be recommended for your own health protection depending upon what health risks you'll encounter.
   — Chapter 3 provides detailed information on vaccinations for travelers.
3. Determine if you will be exposed to malaria or other tropical diseases.
   — If you will be exposed to malaria, determine whether or not it is the chloroquine-resistant type.
   — Obtain the appropriate antimalarial medications.
   — Chapter 9 provides detailed information on preventing malaria and other tropical diseases.
4. If you will be at risk, determine the precautions you'll need to protect your intestinal health.
   — Learn about food and water safety.
   — Determine which method you'll use to prevent travelers' diarrhea.
   — Know how to safely treat diarrhea if it occurs.
5. Plan to travel well. Anticipate the health problems you might encounter, and be prepared to prevent them.

## SOURCES OF HEALTH INFORMATION FOR TRAVELERS

A vaccination and health risk guide is provided in appendix A. Since these recommendations can change as fast as new outbreaks of disease can be reported, up-to-the-minute information is often needed. This is especially important regarding chloroquine-resistant malaria, which is spreading rapidly, and new outbreaks are being reported frequently. Use appendix A as a guide to give you an idea of the vaccinations you will need and of the type of health risks you might encounter. Then check to make certain these recommendations still stand. There are several sources of health information where travelers can find out the most current status of vaccinations and health risks.

## Your Personal Physician

A good reason for getting a pre-trip medical checkup is to ask your physician what vaccinations you will need and what disease risks you might encounter. If given enough notice, your doctor should be able to provide you with current recommendations.

## Travel Clinics

Clinics that specialize in health care for travelers have opened in several areas of the country. These clinics can provide information about vaccinations, the risk of getting malaria, and the medicines you may need while traveling. Travel clinics, often affiliated with university medical centers, are located in most major cities.

## State Departments of Health

Your state department of health is a valuable source of health information. Health departments maintain a list of vaccination requirements for each country in the world, and they maintain a constantly updated list of disease outbreaks. To find out if you will need a required vaccination or if you will be exposed to malaria, a phone call to your local health department is often all that is required. A list of state health departments is included in appendix B.

# 2

# Health Insurance for Travelers

Health insurance is an important consideration for all travelers. Many health insurance programs, including Medicare, do not provide adequate overseas coverage. In addition, the cost of medical care has spiraled worldwide, and you can generally count on it being expensive wherever you go. In France, for example, the cost of intensive care is around $800 a day. The cost of a medical evacuation back home is nothing short of staggering. One of the most important preparations you should make before you leave is to check whether you will be adequately covered by health insurance while traveling abroad.

## DO YOU HAVE ADEQUATE COVERAGE?

For persons planning to travel overseas, the minimum a health insurance program should provide is assurance that all medical expenses for an illness or accident will be covered. Most employee insurance programs and private health insurance plans provide reimbursement for medical expenses incurred anywhere in the world. A few,

15

however, do not, and you should carefully check your personal policy before you leave.

Medicare provides almost no coverage outside the United States. Exceptions are made, in very limited circumstances, for citizens traveling in Mexico and Canada. This information is printed in the back of your U.S. passport. If you rely on Medicare at home, do not expect to do so abroad. Privately funded health insurance will be necessary to adequately protect you while you travel outside the country.

Another important point to consider is the astronomical cost of a medical evacuation back home or to a major medical center in the event of a serious illness or injury. An American tourist who suffered a heart attack in Tahiti was informed that a medical evacuation via U.S. military transport would cost $72,000. By making arrangements through private air carriers, the cost was reduced but was still a hefty $20,000. The average cost of a medical evacuation, worldwide, is around $10,000. These costs, unfortunately, are not often covered by privately funded health insurance policies (and never by Medicare). When determining if you have adequate overseas coverage, consider whether payment of emergency medical transportation is provided.

Even when health insurance programs do provide overseas medical coverage, the terms under which they will pay for medical bills are very often inconvenient. For example, of the major insurance plans that do provide overseas coverage, particularly Blue Cross and Blue Shield, most require that you pay foreign doctor and hospital bills directly and then be reimbursed later. To be reimbursed, you will need to produce an itemized bill—something that may not be readily available overseas. In addition, you may be expected to pay your doctor and hospital bills in full before you are discharged. U.S. embassy officials can assist you with the transfer of private funds, but the whole process can be a time-consuming and unwanted aggravation if you are unprepared. And, while you are recovering from a medical emergency in a foreign hospital far from home, you may be confronted with a financial emergency as well.

In summary, an adequate health insurance program for travelers would be one that guarantees full coverage for accidents and illnesses that occur while abroad. In addition, it should guarantee full coverage of the cost of an emergency medical evacuation. And, finally, if you need it, it should provide direct payment to foreign doctors and hospitals. Luckily, there are a growing number of specialized insurance programs for travelers that offer these provisions.

## GETTING ADDITIONAL INSURANCE

If you need additional insurance, you can either add a temporary extension to your current policy or purchase a separate travel policy with another company. Check with your insurance agent. Most travel agencies also have information and applications for special health insurance policies for travelers. Evaluate these policies carefully before you buy. Some policies exclude coverage for preexisting health conditions or for pregnancy. And, while some offer emergency evacuation coverage, it is sometimes very restricted. Compare two or three policies before you commit yourself to any of them.

If you will be traveling on a package tour that offers additional health insurance, you should consider purchasing it, especially if it covers the price of a ticket back home. If you become sick or injured while with a tour group, you may be left behind—the tour must go on. In addition to having to pay for the unused portion of the package tour, you would have to pay for a new ticket back home. The cost of this additional insurance is low and is usually well worth the protection it provides.

Listed below are several insurance companies that provide special services for overseas travelers. In addition to providing financial coverage, some of these organizations will assist you in locating medical care abroad and in the transfer of important medical information to overseas hospitals.

## SPECIAL HEALTH INSURANCE FOR TRAVELERS

1. NEAR (Nationwide-Worldwide Emergency Ambulance Return), 1900 McArthur Blvd., Oklahoma City, OK 71327. Telephone: 800-654-6700. NEAR is a membership organization that provides comprehensive health services to travelers. Membership entitles you to cost-free hospitalization and medical evacuation anywhere in the world. NEAR arranges for the direct transmittal of funds to hospitals, doctors, ambulance companies, and other medical services. It will also transmit personal medical information to foreign doctors in both English and the appropriate foreign language. NEAR will also provide a means of communication between you and your family at home. Cost for an individual membership is $180 a year. A thirty-day membership program is $60. Also available are fifteen-, twenty-, and twenty-five-day memberships priced at $45, $50, and $55, respectively.

2. Assist Card Corporation of America, 745 Fifth Avenue, New York, NY 10022. Telephone: 800-221-4564. Assist Card offers emergency medical assistance to travelers in sixty-two countries, including Hong Kong, Singapore, Thailand, and Japan. After they are contacted through a twenty-four-hour assistance service telephone number, they will dispatch a local doctor or refer you to a local health care facility. They will assume medical costs up to $3,000 and will assume the

full cost of a medical evacuation back home. Rates are based on length of stay abroad, for example, $50 for ten days of coverage abroad.

3. Health Care Abroad, International Underwriters/ Brokers, Inc., 1511 K Street, N.W., Washington, DC 20005. Telephone: 800-336-3310. Health Care Abroad, formerly Med Help Overseas, provides a $100,000 health insurance policy that includes medical evacuation. The company provides a directory of medical services and English-speaking doctors in over 1,100 cities in 128 countries. If a problem arose, you would be instructed to contact one of these physicians. The company will reimburse participating doctors and hospitals directly, so that you will not be billed. There is a $50 deductible. Coverage is available for $2.50 a day, with a twelve-day minimum charge of $30.

4. TravelSafe of Miami, 300 71st Street, Suite 520, Miami, FL 33141. Telephone: 800-327-9966 outside Florida; 800-432-1009 in Florida. TravelSafe offers a plan that pays up to $10,000 in benefits for an illness or an injury overseas. There is a $50-deductible clause, and the premium is $29.50 for the first week of travel and $20 per week thereafter. There is an exclusion for medical conditions that existed up to ninety days before the policy was issued. TravelSafe also provides benefits for lost baggage, baggage delay, theft of valuables, and trip cancellation.

5. ARM Coverage of New York, 9 East 37th Street, New York, NY 10016. Telephone: 212-683-2622. ARM Coverage will pay up to $1,000 in medical expenses for either illness or injury incurred overseas whether or not hospitalization is required. Coverage for a seven- to ten-day period, which includes accidental death and dismemberment and baggage coverage (up to $500 if lost, $100 if delayed), costs $29.50. ARM Coverage also offers a Trip Contingency Protection policy that costs $4 for each $100 worth of insurance. The same company's

EVAC (for Emergency Evacuation Services) policy costs $10 per week.

6. The Travelers Insurance Company, Ticket and Travel Plans, 1 Tower Square, Hartford, CT 06118. Telephone: 800-243-3174. The Travelers will pay up to $5,000 in hospital expenses if the bills result from an accident and not an illness. This policy costs $11.90 for eight days. The Travelers also offers a trip cancellation policy, which costs $4.50 for each $100 in coverage and is good for the duration of your trip. They will pay up to ten times the face value of the policy, up to a maximum of $25,000, for an emergency medical evacuation.

# 3

# Vaccinations for Travelers

Vaccinations are a frequent source of confusion for travelers. It often seems that, no matter whom you ask, no one knows exactly which ones you need. But, by planning ahead, you will not find it difficult to find out. This chapter will guide you through the maze of vaccinations needed for international travel and will help you determine the ones you need for your specific journey.

Vaccines are designed to produce immunity to specific diseases. Because vaccines are prepared in various ways from various ingredients, some work better than others, and some are safer than others. You should ask your doctor to help you weigh the risk of side effects against the protective benefits of any vaccinations you might need.

Vaccinations for travelers are divided into three categories:

1. Routine vaccinations. All travelers, regardless of their destination, should have up-to-date vaccinations against tetanus, diphtheria, polio, and sometimes measles.
2. Required vaccinations. International Health Regulations allow countries to require certain vaccinations in

21

order to gain entry. Whether or not there are vaccinations required for your journey depends upon your specific itinerary.

3. Recommended vaccinations. Additional vaccinations may be recommended for your own safety when you are planning to travel to or live in rural regions in developing countries.

## ROUTINE VACCINATIONS

All travelers, regardless of destination, should have their routine childhood series of vaccinations up-to-date. The diseases these vaccines protect against are still major health problems in much of the world, and you could be at significant risk if you are unprotected. These are the routine vaccinations.

### Tetanus and Diphtheria Vaccines

The tetanus and diphtheria vaccines are routinely administered together as a single injection. Most Americans receive these vaccines during childhood, and it is recommended that everyone, whether traveling or not, receive a booster injection every ten years. If you have not been previously immunized, or if you have not received a booster within ten years, see your physician.

### Polio

Polio still exists. And it is a major health problem in developing, and in tropical, countries. Taiwan is currently experiencing a large outbreak of this dreaded disease. All travelers, regardless of destination, should be fully immunized against polio. This means completion of the primary vaccination series that is usually administered during childhood. If you have not been vaccinated against polio, you should receive the full series, unless your doctor advises against it because of other existing health conditions.

In addition to the primary vaccination series, travelers to tropical and developing countries, where the risk of polio is high, should receive a single booster injection before they leave—again, unless other health reasons interdict.

## Measles

Measles can be a serious illness, and if you are not immune to it, the risk of acquiring an infection abroad is significant. Because of control efforts in this country, many adolescents and young adults have never been exposed to measles and are still susceptible (once you've had a case of measles or been vaccinated against it, you are immune for life). Anyone born after 1956 who has not received a measles vaccination or had a physician-diagnosed case of measles should receive the vaccination before traveling.

Most people born before 1957 are likely to have been exposed to measles naturally and are considered immune to another infection. Women who are pregnant or who may become pregnant within three months should not be vaccinated against measles.

## REQUIRED VACCINATIONS

Under International Health Regulations, a country may require a certificate of vaccination against cholera or yellow fever as condition for entry. These regulations are designed to prevent the importation of disease into a country; they are not designed for your own health protection. Whether or not you will be required to produce

evidence of vaccination depends upon the specific vaccination requirements of the countries you plan to visit and
upon the prevailing local health conditions in other countries on your itinerary. With only a few exceptions, no
vaccinations are required to gain entry into countries when
traveling directly from the United States. Vaccinations may
be required, however, if you have stopped in other countries along the way.

For example, an American traveler was denied entry
into India last year because he had not received a yellow
fever vaccination. There is no yellow fever in that country, and Indian customs officials plan to keep it that way.
They demanded proof of vaccination because the traveler's plane had refueled in Nairobi, Kenya, where there is
a potential, albeit small, risk of acquiring a yellow fever
infection. Had his plane flown directly from London or
stopped to refuel in a country further north where there
is no risk of acquiring yellow fever, no vaccination would
have been required. So, when you are determining which
vaccinations, if any, are needed for your trip, it is essential to consider your exact itinerary, including any stop-
overs.

There are three types of entry requirements for cholera and yellow fever vaccinations:

1. A vaccination certificate is required for entry for all
   travelers entering from all countries. Only a few
   countries maintain this absolute—and arbitrary—
   requirement.
2. A vaccination certificate is required for entry only for
   travelers arriving from countries known to be infected
   with cholera or yellow fever.
3. A vaccination certificate is required for entry only for
   travelers arriving from regions of the world considered
   to be potentially infected with yellow fever. This requirement pertains specifically to travelers arriving from
   yellow fever endemic zones.

## Plan Ahead for Required Vaccinations

No matter how complicated vaccination requirements may seem initially, it is much better to figure them out and obtain all required vaccinations before you leave. If you have not received a vaccination that is required for entry to a country, when you get to the border or customs office, one of three things could happen: (1) you may be refused entry; (2) you may be instructed to receive the vaccination then and there; or (3) you may be asked to undergo a medical examination or a period of quarantine. The following steps will help you avoid all three possibilities.

- List all the countries you plan to visit in the order in which you will visit them. Include all stops, no matter how brief, that you will make along the way.
- Check the vaccination requirements listed in appendix A for each country.
- If a vaccination is required of all travelers regardless of their previous itinerary, then, to gain entry, you must be vaccinated.
- If a vaccination is required only if you will be arriving from an actively infected country, then you will need to determine if any of the preceding countries on your itinerary are known to be infected with cholera or yellow fever. That information can be obtained by calling your local department of health (see below).
- If a vaccination is required only if you will be arriving from a potentially infected area—which means the yellow fever endemic zone—you will need to determine if any of the preceding countries on your itinerary are so considered.
- You can ask your physician or local health department for assistance.

## Information from Your State Department of Health

The local office of your state department of health not only has up-to-date information concerning international vaccination requirements; it can also tell you which countries on your itinerary are infected with cholera or yellow fever. Since regulations can change as fast as new outbreaks of disease can be reported, be sure to check with your local department of health for the latest information. A list of state departments of health is provided in appendix B.

## Necessary Documentation

In order to be accepted by customs officials, any yellow fever or cholera vaccinations you receive must be documented on an International Certificate of Vaccination—the standard yellow card—which is available from your local department of health or from your physician. Without the proper documentation, it will be assumed that you have not been vaccinated and no amount of arguing will convince customs officials otherwise. More than a few travelers have been vaccinated against cholera and yellow fever more often than was necessary only because they could not produce their yellow card when it was needed.

## Yellow Fever Vaccination

Although yellow fever is endemic only to the equatorial regions of the Americas and Africa, the yellow fever vaccination is frequently required to gain entry into tropical and subtropical countries worldwide. This vaccination is only infrequently required for entry for all travelers. More commonly, it is required only if you have previously visited either a country reported to be actively infected or a country in the yellow fever endemic zone.

Countries actively infected with yellow fever are monitored by the World Health Organization, and weekly reports are issued to state health departments. Active outbreaks of this disease are primarily located in a few countries in Africa and in South America. A phone call to your local health department will provide you with up-to-date information.

Countries considered to have the potential to be infected with yellow fever, as opposed to having a known active outbreak, are classified as comprising the yellow fever endemic zone. In these countries, the risk of an outbreak is continually present. The yellow fever endemic zone includes much of equatorial Africa and South America.

To be accepted for international travel, the yellow fever vaccine must be administered at a designated Yellow Fever Vaccination Center and must be recorded on the International Certificate of Vaccination. Locations of centers near you can be obtained from your physician or local health department.

Not only is yellow fever vaccine effective in preventing an extremely serious disease; it is generally regarded as a safe vaccine. It has few side effects, and it offers protection for at least ten years. For international vaccination requirements, a documented yellow fever vaccination is good for ten years from the date you received it.

Regardless of international vaccination requirements, you should be vaccinated against yellow fever for your own health safety if you will be traveling to an area actively infected with the disease. It is also recommended that you be vaccinated if you plan to travel or to live in rural regions in countries located within the yellow fever endemic zone. Travelers to large cities and tourist centers in the endemic zone are not considered to be at significant risk.

The yellow fever vaccine should be avoided during pregnancy. But a pregnant woman who must travel to an area actively infected with yellow fever will have to weigh the relatively small risk to the mother and the fetus from the vaccine against the serious consequences of a yellow fever infection. In this instance, it may be safer to receive the vaccine. The safest way to protect yourself during pregnancy, of course, is to postpone travel to infected areas. Consult with your physician.

## Cholera Vaccination

The cholera vaccine is a nuisance for travelers because, in the first place, the currently available vaccine is not very effective in preventing the disease, and, in the second place, the only reason to be vaccinated at all is to fulfill the entry requirements of a few countries. At present, only Mozambique requires all entering persons to be vaccinated against cholera; several other countries require a vaccination only if you are entering from an infected area. The current international regulations concerning cholera vaccination are listed in appendix A.

Countries reported to be actively infected with cholera are usually developing nations in Asia and Africa. Since new outbreaks are reported frequently, be sure to check with your local health department to see if any of the countries on your itinerary are reported to be infected with cholera. Often, after you have visited a country that is reported to be infected, other countries on your itinerary will require proof of vaccination in order to gain entry.

Cholera vaccinations are often accompanied by pain and swelling at the site of the injection and are followed by one or two days of flulike symptoms. Because the safety of this vaccine during pregnancy has not been established, pregnant women should avoid being vaccinated. If you will be traveling during pregnancy and a cholera vaccination may be required along the way, ask your physician for a written statement stating that this vaccine cannot be given because of health reasons.

Travelers should keep in mind that, since the cholera

vaccine is only partially effective in preventing the disease, the best way to keep from getting cholera is to avoid contaminated food and water.

## Smallpox Vaccination

The good news about smallpox is that the disease no longer exists. The bad news is that overzealous customs officials in developing countries sometimes still demand proof of a smallpox vaccination in order to gain entry. So it needs to be briefly discussed here.

Since the World Health Organization certified in December 1979 that the world is free of smallpox, there is no longer any medical reason to be vaccinated against this disease. Without a disease to protect against, the vaccination itself becomes an unacceptable health risk.

If there is any chance you may be asked for proof of vaccination against smallpox, ask your physician for a letter stating that the vaccination is "contraindicated for health reasons." In most instances, customs officials will accept such a letter as substitute for the vaccination.

## VACCINATIONS RECOMMENDED FOR SOME TRAVELERS

Certain vaccinations are recommended for travelers who will be living, working, or traveling in rural areas of developing countries where sanitary conditions are poor. These vaccinations are not required by International Health Regulations and are generally not needed for travel to tourist and resort areas.

## Hepatitis

Although it is not a true vaccination, hepatitis immune globulin is an agent that offers some protection against infectious hepatitis. Immune globulin is recommended for travelers who plan to leave the usual tourist routes in developing and tropical countries and for travelers who plan to stay in these countries for longer than three months.

An injection with immune globulin offers a partial protection against infectious hepatitis that lasts for four to six months. Repeated injections are necessary for travelers staying overseas for longer than six months.

For most travelers, however, the risk of acquiring hepatitis while abroad is no greater than it is in the United States. As with cholera, the best protection against this disease is good food and water hygiene. A new vaccine against hepatitis B (serum hepatitis) has recently been introduced, but at the present time it is not recommended for travelers abroad.

## The Plague

The dreaded plague of the Middle Ages still exists in parts of the world (including the scenic mountains of northern California). However, the risk to the average traveler of acquiring the plague is almost nonexistent. Vaccination against the plague is recommended only for persons who will have direct contact with wild rodents and rabbits in plague-infested areas, particularly Vietnam, Democratic Kampuchea, and the Lao People's Democratic Republic. Other travelers do not need to be vaccinated.

## Typhoid

Typhoid fever is still a serious health problem in many parts of the world, but the risk to most travelers is small. Currently available vaccines offer only limited protection. The best protection against this illness is good food and water hygiene. Vaccination is not routinely recommended for the average traveler.

Vaccination is recommended, however, for those people traveling to rural areas off the usual tourist routes in developing countries where sanitary conditions are poor. The injection often causes one or two days of pain at the injection site and may be followed by fever, nausea, and headache. It must be repeated every three years. Recently, a new oral vaccine has been introduced, and it is reported to be just as effective as the injection but without the side effects. Ask your physician about its availability.

## SUMMARY OF VACCINATIONS FOR TRAVELERS

### Vaccinations for Travelers to Western Nations

- Routine vaccinations should be up-to-date and include tetanus, diphtheria, polio, and sometimes measles.
- Generally no other vaccinations are required or recommended.

### Vaccinations for Travelers to Developing Nations

- Routine vaccinations should be up-to-date.
- A booster dose of polio vaccine is recommended.
- Yellow fever vaccine is frequently required and is recommended for travel in areas where risk of infection exists.
- Cholera vaccination should be obtained only to fulfill entry requirements.
- For travelers planning to visit rural areas where sanitary conditions are poor, hepatitis immune globulin and typhoid vaccine are recommended.

## Vaccinations for Travel from and to the United States

- With only a few exceptions, no vaccinations are required by International Health Regulations for travel directly from the United States.

- Without exception, no vaccinations are required to gain entry back into the United States, no matter where you have traveled.

# Travel for All Ages

## TRAVELING WITH CHILDREN

It has been said that there are two kinds of travel—first class, and with children. Indeed, traveling with children is a remarkable experience. Seeing the world reflected in the eyes of a child is refreshing, and the education you and your family will receive can be obtained in no other way. But when the children are coming along, a lot of planning needs to be done.

### Should You Bring the Kids?

There is no convincing reason not to bring your children along—assuming they will stay healthy and well-behaved and are always a pure delight to be with. So much for fantasy! Consider the reality. Before you decide, you should examine your own expectations. Forget visions of your single years when trips were planned spur-of-the-moment, museums were appreciated at a leisurely pace, and dinners were savored through five courses. Be realistic and try to envision scenes of bored, restless, and impatient children asking when is it time to go home. Don't feel guilty if you and your spouse need time alone with each other to renew yourselves and your relationship. The children can come along on the next trip.

On the other had, traveling with children can be wonderful. A trip can be a chance to bring your family closer together. The educational benefits of travel for children will be obvious as the pages of their textbooks come alive. It takes planning and flexibility on your part, but traveling with children can be rewarding for you and your whole family.

## Planning for Travel with Children

From the very beginning, include your children in the planning stages of your vacation. Talk to them about your travel plans, show them maps and brochures, and read to them stories about the countries you plan to visit. Let them be a part of it from the start.

Boredom is the traveling parent's nemesis. It breeds ill temper and restlessness in children. To keep boredom at bay during traveling times, bring along a few transportable toys (but avoid ones with small pieces that can be misplaced) and other forms of entertainment like comic books, children's books, and games. Food is another antidote to boredom, and packing picnic-style lunches that can be readily dispensed to restless and, hopefully, hungry children may buy you a little quiet time en route.

Before undertaking a long overseas family journey, you may want to consider taking a short weekend trip together first. It will introduce your children to what travel is all about, and you to what travel with children is all about.

## Health Considerations for Children

Aside from their bouts of boredom and restlessness, children are generally hearty travelers. Providing your children have enjoyed good health and their routine series of vaccinations are up-to-date, there are few special problems they might encounter. Here are a few additional words of caution for traveling with children.

**Accidents.**   Accidents will be the biggest threat to your children's health while traveling abroad. So be careful. Keep all medicines out of their reach. Watch toddlers in hotel rooms—your own house may be "childproofed," but hotel rooms may have tangles of electrical cables and cords that a curious child could get into. Check under tables, desks, and beds for potential hazards.

**Water and Food Safety.**   You may be able to remember the precautions concerning water and food safety discussed in chapter 10, but don't expect that your children will. Children need repeated warnings about the safety of drinking water. Carry a container filled with purified drinking water to quench your child's thirst when touring away from your room.

**Vaccinations.**   All children, traveling or not, should have their routine series of vaccinations up-to-date. Measles, mumps, and rubella are still widespread in developing countries, and your children's physician may recommend these vaccinations before going abroad. Polio vaccination is especially important because this crippling disease is still a major health problem in much of the world.

International vaccination requirements are often waived for children less than one year of age. Since the currently available cholera vaccine is not very effective, your physician may provide a letter exempting even older children from this vaccine. The yellow fever vaccine is recommended for all children over the age of six months who will be traveling to an infected area.

## Flying with Children

Air pressure changes during ascent and descent can produce ear pain in infants and children, making them restless and uncomfortable. To prevent this, encourage older children to chew gum during a flight, and provide younger babies with frequent sips of formula, water, or juice from a bottle. Fluids are also important to prevent the dehydration caused by the low cabin humidity.

## SENIOR CITIZENS

The "golden years" are often the ideal time to travel. With the obligations of career and parenting behind you, ahead lies the freedom to explore the world at your own pace. And the key to successful and rewarding travel for the senior citizen is exercising that freedom to travel at your own pace.

Combined with the wisdom to truly appreciate foreign travel, most seniors have the experience and common sense to plan their trips to meet their own needs and interests, and they are often considered to be the world's best travelers. However, advancing age does diminish the body's ability to adapt to the physical stresses of travel. So, when you are planning your next trip, here are some points to remember.

- The effects of jet lag will be more pronounced in older travelers. Allow yourself plenty of time to adjust after a long flight. Or, if possible, break your journey into short legs, and schedule two or three days for rest after each stop.

- Extremes in climate—cold, heat, and altitude—can cause pronounced physical stress. It is important to allow plenty of time to adapt to warmer or more humid climates and to increases in altitude.

- Enjoy the freedom to set your own pace. Instead of frantically rushing around, adopt a more leisurely pace and take time to appreciate the finer and more subtle aspects of life that are so often bypassed during youth.

- Be realistic when planning your itinerary. It makes little sense to join a whirlwind tour group or to plan to go helicopter skiing in Canada. Instead, set your sights on activities and destinations you will personally enjoy, both intellectually and physically.

- Travel stimulates the mind, adds to the enjoyment of life, and can be a benefit to your health. Don't be afraid to go abroad, even if it's for the first time. The common physical infirmities that go along with aging are little problem in today's age of modern transportation. If it is at all possible to go, do it. Travel definitely can be good for you.

## Health Considerations for Senior Travelers

Schedule a visit with your personal physician to go over your travel plans and get a complete medical checkup before you leave. Get off to a good start by taking care of any health problems that have been nagging you.

Be sure to double-check your health insurance policy to determine how well you are covered while traveling overseas. Remember that Medicare will not cover you anywhere outside the United States, except for Puerto Rico, the U.S. Virgin Islands, Guam, and American Samoa. Insurance is discussed in chapter 2.

## Organizations for Traveling Seniors

Senior citizens are a growing part of the travel population, and the travel industry knows it. Many privileges and advantages are available to older travelers through senior groups and tour operators—even European governments offer special discounts and itineraries.

Your local travel agency and senior citizens' group should be able to give you information about special tours and individual discounts. Additional sources of information are:

— National Council of Senior Citizens
  1511 K Street N.W.
  Washington, DC 20005

— National Association of Mature People
  2000 Clausen Center
  P.O. Box 26792
  Oklahoma City, OK 73126

— Gadabout Tours
  700 East Tahquist
  McCallum Way
  Palm Springs, CA 92262
  202-347-8800
  For Travel Services: 202-296-4670

— Groups Unlimited
  422 Madison Avenue
  New York, NY 10017
  212-838-4730

— American Association of Retired Persons
  555 Madison Avenue
  New York, NY 10022
  212-758-1411

# SECTION II

# Getting There Well

# 5

# Avoiding Motion
# Sickness

It has been said that there are two stages of motion sickness: "The first is when you feel like you are going to die; the second is when you wish only that you could." Getting there is supposed to be half the fun, but motion sickness has taken some of the fun out of travel ever since voyagers first set out to sea, then into the air, and now up into space! In fact, motion sickness can ruin a good trip no matter how you travel. I have heard that travelers have even become sick riding camels around the pyramids of Giza.

The symptoms of motion sickness—cold sweats, weakness, nausea, vomiting, and dizziness—are all too familiar to many travelers. These symptoms result when the equilibrium centers in the inner ear get out of balance with what the eyes are actually seeing—an imbalance that can be produced by any kind of rocking, shifting, or angular motion. Whatever kind of motion causes it, the result is the same, and it makes us feel lousy.

Motion sickness can happen to anybody (and sooner or later usually does), but some travelers are more susceptible than others—and nobody knows why. Children aged ten to twelve are the most susceptible of all; the older we get, the better we seem to tolerate motion. Previous travel experience also helps; veteran travelers are less likely to get sick than first-timers, perhaps because there is an element of apprehension involved. But in truly turbulent conditions, anybody can get sick.

Motion sickness can usually be prevented. A few general precautions will help you stay well, and if these aren't enough, you can take one of several effective antimotion-sickness medications.

## PREVENTING MOTION SICKNESS

Reduce your chances of becoming ill by eating lightly before and during the time you travel. Although the temptation to do the opposite is often great, abstain from alcohol while traveling (alcohol can produce symptoms similar to motion sickness even when you're standing still!). Overindulgence of food and spirits will increase the risk of motion sickness and eventually make getting there miserable.

### In Flight

To minimize airsickness, wear loose-fitting and comfortable clothing during the flight. You can don tight jeans and three-piece suits when you arrive. For a smoother flight sit near the wing, where the plane is more stable. And, if you are concerned about airsickness, stay away from the smoking section.

When air turbulence is expected (typically understated by the flight crew), skip the in-flight meal, recline your seat, close your eyes, and try to relax. If you know you are susceptible to motion sickness, consider using an antimotion-sickness medication.

## At Sea

To reduce the chance of seasickness, select a cabin close to midships and near the waterline where the ship's rocking motion will be least noticeable, and go easy on food and spirits until you have your sea legs under you.

If you begin to feel queasy, the first thing to do is get out on deck. Fresh air is one of the best remedies for seasickness. To ward off symptoms in your cabin, lie quietly on your back with your eyes closed. Do not try to read. (Even if you are reading this in your cabin now and are feeling a bit ill, close the book, close your eyes, lie back, and try to sleep. You will feel better soon.)

If rough weather is forecast, and you are susceptible to seasickness, consider using an antimotion-sickness medication. Once you stop traveling, the major symptoms will pass in a few minutes, but you will probably feel run-down for several hours.

## TWO TYPES OF ANTIMOTION-SICKNESS MEDICINE

Two types of drugs are available for preventing motion sickness: antihistamines and scopolamine. Each one is most effective when it is taken one or two hours before departure. Once you are traveling and the symptoms of motion sickness appear, it is often too late for these drugs to be of much help.

### Antihistamines

Antihistamine drugs are generally safe and effective when used for preventing motion sickness. Several types of antihistamines are available under a variety of brand names. The following ones are the most useful in preventing motion sickness:

**Promethazine (Phenergan).**   The adult dose is one twenty-five-milligram tablet taken twice daily. The initial dose should be taken one hour before travel and repeated eight hours later if necessary. On succeeding days of travel, take one dose on arising and one again before the evening meal. Phenergan may be given to children in tablet or syrup form at half the adult dose. A prescription is required.

**Dimenhydrinate (Dramamine).**   The adult dose is one or two fifty-milligram tablets every four to six hours, not to exceed eight tablets a day. The initial dose should be taken one hour prior to travel. For children aged six to twelve, the dose is one-half to one tablet every six to eight hours; for children aged two to six, up to one-half a tablet every eight hours. Children may also be given Dramamine cherry-flavored liquid according to directions for its use. No prescription is required.

**Cyclizine (Marezine).**   The adult dose is one fifty-milligram tablet taken every four to six hours as needed; for children aged six to twelve, one-half a tablet taken up to three times daily. The initial dose should be taken one hour prior to travel. No prescription is required.

**Meclizine (Bonine).**   The adult dose is one or two twenty-five-milligram tablets taken one hour prior to traveling. The dose may be repeated every twenty-four hours for the duration of the journey. This is a convenient medication as it needs to be taken only once a day. Since its safety for children has not been established, it is not recommended for children under age twelve. No prescription is required.

**A Combination of Promethazine and Ephedrine.**   For travelers needing more potent antimotion-sickness medicine, a combination of promethazine, one twenty-five-milligram tablet (as discussed above), and ephedrine (a common decongestant), one fifty-milligram tablet, work very well in preventing motion sickness. Discuss the use of both drugs with your physician.

A word of warning about antihistamines: Because their main side effects are drowsiness and loss of alertness, these drugs should not be used by people who operate automobiles or other hazardous machinery. They should not be mixed with alcohol, tranquilizers, or any type of sedative. People who are prone to motion sickness and are under treatment for other medical conditions, including pregnancy, should consult their physician before using antihistamines.

## Scopolamine (Transderm-V)

Transdermal scopolamine is an innovative way to administer a well-known drug to prevent motion sickness. The drug scopolamine is contained in a small plastic disk that is placed on the skin behind the ear. It is slowly absorbed into the body, where it acts to quiet the sensory organs in the inner ear.

Each disk will last for three days, making this a practical method of preventing motion sickness on long journeys and ocean voyages, and new disks can be applied every three days if needed. In addition to the frequent side effect of a dry mouth, occasional drowsiness and blurred vision occur. Therefore, if you use scopolamine, do so with caution, at least until you are familiar with its effects and especially if you have to maintain alertness for driving or other activities.

Many travelers find Transderm-V a useful way to prevent motion sickness when long-term protection is needed. However, Transderm-V has not been proven safe for children. In addition, it can complicate bladder and eye problems, and its side effects can be pronounced in some elderly travelers. All travelers should consult their physician before using it. A prescription is required.

*Note:* Antihistamines and Transderm-V won't be very helpful once symptoms have occurred, but it is sometimes worth giving them a try. More powerful antinausea medications such as Compazine and Tigan may bring some relief, and veteran motion sickness victims often bring one or the other along. You can ask your physician about adding one of these medications to your medical kit.

## OLD AND NEW REMEDIES FOR MOTION SICKNESS

Old remedies for motion sickness—like eating raw onions and drinking straight gin—have largely gone by the wayside, and they have been replaced by the newer medications discussed above. One old remedy, however, seems to work after all.

A prestigious medical journal, *The New England Journal of Medicine,* recently reported that ginger root is effective in preventing motion sickness. The authors recommend two or three capsules of the powdered herb, available in health food stores, to be taken fifteen minutes before departure. The herb is supposed to work directly on the stomach to reduce nausea, and it does not cause drowsiness. The dosage can be repeated every four hours if it is needed. Ginger root appears to be a simple and safe method, and if it works for you, great!

## SUMMARY

Reduce the likelihood of motion sickness by dressing comfortably, eating lightly, and avoiding alcohol.

Select one of the antimotion-sickness medications and

bring it along. If you think you are going to be sick, take it before you begin to travel.

As a last resort, you can follow the advice Snoopy gave in a recent comic strip: "How to avoid carsickness, seasickness, and airsickness. . . . Be careful what you eat. And stay home."

# 6

# Flying Well

The modern jet has revolutionized travel. All you have to do is climb on board, and in a few hours you can be anywhere in the world. But jet travel carries with it a number of twentieth-century health problems. Knowing how to avoid these problems will help keep you flying well.

## BEING COMFORTABLE ALOFT

Jane Morse, a syndicated travel writer, coined a Confucian saying: "He who does not prepare for a long time aloft can expect deep trouble back on the ground." Anyone who has spent several hours cramped in a cabin seat 35,000 feet above the ground knows exactly what she means. An unprepared flyer can expect stiffness and fatigue and a less-than-cheerful disposition when the flight is over.

There are several ways you can prepare to be comfortable aloft. The first is knowing how to dress. There is no reason to wear anything on board but loose-fitting and comfortable clothing. Tight-fitting pants, boots, and undergarments, and cumbersome three-piece suits lead to an uncomfortable flight and discomfort when you land. The time for haute couture is later. And, because in-flight temperatures can get chilly, wear clothing that keeps you warm while aloft.

How well you spend your time in flight will largely determine how well you feel when you land. The key to a successful flight is to take it easy and try to rest. Eat lightly; heavy meals will add to your discomfort and interfere with sleep (and airline food is rarely regarded as something worth losing sleep over). Avoid alcohol; drinking is a popular way to kill time in flight, but the aftereffects can be devastating. Heavy meals and alcohol not only lead to fatigue when you land, they promote motion sickness and jet lag as well. Moderation is essential to flying well.

Do drink plenty of juices and other nonalcoholic beverages while in flight. The air is extremely dry in most passenger compartments, and after several hours it can produce a mild dehydration, especially in young children. Also, get up and walk the aisles for five minutes every hour to keep your blood circulating. Sitting for prolonged periods of time will lead to mild ankle-swelling, so don't be surprised if your shoes feel tight when the flight is over.

Bring along enough things to occupy your time. Light novels and magazines are easier to digest in flight than textbooks on world economic theory. Board games, cards, and Scrabble are popular pastimes and a good way to meet fellow passengers. When you don't feel like reading or playing games, write letters or postcards to your friends. You can post them from your destination and spend the time you've saved sightseeing.

Sleeping is probably the best way to pass the time during a long flight, and that is why some travelers prefer to fly at night. Sleeping medications are used by a few veteran air travelers, but, like alcohol, the aftereffects may make you feel less than ambitious when you land. However, the aftereffects may be preferable to sitting awake during an entire twelve-hour flight. Whether you should use sleeping medications or not is something you should discuss with your physician. The most important thing is to be relaxed and comfortable during your flight. It is the best way to get off to a good start when you land.

## COPING WITH JET LAG

Jet lag has been aptly described as the world's longest hangover; it has been less aptly described as transmeridian dysrhythmia, circadian rhythm desynchronosis, and a transient state of dyschronism. Whatever it is called, it occurs when we fly across three or more time zones, and its effects can take the edge out of anybody's performance back on the ground.

Jet lag happens when your body's internal time clock, which regulates sleeping, eating, and hormonal cycles, falls out of "sync" with the earth's twenty-four-hour, day-and-night cycle. The result is insomnia, loss of appetite, irritability, poor memory, and fatigue—symptoms that typically last two or three days, longer in older travelers. Jet lag is more pronounced traveling from east to west than west to east, and it is nonexistent on northward and southward flights (although fatigue is common after any long flight).

There are several ways to reduce the effects of jet lag. First, get plenty of rest before you leave, and eat very lightly on the day of departure. In flight, try to be as comfortable as possible (see pages 48 to 50). Heavy meals and alcohol will definitely make jet lag worse. And try to sleep as much as possible while aloft.

When you arrive at your destination, check into your hotel and immediately take a three- to four-hour nap. When you awake, reset your watch to the local time, and

cautiously get into step with your new environment. Re-
tire at local bedtime, and try to get eight or nine hours of
sound sleep. In the morning, you should feel better, but
it is still wise to avoid strenuous activity for the first two
or three days, while your body takes the time it needs to
further adjust.

## The Anti-Jet Lag Diet

An easy way to prepare in advance to reduce the effect
of jet lag and adapt your body to new time zones is the
anti-jet lag diet. Developed by scientists at the Argonne
National Laboratory, the diet calls for travelers to follow
a feast-fast-feast-fast eating pattern for four days prior to
departure. On day one, four days before you will arrive
at your destination, *feast* on a high-protein breakfast and
lunch and a high-carbohydrate dinner. Drink no coffee,
except between 3:00 and 5:00 P.M. On day two, *fast* on light
meals of fruits, salads, juices, and light soups. Again, drink
no coffee except between 3:00 and 5:00 P.M. On day three,
*feast* again. And, on day four, the day you will be traveling, *fast*. Break the final fast at breakfast time at your destination. The anti-jet lag diet is thoroughly explained in
*Overcoming Jet Lag* by Charles Ehret and Lynne Scanlon
(New York: Berkley Books, 1983). For a wallet-sized card
that summarizes the diet, send a stamped, self-addressed
envelope to:

— Anti-Jet Lag Diet
   OPA
   9700 South Cass Avenue
   Argonne, IL 60439

For truly self-disciplined travelers, the effects of jet lag
can be reduced by actually readjusting your internal time
clock before you leave. On each of the three nights prior
to your departure, go to bed one hour earlier for each time
zone you will cross going east, or one hour later for each

time zone you will cross going west. This means going to bed in the late afternoon for transatlantic flights and in the early morning for transpacific flights. Mealtimes should be adjusted accordingly. This method works well, but many travelers understandably find it difficult to follow.

Because of the negative effects of jet lag on judgment, international companies often do not allow their traveling executives to make important decisions during the first two or three days after arrival overseas. When time is essential, experienced business travelers will wear two watches: one set to home time, by which they eat and sleep, and the other set to local time, for business appointments.

## WHAT TO DO ABOUT FEAR OF FLYING

Fear of flying is a common problem. It ranges from mild anxiety during a turbulent flight to full-blown panic at just the thought of boarding a plane. Symptoms, varying in severity, include weakness, sweating, dizziness, nausea, and trouble with breathing. Victims get little comfort from being told that flying is by far the safest way to travel, safer than trains, automobiles, or even walking across the street.

Fear of flying is actually a form of agoraphobia—which is the fear of losing control of oneself in public. Victims are afraid of becoming panic-stricken and embarrassing themselves while trapped on board a plane. It is an understandable feeling—once the plane is airborne it really is impossible to get off. But when the fear becomes so great that it prevents you from getting out and enjoying the experience of travel, it is probably time to seek help.

And help is available. Start by asking your physician to refer you to counseling centers specializing in agoraphobia and the fear of flying. Local airports and airline offices sometimes sponsor courses for fearful flyers. In-

formation and a special cassette tape program on overcoming the fear of flying is available by writing or calling:

— CHAANGE (Center for Help for Agoraphobia/
Anxiety Through New Growth Experiences)
2915 Providence Road
Suite 310
Charlotte, NC 28211
704-364-5026

Several books about the fear of flying are available in
bookstores and libraries

Angel-Levy, Penny, and Levy, George, *The Complete
Book of Fearless Flying*, Wetherall Publishing, 1981.
Forgione, Albert, and Bauer, Frederic, *Fearless Flying*,
Houghton Mifflin Co., 1980.
Lafferty, Perry, *How To Lose Your Fear of Flying*, Price,
Stern, Sloan, 1980.

## AVOIDING A PAINFUL DESCENT

As an aircraft descends for landing, atmospheric pressure
increases, and you may experience sharp ear pain or sinus
pain, called barotitis or barosinusitis, respectively. The
problem occurs when the air passages leading to the inner ear and sinuses are blocked by colds, hay fever, or
sinus infections. The pain is often excruciating, but, if you
are prepared, it can be prevented.

The surest way to prevent this problem is to postpone
air travel during the early stages of a cold, a flare-up of
hay fever, or a sinus infection. When flying is necessary,
however, barotitis and barosinusitis can be prevented by
using a nose spray, available at drugstores, to keep your
air passages open (this is one of the few instances when
nose sprays are recommended). Decongestant pills will also
be effective if taken at least one hour before descent. (An-

tihistamines work well as decongestants and can be used for this purpose also.)

What should you do if ear pain or sinus pain develops suddenly during flight? If you have a nose spray available, use it immediately. Otherwise, relief may be obtained by performing Valsalva's maneuver. This is accomplished by pinching your nose closed with your thumb and forefinger and then trying to steadily exhale through your nose (the pressure you generate will help open the air passages). Drinking liquids, chewing gum, and crying will also help keep air passages open.

Changes in air pressure during flight may cause dental problems for people with defective fillings or abscessed teeth. Air that is trapped inside the tooth may expand and cause pain—an additional reason for visiting the dentist before you leave.

Scuba divers can develop the bends if they fly too soon after diving, even if they have followed the U.S. Navy Diving Table limits. Scuba divers should allow at least twelve hours between their last dive and an air flight.

People with ongoing medical problems should consult with their physician before flying. Some of the medical reasons for not flying are listed in chapter 16.

# 7

# Traveling by Land and Sea

## WALKING WELL

Pedestrian as it seems, especially when compared to traveling on jets, trains, or modern ocean liners, walking is, in fact, our basic means of travel. Yet, at times, walking is not easy. Seemingly minor problems, like foot blisters, can arrest an entire expedition. To make sure you keep walking well, there are two requirements: good shoes and foot hygiene.

### Good Shoes

Well-fitting and comfortable shoes are essential for trouble-free walking. New shoes should be purchased several weeks before your departure and be well broken in by the time you leave. Only tenderfoot travelers bring new footwear along, and it is usually they who develop tender feet later on.

Your footwear needs will depend upon the type of journey you are planning. Most trips involve walking on pavement and short hikes, and running or jogging shoes, lightweight and flexible, are excellent choices. A well-constructed leather walking shoe with a soft crepe sole is also a very good selection for the average traveler.

When heading off the beaten path, the support offered by a good leather boot is needed. Select a boot that is sturdy enough to protect your feet and ankles but light enough to keep you from being unnecessarily weighted down. Basically, the harsher the terrain, the heavier the boot you will need.

In wet and tropical climates, a pair of sandals will protect the bottoms of your feet and allow them to stay dry. Rubberized sandals are handy for communal showers and bathrooms.

## Foot Hygiene

Along with good shoes, foot hygiene is essential to walking well. Hygiene starts with conditioning, and the best conditioning for your feet is walking. So start walking regularly before you leave.

Go easy on your feet during the first few days of your trip. Make frequent stops to rest them. And remember the cardinal rule for walkers: Stop walking when your feet feel sore. If you ignore the pain, you can count on being sharply reminded later.

Blisters are heralded by the onset of pain. They are caused by friction on the skin, usually from ill-fitting shoes and socks. If a sore spot develops, take care of it immediately. Protect the tender area with adhesive tape, gauze, or moleskin. These materials should be part of your medical kit.

When a blister forms and remains unbroken, leave it alone. The overlying skin will protect against infection. If the blister breaks open, an antibacterial ointment—also part of your medical kit—should be applied to the area. A blister should be protected from further friction, and walking should be limited for several days until it heals.

Wet feet will lead to blisters and skin irritation, so try to keep your feet dry. Cotton and wool socks absorb moisture and will help keep your feet dry. Carry an extra pair of dry socks to change into when you need them.

## Pedestrian Safety

While walking, don't let yourself be so distracted by the sights that you ignore your own safety. Driving customs vary widely abroad, and rules allowing pedestrians the right-of-way may not even exist, much less be respected. In countries like England where they drive on the left side of the road, be especially careful. Wherever you are, always exercise the same precaution you would walking around Chicago, Boston, or New York City: Stop, look, listen, and be ready to jump out of the way.

## DRIVING WELL

The greatest danger you will face abroad is automobile accidents. They are the leading cause of serious injury and disability among travelers. Most fatal accidents occur at night, and, as in this country, alcohol is usually involved.

In developing countries, aggressive drivers on poorly maintained roads are especially dangerous. Defensive driving is an unfamiliar concept, and the highways are literally strewn with wreckage. It's ironic that a journey to the great dark continent of Africa presents as its greatest danger the modern automobile.

What to do? Drive defensively yourself, and always use seat belts. Avoid driving at night and after local "social" events, when the risk of a collision is highest. And, in case you find yourself a nervous passenger in a speeding taxi, it's helpful to know the local words for "slow down" and "stop."

## SAILING WELL

Whether your keel is twenty feet or two hundred, sailing is one of the most satisfying ways to travel—but only when you can avoid the ignominy of turning green at sea. More than anything else, seasickness will drain the fun out of an ocean voyage. But, with the proper precautions, it can be prevented. Avoiding motion sickness is discussed in chapter 5.

Commercial cruise ships are required to have medical facilities on board; these range from sophisticated mini-hospitals to rudimentary dispensaries. Ship's doctors are prepared to take care of most common ailments, and for more serious problems, they can arrange for transportation to shore. However, it is unfair and unwise to expect them to provide the same level of care you can receive at home. If you have an existing medical problem, check in with the ship's doctor when you board so, in case of emergency, medical personnel will be aware of your condition.

### Sanitary Conditions On Board

The U.S. Public Health Service conducts regular inspections of the galleys and food services of ships calling on U.S. ports. The reports are available to the public, and it is interesting to note that, at one time, two of the better-known cruise ships repeatedly failed sanitary inspection. Just as in any restaurant, the likelihood of staying healthy is better on a ship that meets PHS standards.

To receive a free summary of the PHS's most recent

inspections or a copy of the latest report on a particular ship, write to:

— Office of the Chief
  Sanitation and Vector Control Activity
  Quarantine Division
  105 North America Way
  Room 107
  Miami, FL 33132

# III

# Staying Well Abroad

# 8

# Finding Health Care Abroad

Knowing how to locate competent medical care, wherever and whenever you may need it, is the most valuable health protection you will have while abroad. Your health preparations should include a thorough consideration of the quality of health care available at your planned destination and how you will locate good medical care if the need arises. When an injury or illness does occur, there is often little time to search for the best care. So know in advance where you will turn for medical help if a problem arises.

## HOW TO FIND A DOCTOR OVERSEAS

The quality of medical care varies greatly overseas, from internationally recognized expertise to aboriginal folk remedies. Since all doctors learn much about your ailments through talking with you, language barriers can interfere with the care provided by the best practitioners. One important aspect of traveling well, therefore, is knowing how to locate qualified, English-speaking physicians in the countries you plan to visit. And this is not difficult to do.

There are several ways to locate good medical care abroad, through private organizations, the U.S. embassies and consulates, and direct referrals.

## Organizations

Several organizations provide travelers with assistance in locating qualified physicians overseas. This assistance can either be in the form of directories of English-speaking physicians overseas or a direct telephone referral. If you needed a doctor, you would call a special number, and the operator would get you in touch with a qualified doctor or clinic. Some of the special health insurance programs for travelers, discussed in chapter 2, provide this information as part of their services. Two additional organizations are:

- IAMAT (International Association for Medical Assistance to Travelers), 736 Center Street, Lewiston, NY 14092. Telephone: 716-754-4883. IAMAT is a nonprofit organization founded twenty years ago by Dr. Marcolongo, a physician practicing in Toronto. The aim of IAMAT is to make competent medical care available to travelers around the world, even in very remote places. IAMAT provides a directory of English-speaking physicians located in over 300 cities around the world. Standard fee schedules are established, so you'll know in advance what you will be charged. And these doctors are on call to IAMAT members 24 hours a day. In addition, IAMAT provides information on vaccinations, malaria risk and prevention, and water and food safety. Anyone can belong to IAMAT and there is no charge for membership, although a donation is requested to help support its work. Additional information can be obtained by contacting IAMAT directly.

- Intermedic, 777 Third Avenue, New York, NY 10017. Telephone: 212-486-8974. Intermedic provides a directory of over 200 physicians in over 90 countries around the world and gives information about each doctor's professional training and fee schedules. The one-year membership fee is $6 for individuals and $10 for a family.

Before you leave home, contact one or two of these organizations and obtain the names, addresses, and phone numbers of several physicians in the countries and cities you plan to visit. Carry this information with you at all times.

## U.S. Embassies and Consulates

A valuable resource for American travelers is the 133 U.S. embassies, the 33 U.S. consulates, and the 34 consular agencies scattered throughout the world. They can be a powerful ally in times of personal trouble away from home. While these facilities are often staffed with medical personnel, it is important to realize that embassies and consulates cannot and will not provide direct medical services. They will, however, provide valuable assistance in locating qualified medical care.

U.S. consular and embassy personnel have a prepared list of the medical services available in their foreign community. This list includes the names and addresses of local English-speaking physicians, as well as information about their specialty, training background, and fee schedules. Information is available from consulates and embassies during regular business hours. After hours, the duty officer can provide the names of three physicians in the local area. If an embassy or consulate is not located in an area where help is needed, contact the nearest U.S. facility.

Information about the U.S. consular services can be obtained in the United States by calling 202-632-3444. A complete list of U.S. embassies and consulates around the world is provided in appendix D. Consular and embassy personnel can also provide information about arranging a medical evacuation back home, about what to do in the event of a death abroad, and about other legal and financial problems that may arise.

## Direct Referrals

If it is possible that you may require specialized health care abroad for a chronic medical condition or disability, your personal physician may be able to refer you directly to a specialist in the area you plan to visit. Another source of direct referrals, once you are abroad, is the hotel physician at the place you are staying.

## Other Sources

Other sources abroad that you can contact to locate an English-speaking physician include American church missions, the Red Cross, foreign-based U.S. companies, hotel managers, airline offices, travel agencies, tourist bureaus, pharmacists, and dentists. Other national consulates, especially British and Western European, may be willing to offer help in the event of an emergency.

# IN CASE OF AN EMERGENCY

## Overseas Citizens' Emergency Center

Another source of help to Americans in trouble abroad is the Overseas Citizens' Emergency Center in Washington, maintained by the U.S. State Department. In the event of a serious illness or injury, the center will direct you to the nearest U.S. embassy or consulate (where information about local medical services can be obtained), contact and inform relatives and close friends at home, gather and transmit necessary medical information to physicians overseas, and expedite the transfer of emergency funds. The center's telephone number is 202-632-5225. Write it down and carry it with you.

## In the Event of a Life-Threatening Medical Emergency

When time spent searching for a physician cannot be spared, head directly for the emergency room of the largest nearby hospital. If a medical school or a university-based hospital is nearby, that should be your first choice. Calling the emergency number listed in the front of many telephone directories in foreign countries may bring the single most rapid response to an emergency situation.

## To Arrange a Medical Evacuation

If a serious illness or injury occurs, and you need to arrange a medical evacuation back home, contact the nearest U.S. embassy or consular office for assistance. Or call the Overseas Citizens' Emergency Center.

## In the Event of a Death Abroad

Again, the nearest U.S. embassy or consular office should be contacted.

# 9

## Malaria and Tropical Diseases

Once on the verge of eradication, malaria has staged a dramatic global resurgence, and travelers are being exposed to it in record numbers. It is now the most common life-threatening illness acquired abroad. Too many travelers leave home unaware of the growing risk of malaria—or worse, ignore it. One of the most important health preparations you should make is to find out if you will be exposed to malaria. Through the use of antimalarial medications, this serious disease can almost always be prevented.

Travel to the tropics can appear intimidating when the traveler is confronted with an array of exotic and mysterious diseases—loa loa, schistosomiasis, blackwater and breakbone fevers, river blindness, sleeping sickness, elephantiasis, and a host of flukes, worms, and parasites. But, in fact, the risk of acquiring a tropical illness other than malaria is actually quite small. To be sure, traveling far off the beaten path or settling down in a remote village will require certain precautions if you hope to avoid becoming the victim of a disease whose name you can't even pronounce. But, in most instances, a few common-sense guidelines will keep you out of harm's way. Tropical diseases that merit special mention are discussed below. Appendix A lists countries with a known risk of malaria and other tropical diseases.

## MALARIA

Malaria is a formidable disease. It has plagued mankind for thousands of years, and it is the world's foremost health problem today. Its name, *mal aria*, means "bad air," believed for centuries to be the cause of the disease. It is what Shelley meant when he wrote, "the earth's breath is pestilence." At the end of the last century, we learned that what was wrong with the air was actually flying in it— the mosquito.

Armed with this knowledge and the powerful insecticide DDT, in the 1950s the World Health Organization launched a massive worldwide attack aimed at eliminating malaria once and for all. Initially, much progress was made. Malaria loosened its grip, and it disappeared from many parts of the world, including the United States and Europe. But the mosquito became resistant to DDT and began to flourish once again. Over the past ten years, the the world has experienced a resurgence of malaria. It is now estimated that over 300 million people suffer from it annually. To make matters worse, a strain of malaria that is resistant to common antimalarial drugs is gaining ground. This ancient disease remains a formidable health problem today.

### What is Malaria?

Malaria is a disease caused by a group of parasites named *Plasmodium,* of which four species are able to infect people: *P. falciparum, P. vivax, P. ovale,* and *P. malariae.* Each species has its own disease characteristics. The falciparum strain is the most deadly. It causes the most fatalities, and it is the one strain that is developing resistance to certain antimalarial medications. The vivax strain is by far the most common. It is much more benign than falciparum, but, if untreated, can cause relapses for years. The other two strains are quite rare.

The malaria-causing parasites are spread by infected anopheles mosquitoes. When the mosquito feeds, it passes the parasite into the bloodstream, where it flourishes inside red blood cells, destroying them in the process. Symptoms initially consist of fever, shaking chills, headache, and body aches, which are followed in a few hours by intense perspiration and a sense of relief. With vivax malaria, this pattern of symptoms occurs daily for the first few days, and then every two or three days as the disease progresses. With falciparum malaria, however, the initial symptoms persist unabated.

## Who Should Be Concerned?

All travelers should be concerned enough about malaria to determine whether or not their travels will expose them to this disease and, if they will be exposed, to know how to prevent it. Malaria currently infects large regions in Africa, South and Southeast Asia, the Mideast, Central and South America, and parts of Mexico, Haiti, the People's Republic of China, the Malay archipelago, and Oceania.

Different strains of malaria are found in different parts of the world. Determine whether or not you will be exposed to the drug-resistant strain of falciparum malaria so that you are able to protect yourself with an alternative medication (see below). The risk of malaria may vary widely within a country and may be affected by seasonal changes, altitude, and whether you will be traveling in an urban or rural area. For example, while malaria exists in several inland and remote areas of Mexico, Mexico City and the major tourist areas along the Gulf and Pacific coasts are risk free.

No matter how briefly you stay in a malarious area, even if you never leave the airport, protection is needed. A few years ago, a Swiss traveler spent only four hours in Africa, when his plane landed during a flight home. Several days later, when safely back in Switzerland, he developed symptoms of malaria. The moral is that it takes only one unwary traveler, and one mosquito bite, to cause serious infection with this otherwise preventable disease.

## PROTECTION AGAINST MALARIA

Most cases of malaria can be prevented. Although you can, and should, reduce your chances of becoming infected by protecting yourself from the mosquito, the most important way to protect yourself is by taking the right antimalarial medicine. Chloroquine is the antimalarial drug most often used, and it is still effective in most parts of the world. Where drug-resistant strains of malaria—called chloroquine-resistant malaria—are present, another antimalarial medicine is needed.

### Avoiding the Mosquito

Protecting yourself from the bite of infected mosquitoes is an important way of reducing your chance of acquiring malaria. There are several precautions that you can take.

- Since the anopheles mosquito feeds primarily at night, this is the time when the most protection is needed. When outdoors after dusk, wear long sleeves and long trousers. Apply insect repellent to exposed skin. Anopheles mosquitoes attack silently. Don't expect to be warned by the familiar "buzz."

- The most effective insect repellents are made with an ingredient named N,N, diethyl-meta-tolumide (deet). Several such preparations are commercially available. Avoid the use of colognes, perfumes, or after shaves. Since mosquitoes are attracted to these fragrances, there is no need to advertise yourself.
- Living quarters should have well-screened doors and windows. They should be sprayed with insecticides as often as needed to get rid of lingering mosquitoes. Sleep under a mosquito netting that is in good repair, making sure it fits tightly around the edges of the bed.

## Protection with Chloroquine

Chloroquine phosphate (Aralen, Avlochlor, Resochin) is the antimalarial drug most widely recommended and used for the prevention of malaria. When taken properly, it can protect against all types of malaria except the chloroquine-resistant strain of falciparum malaria. Chloroquine is generally recommended, unless otherwise advised by a physician, for all travelers to malarious regions.

Chloroquine has been in use for over thirty years, and it is a very safe drug. But, since a prescription is required, you should discuss its use with your physician. The adult dose is 500 milligrams of chloroquine phosphate (equivalent to 300 milligrams of the base drug chloroquine) to be taken once a week. The drug should be started one or two weeks before entering a malarious region, and it should be continued for six weeks after you leave. Children should receive a reduced dosage of chloroquine as noted below.

Chloroquine has a distinctly bitter taste, and it occasionally causes mild symptoms of nausea, headache, or dizziness. Its side effects are short-lived and can be minimized by taking the drug with a full meal. A few travelers, however, will find these symptoms troublesome. The reason for starting the drug one or two weeks before you enter a malarious region is to avoid the untimely realization, amidst a swarm of hungry mosquitoes, that you are unable to take the drug at all.

Chloroquine must be continued for a full six weeks after you leave an infected area. It is not uncommon for travelers to return home and forget this admonition. (Who worries about malaria after the slides are developed and shown to everyone who will sit through them?) But it is also not uncommon for travelers to come down with malaria several weeks after returning home. This is because, if medication is discontinued, parasites are able to live in a dormant state inside the body for weeks, months, and even years in some instances. The six weeks of continued treatment with chloroquine are designed to eliminate these lingering parasites.

Remembering your weekly dose of chloroquine is easier if you select one day of the week on which to take your medicine. Members of your traveling party can help remind each other if everyone uses the same day. For years, people living in malarious regions have designated Sunday as the day of the week on which to take their medicine. And, if you decide to follow suit, you will be taking part in the long tropical tradition of "Sunday Medicine."

## Protection from Chloroquine-Resistant Malaria

The chloroquine-resistant strain of falciparum malaria is widespread in South and Southeast Asia, and it is gaining ground in Central and South America, parts of East Africa, and some of the South Pacific islands (appendix A). Travelers to these areas should be aware that chloroquine may not provide adequate protection by itself. Another antimalarial drug, Fansidar, to be taken in addition to chloroquine, is needed for adequate protection.

Fansidar has only recently become available in the United States, although it has been in use in other parts of the world for much longer. It is a combination of two drugs (each tablet contains 500 milligrams of sulfadoxine and 25 milligrams of pyrimethamine), and the adult dose is one tablet once a week. Like chloroquine, Fansidar should be started one or two weeks before entering a malarious region, and it should be continued for six weeks after you leave. Since other strains of malaria are likely to be present where chloroquine-resistant falciparum is found, the U.S. Public Health Service recommends taking both chloroquine and Fansidar in areas where chloroquine resistance occurs. Since Fansidar has the potential for causing serious side effects, its use should be discussed with your physician.

## Malaria Protection in Children

Children should be protected from malaria as adults are, except that the dose of antimalarial drugs should be reduced. The dose of these drugs in children is determined by the child's body weight. Your pharmacist or physician can help you determine the correct amount for your children.

**Chloroquine Phosphate.** Chloroquine phosphate should be administered to children in a dose of five milligrams of the base drug chloroquine per kilogram of body weight (one kilogram equals 2.2 pounds), up to a maximum dose of 300 milligrams of base drug. For example, if your child weighs sixty pounds, this is equal to approximately twenty-seven kilograms. At five milligrams of drug for each kilogram of weight, the dose would be 135 milligrams each week. Chloroquine phosphate is available only in solid form and has a distinctly bitter taste. So a practical solution for getting your child to take it is to have your pharmacist prepare premeasured gelatin capsules that can be mixed into food or chocolate syrup.

**Chloroquine Sulfate.**  Chloroquine sulfate is a drug very similar to chloroquine phosphate, and it has the advantage of being available in certain countries overseas in a pediatric liquid suspension (Nivaquine). The dose of chloroquine sulfate for children is five milligrams of base drug for each kilogram of body weight up to a maximum of 300 milligrams.

**Fansidar.**  When this drug is needed for protection against chloroquine-resistant malaria, the dosage in children is one-eighth of a tablet for those weighing four to nine kilograms; one-quarter of a tablet for those weighing ten to fourteen kilograms; one-half for those weighing fifteen to twenty-nine kilograms; three-quarters for those weighing thirty to fifty kilograms; and 1 tablet for those weighing over fifty kilograms.

All antimalarial drugs for children should be taken on the same schedule as recommended for adults: once a week starting one or two weeks before entering a malarious region and continued for six weeks after leaving.

## Malaria Protection During Pregnancy

An infection with malaria poses a serious health threat to both a pregnant woman and her unborn child. In all its years of use, chloroquine phosphate has not been found to have any harmful effect on the fetus when used in the recommended dose for malaria prevention. For these reasons, if you are pregnant and will be traveling in a malarious region, chloroquine is recommended.

Fansidar has not been proven safe during pregnancy, and it should be avoided. In fact, there is evidence that Fansidar may be potentially harmful to the fetus when taken either early or late in pregnancy. Therefore, women who are pregnant or who are likely to become pregnant should avoid travel to areas known to be infected with chloroquine-resistant malaria. Pregnant women who cannot avoid travel to these areas should discuss the risks with their physician.

Tetracycline, other tetracycline-related drugs, quinine, and primaquine—all of which are occasionally used for the treatment of malaria—should all be avoided during pregnancy, unless they are required to treat a life-threatening infection in the mother.

## Precautions Concerning Antimalarial Drugs

For the great majority of travelers, taking an antimalarial medication is much safer than running the risk of acquiring malaria. But all antimalarial drugs should be regarded as potent medicines with the potential for serious side effects and reactions. People with known drug allergies, certain chronic blood conditions, or other medical problems should consult with their personal physician before taking any antimalarial medication.

## Malaria Precautions After Returning Home

After leaving a malarious region, you must still protect yourself from this disease. The most important precaution is to continue taking your antimalarial medication for a full six weeks after your immediate exposure is over. For most travelers, this will eliminate any chance of persistent, or latent, infection. But even this precaution is no guarantee; there is a remote possibility that a few lingering parasites may live on, silently, with the potential to flare up and cause symptoms weeks, months, and even years later.

Because of the possibility of a persistent infection, even after a full course of medication, some physicians will prescribe what is called a radical cure, to insure that there are no living parasites left in the body. This is accomplished with a drug called primaquine, which is taken after you return home. Primaquine, however, like all antimalarial drugs, is a potent medicine, and most doctors today reserve its use for patients only after they have developed an active, full-blown case of malaria.

My own case of malaria, vivax in nature, occurred a full two months after I returned home from Africa. The symptoms, much like a severe case of the flu, came on suddenly and caught me by surprise. But, because I had recently been in a malarious region, I requested that blood smears be taken, and the diagnosis was made promptly. Once malaria is diagnosed, the treatment is generally simple and effective.

My own experience with malaria is becoming more common. American travelers are bringing the disease home with them in increasing numbers. American physicians, many of whom have never seen an actual case of malaria, may have difficulty diagnosing it unless you alert them to your recent exposure. After returning home from a malarious region, should you experience any symptoms suggestive of malaria—fever, chills, body aches, or a flu-like illness—see a physician and make certain you mention the possibility of malaria, even if your exposure was several months earlier. Keep in mind that malaria is indeed a formidable disease.

## TROPICAL DISEASES

### Preventing Tropical Diseases

Most tropical diseases are spread by insects or contaminated food and water. For diseases other than malaria, medications that may be available for prevention are not generally recommended for the average traveler, because the risk of acquiring an infection is low, and the chance of a toxic drug reaction is considerable. The following precautions will protect you from exposure to most tropical illnesses.

**Protection From Insects.**   The steps described earlier for protecting yourself from mosquitoes will generally protect you from other biting insects as well. Wear long-sleeve shirts and long trousers, especially outdoors at night. Use insect repellents and mosquito netting, and make sure your living quarters are free of insects.

**Food and Water Hygiene.**   Contaminated food and water transmit many infections—typhoid, cholera, hepatitis, giardiasis, and dysentery—and good food and water hygiene will help protect you from them all. Food and water hygiene are discussed in chapter 10.

**Foot Protection.**   It is unwise to go barefoot in the tropics. The soil can be the source of several infections— schistosomiasis, mites, sand flies, hookworms, and Chagas' disease—all of which can be prevented with a pair of sandals.

## Schistosomiasis

Schistosomiasis, also known as bilharziasis, is a parasitic infection that is acquired by swimming in fresh water in certain areas of the tropics. It is considered to be second only to malaria as a major worldwide health problem. And, like malaria, it can be a significant health hazard to unwary travelers. It also can be prevented.

Schistosomiasis is a disease as old as mankind, and evidence of this infection has been found in mummies of the ancient pharaohs. The infection is caused by a parasite that first develops inside minute snails inhabiting freshwater lakes and streams. In the water, the parasite can pass from the snails and penetrate human skin, where it migrates to the blood vessels of the bladder or intestines. People contract this disease by washing, bathing, swimming, or drinking water contaminated by infected snails.

Schistosomiasis is found in various locations throughout the world (appendix A). The major areas of infection are located in Africa, Saudi Arabia, India, Indonesia, China, Japan, Puerto Rico, Brazil, Martinique, Antigua, Dominican Republic, St. Martin, and St. Lucia.

**Preventing Schistosomiasis.** Travelers can avoid the dangers of schistosomiasis by avoiding all contact with contaminated fresh water (salt water is free of the parasites that cause this disease). Most infections in unwary travelers occur when they succumb to the appeal of a cool tropical stream or pond, without first checking with local health authorities to determine if it might be contaminated. Your best protection from schistosomiasis is your own precaution—assume no tropical fresh water is safe for swimming, bathing, washing, or drinking, even if you see others using the water for similar purposes. If you must use fresh water for washing yourself, purify it as described in the next chapter.

There are no preventive drugs or vaccines for schistosomiasis, but a new drug is available that is able to stop the spread of parasites once they are inside the body. But, by the time this disease is diagnosed and treatment is started, much damage will have already occurred. Schistosomiasis is truly a tropical-disease hazard for travelers, but by following a few precautions it is entirely preventable.

## Chagas' Disease

For travelers in Latin America, Chagas' disease can pose a serious health threat. There is no drug or vaccine to prevent it, so some knowledge of the illness and how to protect yourself is essential. Chagas' disease is a parasitic disease that occurs primarily in rural and forest regions of South and Central America. Hikers and campers in these regions are particularly vulnerable. Also at risk are missionaries, geologists, and other field workers.

The parasite, called *Trypanosoma cruzi*, is transmitted by the reduviid bug. Also called the vinchuca, kissing bug, and, more appropriately, the assassin bug, the insect likes to reside in crevices and palm fronds. The bug is large, about two centimeters in length, and once you see one, you won't forget its appearance. It feeds at night, and that is when most bites occur. The bug depends on blood for survival, and in the process of feeding transmits the infection. Exposed parts of the skin, especially the face, are most commonly attacked.

Once the bite occurs, a hard, violet-hued swelling appears at the site in about a week. Some of the parasites enter the blood stream and invade the heart, brain, liver, and spleen. In adults, the infection of the heart is the most serious consequence, and heart failure can be the result. This can occur suddenly, or the condition can take as long as ten years to develop. The symptoms of heart failure are identical to the much more common arteriosclerotic heart disease, and Chagas' disease may never be diagnosed as the cause.

**Who is at Risk?** Chagas' disease exists in Latin America. Travelers to remote areas in these countries are primarily at risk. Business travelers and tourists visiting the outskirts of cities should be aware of the risk and of how to avoid being bitten. The risk in developed areas and large cities is small.

**How to Avoid an Infection**

- Since the reduviid bug lives in the palm-frond roofs and the crevices of walls of natives' huts, do not take up lodging in rural dwellings.

- Search your hotel room for hidden insects—under the mattress, behind pictures, in drawers, or in dark corners—especially in modest establishments in rural areas.
- To help keep the insects away during the night, apply insect repellent to all exposed areas of skin when retiring.
- Use insecticides, preferably pyrethrin-based, to kill insects in your living quarters. Do not directly handle the insects that you find.
- Use insect netting to protect your bed.
- If you are sleeping outdoors, stay away from palm trees, and do not pitch your tent near rock formations where insects may be hiding.

## Typhoid Fever

Typhoid fever is a bacterial disease that is transmitted by contaminated food and water. It is found throughout the world and is especially prevalent in the areas of Central and South America, Africa, and Asia where food and water sanitation is poor. For the average traveler, the risk of typhoid fever is small.

The best way to protect yourself from this infection is to practice good food and water hygiene. A vaccination is available, but it offers only partial protection from the disease. The typhoid vaccine is recommended only for travelers who plan to visit small, rural villages off the usual tourist itinerary and for travelers to areas experiencing an outbreak of disease (see chapter 3).

## Trypanosomiasis (Sleeping Sickness)

Sleeping sickness is caused by a protozoan organism transmitted by the infamous tsetse fly, which is found in the central regions of Africa. The disease produces a persistent fever followed by gradually increasing weakness and fatigue. The risk to travelers in the tropics is small, and very few cases have ever been reported in Americans.

There is no vaccination available against this disease. There are medicines that can be taken for prevention, but, since the risk of infection is so low, they are not recommended for the average traveler. The safest protection is to guard yourself from the tsetse fly by following the same precautions you would use to avoid the mosquito.

## Dengue Fever

Dengue fever is a viral illness with symptoms much like influenza. It is transmitted by the *Aedes aegypti* mosquito, which is found in tropical and subtropical regions worldwide. Unless you are traveling to an area experiencing an outbreak of this disease, the risk of acquiring dengue fever is usually quite low. And only rarely is it a life-threatening illness.

Also known as "breakbone fever," dengue fever usually appears with an abrupt onset of fever, body aches, muscle pains, joint pain, and headache. Several days into the illness, a rash breaks out. Symptoms last from three to seven days and disappear on their own without treatment. Most cases of this illness are not severe, although initially a victim may feel miserable. Occasionally, a complication called dengue hemorrhagic fever results, which produces easy bruising and bleeding from the nose and gums. This requires prompt medical attention.

Outbreaks of dengue fever have been concentrated in tropical Asia, especially the Philippines, Vietnam, and Thailand, and more recently, in the Caribbean. The southern United States, Mexico, and the Mediterranean are also risk areas. At present, there are no drugs or vaccinations available to prevent or treat dengue fever, although work on a vaccine is underway. The main precaution to take against this illness is to protect yourself from the mosquito, and to avoid regions experiencing major outbreaks.

## Yellow Fever

Yellow fever is a serious, often fatal, disease that gained notoriety during the building of the Panama Canal. Like malaria and dengue fever, yellow fever is transmitted by the mosquito. Unlike the others, however, yellow fever is caused by a virus that produces a severe hepatitis, or inflammation of the liver. Its name refers to the yellow jaundice that results from the damage to the liver. Yellow fever is still a major health problem in equatorial Africa and in Central and South America. A safe and effective vaccine is available that is recommended for all travelers to these areas, and this disease is now entirely preventable (see chapter 3).

# 10

## Water and Food Safety

Attitudes toward water and food safety vary widely among travelers. Some adopt a cavalier "I can eat anything" approach, and sometimes they pay the unsettling consequences. Other travelers adhere to a strict "tea and toast" regimen and deny themselves the pleasures of sampling local cuisines. But contaminated water and food are the primary cause of travelers' diarrhea, as well as more serious intestinal infections like cholera, typhoid fever, dysentery, and hepatitis. And, no matter where you are going, knowing what is safe for consumption, and what isn't, is an essential part of traveling well.

### WATER SAFETY

America is one of the few countries in the world where you can drink water from almost any tap or drinking fountain without worrying about its safety. Tap water is often safe in most of the large cities in Western Europe, but one wonders why most Parisians bring bottled water with them when they leave their city for vacations elsewhere in France. Water treatment facilities simply are inadequate or do not exist in many cities in the world, and they are notably absent in less developed countries. Facilities may or not be adequate in tourist resort areas. Be critical of the safety of the water in every new area you visit. Always assure yourself that it's safe before you drink.

## Water to Avoid

- Avoid all tap water unless you are absolutely sure it is safe for drinking.
- Avoid locally bottled, uncarbonated water, especially if it is served uncapped. It is a fairly common practice for restaurants to refill brand name bottles with local tap water—and sometimes they even recap them on the premises!
- Avoid ice cubes, since they undoubtedly have been prepared from local tap water.
- Realize that drinking glasses have been washed in local tap water.
- Do not use tap water for brushing your teeth.

## Water That Is Safe

- Commercially bottled carbonated water and name-brand soft drinks are safe to drink, providing the containers they are served in are also safe.
- Beer and wine are safe to drink. It is safer to drink beer and soft drinks directly from the container, wiping it dry first.
- Hot beverages prepared with boiling water, such as tea and coffee, are safe.
- Freshly prepared, undiluted fruit juices are safe.
- Alcoholic mixed drinks may or may not be safe. You cannot assume that they are.

## Making Water Safe To Drink

In areas where the water is unsafe or is of questionable safety, it can be purified by the following methods.

- Boil tap water for five to ten minutes and allow it to cool. Remember not to add ice cubes that may be contaminated. Afterward, pour the water several times between two clean containers to improve the taste made flat by boiling.

- A small coil heater, sold specifically for this purpose, can be used to boil water while traveling. Coil heaters are convenient when you travel to areas where pure water may be difficult to obtain.

- Water can also be made safe for drinking by adding commercially available purifying tablets such as Halazone, Potable-Aqua, or Globulin. Purifying tablets are available at drugstores and should be used according to packaged instructions, which usually call for a thirty-minute waiting period after the tablets are added.

- Liquid chlorine laundry bleach (4 to 6 percent chlorine strength) can also be used to purify water. Add two drops of chlorine bleach to each quart of water if the water is clear and from the tap or four drops to each quart if the water is cloudy or non-tap, and wait thirty minutes before drinking.

- Tincture of iodine (from your medical kit) is another purifying agent. Add five drops (make sure it is tincture of iodine) to each quart of water if it is clear and from the tap or ten drops if it is cloudy or non-tap. Again, wait thirty minutes before drinking.

- Tap water that is uncomfortably hot to touch is pasteurized, not purified, and when cooled it is relatively safe to drink if nothing else is available.

## FOOD SAFETY

Sampling the local cuisine is one of the most enjoyable features of any trip. But poorly prepared and contaminated foods are a major source of intestinal infections, and you need to be careful in your selection of what and where you eat.

### Foods To Avoid

- Leafy green and uncooked vegetables, common sources of travelers' diarrhea and other intestinal infections, should be fastidiously avoided.
- Perishable foods such as those made with mayonnaise, custards, and cream dishes should not be eaten, since it is often impossible to determine how well they have been preserved.
- Raw or undercooked meats and fishes, which can be sources of tapeworm and other disagreeable infections, should be avoided.
- Shellfish such as crab, oysters, and shrimp taken out of polluted waters are a common source of hepatitis.
- Fresh milk should not be drunk in the tropics and developing countries unless it has been boiled.
- All foods that have been left standing out in the open should be avoided, as they are likely to be contaminated by insects.

### Foods That Are Safe

- Fresh fruit is safe only if you peel it yourself. If the skin has been punctured, leave it alone.
- Freshly boiled vegetables and well-cooked (and still hot) meats and fishes can be eaten.

- Canned foods such as vegetables, canned milk, and soups are generally safe.
- Milk and dairy products in Western Europe are prepared with the same standards as in the United States and are generally safe, but dairy products elsewhere should be approached with caution.
- Follow the travelers' admonition: "Boil it, cook it, peel it, or forget it."

## Choosing a Restaurant

Travelers depend heavily on restaurants as sources of food, and your intestinal health is often entirely at the mercy of the kitchen staff. While you are more likely to be safe at established restaurants in large cities, hygienic standards cannot be guaranteed anywhere. Food poisoning has occurred in some of the world's most expensive restaurants, on board the most famous cruise ships, and even while in flight.

How do you select a safe place to eat? Essentially, you have to rely on the general appearance of the restaurant and on how clean the dining area and waiters appear. You can gain a good insight into the cleanliness of a restaurant by inspecting the restrooms. If you find flies or roaches there, you probably will find them in the kitchen also. Some travelers even resort to an actual inspection of the kitchen, but, if you try this, don't expect to be graciously welcomed by the chef.

An additional health problem in the restaurants of developing countries is the practice of spraying generous amounts of insecticides on stored foods to prevent infestation. If you are concerned about this practice—and you should be, especially if you are traveling with children—you can try the direct approach, and ask your waiter or chef if insecticides are used. Once I was proudly reassured by a waiter in a Kenyan restaurant that their food was the freshest around, because they did indeed take the precaution to spray insecticide on all of their vegetables. Unfortunately for me, I thought to ask him only as I was paying my check.

Generally, the safest restaurants are ones that are attractive and tidy in appearance, have clean restrooms and toilet facilities, are located in well-maintained neighborhoods, and are filled with patrons who appear healthy. The final decision will be yours, and it will be based on your own intuition. If you have any doubts, walk away.

# 11

## Travelers' Diarrhea

It has been noted that, "while travel expands the mind, it loosens the bowels." And travelers' diarrhea, mind-expanding only in its many colorful and descriptive names, is the most frequent cause of loosened bowels. It affects nearly half of all travelers to Mexico and other developing countries. You should know before you leave how to protect yourself from the *tourista*, Montezuma's revenge, the Aztec two-step, the Casablanca crud, the Delhi belly, the Hong Kong hop, the Thai tummy, the Turkey trots, the Jerusalem jumps, the Rangoon runs, and the Trotskys.

Travelers' diarrhea is an intestinal infection that is usually caused by common bacteria found in contaminated food and water. Symptoms range from a mild illness with one or two loose bowel movements a day to an incapacitating illness with profuse watery diarrhea, nausea, cramps, and fever. Without specific treatment, travelers' diarrhea will usually run its course in three to five days. But that often means missing several valuable days of travel.

Your risk of getting travelers' diarrhea is determined to a major extent by your destination and by the precautions you take when you arrive. Mexico is notorious for this problem—an estimated one million Americans become ill in Mexico each year. But a significant risk also exists in other developing countries—most Latin American countries, all of Africa, the Middle East, South and Southeast Asia, and the Mediterranean countries, especially Spain and Greece. For American travelers, the lowest risk of travelers' diarrhea is in northern Europe. But, wherever you go, knowing how to prevent diarrhea and how to treat it when it occurs is fundamental to staying healthy abroad.

## PREVENTING TRAVELERS' DIARRHEA

There are several methods you can use to reduce your chances of acquiring travelers' diarrhea. Which of the methods you should employ will depend on your destination and the likelihood of becoming ill, on your personal state of health, and on the reason you are traveling in the first place—some travelers need to take more precautions than others.

### Food and Water Hygiene

As mentioned earlier, food and water safety should be a concern of all travelers. Avoiding contaminated food and water will reduce your chances of acquiring travelers' diarrhea, as well as other more serious intestinal infections.

### Bismuth Subsalicylate (Pepto-Bismol)

In addition to being an effective treatment for diarrhea, Pepto-Bismol, in heroic doses, will actually prevent travelers' diarrhea. How Pepto-Bismol prevents this intestinal infection is not understood, but, if you take two ounces four times a day during your trip, you can reduce your chances of getting travelers' diarrhea by one-half. The problem with this method is that the quantity of Pepto-Bismol you need to take—a full 240-milliliter bottle for each day that you travel—could require an extra suitcase. Large doses of Pepto-Bismol are safe for most adults, but not for people taking large doses of aspirin. And such dosages may not be safe for people taking certain other medications (especially anticoagulants). Pepto-Bismol tablets are more convenient to use while traveling than the liquid, but it is uncertain whether the tablets are as effective. Remember that Pepto-Bismol will turn your tongue and stools black.

## Antibiotics for Preventing Diarrhea

Certain antibiotics, when started before you leave home and continued during your trip, can prevent travelers' diarrhea from occurring. But the use of antibiotics to prevent diarrhea is not recommended for the average traveler because: (1) travelers' diarrhea is not inevitable; (2) when it does occur it is often mild and can be safely and easily treated; and (3) antibiotics, if used indiscriminately, have the potential for causing serious side effects. Most travelers should reserve the use of antibiotics for treatment of severe diarrhea, if and when it occurs.

A few travelers, however, have valid reasons for taking antibiotics to prevent travelers' diarrhea. These include people with chronic health conditions that would be worsened by the development of diarrhea, and persons traveling for important business purposes or for athletic events who cannot afford to become sick at all. These travelers should discuss antibiotic prevention with their physicians. When recommended, two antibiotics are effective in preventing travelers' diarrhea.

**Doxycycline (Vibramycin).** This antibiotic, which is related to tetracycline, is very effective in preventing traveler's diarrhea. Two 100-milligram capsules are taken on the day of departure, and one capsule is continued daily for three weeks. Its major side effects are photosensitivity reactions—which means the skin becomes very sensitive to being burned by the sun—and stomach upset and diarrhea (which you are trying to prevent in the first place). Because doxycycline, as well as other tetracycline drugs, can stain developing teeth and bones, it should not be taken by pregnant women or by children under the age of eight years. Travelers taking doxycycline should not take Pepto-Bismol, because Pepto-Bismol will prevent the absorption of the antibiotic from the stomach.

**Trimethoprim/Sulfamethoxazole (Bactrim, Septra).** This antibiotic combination is also effective in preventing travelers' diarrhea. It is taken twice daily for two weeks starting on the day of travel. Again, side effects are a potential problem, and its use should be discussed with your physician.

**Vaccinations.** A vaccination against travelers' diarrhea is not yet available, but work on a vaccine is underway, and it may be available soon.

## TREATING TRAVELERS' DIARRHEA

Over the years travelers have been ingenious in their attempts to treat diarrhea. A variety of nostrums have been tried—talcs, gums, plant roots, and reptile parts—and none found effective. As a result, travelers have often resorted to the "grin and bear it" technique, but the grin quickly fades, and bearing it can sometimes last as long as a week.

None of these methods treat the most serious consequence of diarrhea—fluid loss from the body.

## Fluid Replacement

The loss of fluid and salt from the body as a result of diarrhea can produce dehydration, which can be a serious health threat, especially in infants and elderly persons. The most important treatment of diarrhea is fluid replacement.

In mild cases of diarrhea (two to four loose stools a day), fluid replacement and rest are often the only treatments necessary. Stick to clear liquids such as tea, fruit juices, and carbonated beverages. Avoid milk and other dairy products, as they often make diarrhea worse.

In more severe cases of diarrhea (five or more loose stools a day), adequate fluid replacement can be insured by using the following formula, recommended by the U.S. Public Health Service. Prepare two separate glasses of the following:

- *Glass number one.* To eight ounces of fruit juice (orange, apple, or several oranges squeezed into a glass of purified water), add one half teaspoon of honey, corn syrup, or table sugar, and a pinch of table salt.
- *Glass number two.* To eight ounces of carbonated or boiled water, add one quarter teaspoon of baking soda. Drink alternately from each glass until thirst is quenched.

You can supplement these preparations with other safe beverages as desired. If you are experiencing several profuse, watery stools a day, try to drink at least one or two quarts of fluid every eight hours.

## Antidiarrheal Medicines

The use of medicines to decrease cramps and the frequency of stools is popular among travelers—antidiarrheal medicines allow you to travel further than the nearest bathroom. Before using any of them, you should be aware that most physicians view diarrhea as a natural mechanism the body uses to rid itself of noxious and offending material; inhibiting this mechanism could theoretically prolong a diarrheal illness. However, travelers have relied on these medicines for years without experiencing any harmful effects, and it is probably safe to bring one along to use when needed. Ask your physician.

- Bismuth subsalicylate (Pepto-Bismol) is one of the safest and most effective methods of treating the symptoms of diarrhea. In doses of one to two tablespoons every half hour for eight doses, it is effective in alleviating cramps and the loss of fluids from the body. Whether the tablets work as well as the liquid form is not known.

  The active ingredient in Pepto-Bismol is similar to aspirin. Persons already taking large doses of aspirin, anticoagulant drugs, or certain other medicines should check with their physician before taking Pepto-Bismol.

- Diphenoxylate (Lomotil and others) and loperamide (Imodium), which both come in pill form, are popular among travelers for the treatment of diarrhea. Both are effective in reducing cramps and the frequency of diarrhea. A prescription is required, and their use should be discussed with your physician.

- The opiate drugs—tincture of opium, paregoric, and codeine—have long been used for the treatment of diarrhea. They are effective and still prescribed by some physicians. But loperamide and diphenoxylate, which are related to the opiates, are safer, more convenient, and less likely to raise suspicions at customs.

- Kaolin and pectin preparations have never been shown to reduce cramps or the loss of fluids from the body, and are not recommended.

## Antibiotics for Treatment of Diarrhea

In severe cases of travelers' diarrhea, certain antibiotics are useful in reducing symptoms and shortening the course of illness. Taken early after the onset of diarrhea, a combination of trimethoprim and sulfamethoxazole (Bactrim, Septra, and others) taken twice daily is often dramatically effective. This method of treating diarrhea should be reserved for treating only severe cases of travelers' diarrhea (more than five stools a day and a fever). Mild diarrhea is more safely treated without the use of antibiotics. Since this antibiotic combination has potential side effects, its use should be discussed with your physician.

Purchasing antibiotics overseas for the treatment of diarrhea is ill advised. Some antibiotics sold overseas, such as Entero Vioform and Mexiform, are so toxic that they have been banned in the United States. Instead of risking your health by using an unfamiliar drug, ask your physician about using Bactrim or Septra to treat diarrhea and, if they are recommended, take them with you.

**When to Seek Medical Help.**   Most cases of diarrhea that occur while traveling will resolve on their own and need only to be managed by replacing fluids. Travelers' diarrhea can at times be an incapacitating illness, but symptoms normally do not last beyond five days. Medical attention should be obtained when diarrhea persists beyond five days, or when it is associated with high fever or blood and mucus in the stools. These additional symptoms indicate the presence of a serious intestinal infection.

## TRAVELERS' DIARRHEA SUMMARY

### Prevention

- Food and water hygiene will reduce your chance of developing diarrhea.
- Large doses of Pepto-Bismol, although inconvenient to carry, are effective in preventing diarrhea.
- Indicated for business travelers, athletes, and persons with medical conditions, who cannot afford to become sick: trimethoprim sulfamethoxazole (Septra, Bactrim, and others), one double-strength tablet twice a day, or doxycycline (Vibramycin), one 100-milligram tablet once a day.

### Treatment

1. For mild diarrhea (two to four loose stools a day), prevent dehydration by replacing fluids.
2. For moderate diarrhea (four to five loose stools a day with abdominal cramping):
   - Pepto-Bismol: two tablespoons every half hour for eight doses or two tablets every half to one hour, no more than eight a day

     or
   - loperamide (Imodium): two capsules to start, then one capsule after each bowel movement, no more than eight a day

     or
   - diphenoxylate (Lomotil): two tablets four times a day.
   - Prevent dehydration by replacing fluids.

3. For severe diarrhea (more than five loose stools a day and fever):
   - trimethoprim sulfamethoxazole (Bactrim, Septra, and others), one double-strength tablet twice a day for three to five days.
   - Prevent dehydration by vigorous fluid replacement.

## OTHER CAUSES OF DIARRHEA

### Giardia

Giardiasis is an intestinal infection caused by an organism, *Giardia lamblia*, which is found in contaminated water—rarely is it found in food. Giardiasis occurs worldwide, and it has caused outbreaks of diarrhea in such far-ranging places as Aspen and Leningrad. It can also infect campers drinking fresh stream water, which presumably has been contaminated by animals upstream.

Giardiasis can begin with the explosive onset of stomach cramps, nausea, and bloating that evolves into persistent diarrhea, which is then usually mild. Or symptoms can begin several weeks after exposure and may not occur at all until after you have returned home. Any traveler who experiences diarrhea lasting more than seven days or diarrhea that begins after returning home should see a physician for a stool test. Effective treatment is available.

### Cholera

Cholera is a concern to travelers largely because a vaccination against the disease is sometimes required for international travel. There is little likelihood of actually acquiring the disease. During the past twenty years, only ten cases of cholera have been reported in U.S. travelers.

Cholera is an intestinal infection caused by a bacterium called *Vibrio cholerae*. It is spread by water that has been contaminated by sewage; outbreaks of disease are associated with economic and social upheavals and the resulting breakdown in sanitary conditions. Recent outbreaks of cholera have occurred in parts of Asia, Africa, and Oceania.

The best protection from cholera is to follow the guidelines for food and water hygiene, especially in areas with poor sanitation. The cholera vaccine currently available offers little protection from the disease. Unless the vaccine is required to gain entry to a country, the only persons who should consider the vaccination are persons with chronic stomach and intestinal disorders who plan to travel to areas where cholera is present (these persons may be more susceptible to all types of intestinal infections). Other travelers should not be vaccinated.

## Dysentery

Dysentery is a serious intestinal infection that is caused either by an amoeba (amoebic dysentery) or by a bacterium (bacillary dysentery). Both types of infection are spread by contaminated food and water. Severe diarrhea develops, often accompanied by the passage of blood and mucus in the stool. Good food and water hygiene offer the best protection against dysentery. If you develop diarrhea accompanied by the passage of blood or mucus, seek medical attention immediately. Certain antibiotics are helpful in the treatment of this disorder, but they should be prescribed by a physician.

# 12

# Traveling Well Outdoors

Nature, around the world, offers a whole variety of enticing splendors that are often the very reason we travel. Ranging from hot, cloudless skies and warm, tropical evenings to pristine, snow-covered mountains and bitter cold nights, nature challenges us to adapt. And adapt we must. Knowing how to meet the challenges of nature's elements is vital to staying healthy and traveling well outdoors.

## THE SUN

Dreamt of by the snowbound and extolled in travel brochures, the sun draws us from our homes. We'll go almost anywhere to find it. And the mark of a good vacation is often how deep our tans are when we return. But too much of a wonderful thing can be harmful. Probably more travel and vacation days are lost to sunburn than to anything else. So, whether you are flying off to find your place in the sun or just happen to be outdoors on a warm and sunny day, knowing how to protect yourself from too much sun is an important aspect of traveling well.

## Sunburn

There is little doubt that the well-tanned traveler returning home is the image of health and fitness. But there is also little doubt that too much exposure to the sun has harmful effects. Heavy exposure causes premature aging of the skin and leads to skin cancer. And too much exposure also causes sunburn.

Sunburn should be approached for what it is: actual burning of the skin caused by the ultraviolet radiation of the sun. It begins as a first-degree burn, which produces red and painful skin. If exposure continues, the injury may progress to a second-degree burn, with blistering of the skin. If your sunburn is extensive, you may even feel dizzy and weak and run a low grade fever. The risk of sunburn is increased near water and snow, both of which readily reflect the sun's rays. Some people are more susceptible to sunburn than others, but, anywhere we travel and spend a lot of time outdoors, we are all at risk of overexposure to the sun.

## Your Skin Type

Your susceptibility to sunburn depends on your prior exposure to the sun and your skin type. Skin types are determined by the amount of melanin in the skin, a pigment that provides a natural protection from the ultraviolet rays of the sun. Increases in the amount of this pigment result in tanning and in increased protection from sunburn.

Fair-skinned people, especially redheads, freckled people, and those of Irish and Scottish ancestry, have less melanin in their skin and consequently less natural protection from the sun. Darker-skinned people have more melanin and more natural protection.

People can be classified as having one of six skin types. Knowing your own skin type will tell you what degree of protection you will need from the sun.

| Skin type | Examples | Sunburn Potential |
|---|---|---|
| One | Fair-skinned Irish, Scots, redheads | Frequently burn. Rarely tan. |
| Two | Fair-skinned blue-eyed Caucasians | Frequently burn. Slight tan. |
| Three | Darker Caucasians | Some sunburn. Some tan. |
| Four | Mediterranean ancestry | Mild sunburn. Tan well. |
| Five | Spanish, Orientals, Indians | Rarely burn. |
| Six | Black-skinned | Never burn. |

## Sun Protection

There are several ways to protect yourself and your vacation from the harmful effects of too much sun. Lighter-skinned people (skin types one to three) need to take greater precautions than darker-skinned people (skin types four to six).

**Sunscreens.** There are several effective sunscreens available, and choosing the right one depends on your skin type. Sunscreens work by either reflecting or absorbing the sun's ultraviolet rays.

Reflecting screens are made from compounds like zinc oxide, are extremely effective, and usually come in the form of a white paste. Reflecting screens are useful in protecting already burned skin from further damage when staying outdoors is absolutely necessary. However, sunning in Saint-Tropez with your face painted white may not be your image of chic.

Absorbing screens are cosmetically more popular. They are made from compounds such as PABA, PABA esters, and benzophenones. The PABA sunscreens are most widely used, and they are highly effective in preventing sunburn. Their major disadvantage is that they can stain clothing yellow or brown, and they sometimes cause skin reactions, especially if you are taking certain medications.

Sunscreens are classified according to a "sun protection factor," or SPF, which is a measure of the sunscreen's effectiveness in protecting against sunburn. SPF numbers range from two to fifteen—the higher the number the greater the protection.

People with skin types one and two (most susceptible to sunburn) should use a sunscreen with the highest SPF number. Some examples of products commercially available are Pre-Sun 15, Supershade 15, Pabanol, Total Eclipse, and Piz Buin Exclusive. People with skin types three and four should use a sunscreen with a SPF number in the range of four to eight (there are many available). People with skin types five and six will be adequately protected with lower SPF sunscreens.

Sunscreens and tanning creams work by protecting the skin from the ultraviolet rays of the sun. While they help prevent sunburn, they do not promote tanning—a myth propagated by advertising. Sunscreens allow you to spend more time outdoors with less risk of sunburn. Many of these preparations are easily washed off, so they should be reapplied if you swim or are perspiring heavily.

There are additional ways to protect yourself from overexposure to the sun. While traveling, try to avoid outdoor activities between 10:00 A.M. and 2:00 P.M., when the sun is at its brightest. When you do plan to be out in the sun for extended periods of time, wear a hat and long sleeves. Good sunglasses will protect your eyes.

If you want a tan, the only way to tan is to go slow.

Start with ten to fifteen minutes of sun on each side in the early morning and again in the late afternoon. Then increase your tanning time by about five minutes each day.

If you overdo it and begin to burn, you are almost forced to stay out of the sun to avoid further burning. If you must venture outdoors again during the day, cover yourself with clothing and protect exposed skin areas with a reflecting sunscreen like zinc oxide.

Be aware that sand, snow, and concrete surfaces will reflect ultraviolet rays onto parts of the skin that may be unprotected by suntan and sunscreens. And be aware that ultraviolet rays are particularly intense at high altitudes, even on cloudy days.

Certain drugs can make you more susceptible to sunburn. The antibiotics tetracycline, doxycycline, and the sulfa-type antibiotics such as Bactrim and Septra, which are often used by travelers for the prevention and treatment of travelers' diarrhea, can sensitize the skin and increase the risk of sunburn. Other drugs, such as the thiazide-type of diuretics, can also act in this way. If you are taking any of these drugs or plan to use them on your trip, consult with your physician about the possible increased risk of sunburn. When you are taking these drugs, you should protect your skin with a high-SPF sunscreen. But use a screen other than PABA, as this compound may interact with medications and further increase your risk of a reaction to the sun.

## Treatment of Sunburn

- The most important step in treating sunburn is to avoid additional exposure to the sun. Further exposure can lead to severe second-degree burns that require medical attention. So, if you become sunburned, read a good book or write long letters home, but stay out of the sun!

- Sunburned skin should be cooled with wet compresses or a cool bath. Liberal amounts of moisturizing lotions, such as Calamine, should be frequently applied.
- Aspirin is effective in relieving the pain and inflammation of burned skin. An antihistamine drug, part of your medical kit, will help relieve the itching.
- Of course, the best treatment is prevention. Use a good sunscreen to protect yourself when out in the sun. Although you may end up with less of a tan, it will be better for your skin, and your vacation, too.

## THE HEAT

It is assumed that only mad dogs and Englishmen go out in the midday sun, but more than a few intrepid travelers have done so as well. If unaccustomed to hot and humid climates, unwary travelers can frequently develop heat-related problems. Knowing how to prevent these problems and how to stay healthy in the heat is an important part of traveling well.

### Heat Fatigue

Heat fatigue is the mildest manifestation of overexposure to the heat. As in other heat-related illnesses, heat fatigue is caused by the loss of body fluid through perspiration. The result is mild dehydration and a feeling of weakness and tiredness. Heat fatigue should be recognized and remedied promptly. If it is not, more serious heat-related problems are likely to follow. When you begin to feel rundown and tired while outdoors in the heat, stop to rest and drink plenty of fluids before going on.

## Heat Cramps

Heat cramps are painful muscle spasms that usually occur in the abdomen and legs. Heat cramps are also caused by loss of body fluids, and they usually occur following vigorous physical exercise. Avoiding strenuous activities during the first few days of travel in a warm climate will help prevent this problem. Treatment consists of rest and drinking fluids.

## Heat Exhaustion

Heat exhaustion is a common problem in the tropics, especially among newly arrived travelers who have not had time to adapt to the warm climate. Victims of heat exhaustion usually sweat profusely and have lost a large amount of body fluid. If this condition is ignored and goes untreated, it can lead to a life-threatening heatstroke.

Recognize and treat heat exhaustion early. Its symptoms include weakness, nausea, vomiting, dizziness, and headache. When symptoms occur, immediately stop to rest in a shaded area, drink plenty of fluids (especially fruit juices), and wait for the symptoms to pass before going on.

## Heatstroke (Sunstroke)

Heatstroke, the most serious consequence of overexposure to the heat, is a true medical emergency. It often follows on the heels of heat exhaustion, after the body has lost so much fluid that it can no longer cool itself. Body temperature soars, and collapse is imminent.

Symptoms of an impending heatstroke include: gooseflesh, chills, headache, rapid breathing, nausea, vomiting, and a staggering gait. Additional symptoms, which indicate brain involvement, begin with slurred and incoherent speech and progress to delirium and eventual coma. Because the body is so depleted of fluid, sweating is often absent, and the skin is dry. (Physically conditioned people, such as athletes and runners, may continue to perspire even though they are in danger of heatstroke.)

Anybody exposed to the heat long enough may develop heatstroke. People who may be at increased risk are elderly travelers, people who have previously suffered from a heatstroke, and people suffering from other illnesses (colds, flu, and travelers' diarrhea will weaken your resistance to the heat). In addition, certain medicines can increase the likelihood of a heatstroke; important ones are scopolamine (for preventing motion sickness), tranquilizers, and antidepressants.

If you recognize symptoms of an impending heatstroke, either in yourself or in a traveling companion, medical attention should be obtained as soon as possible. In the meantime, measures to cool the victim should be started promptly. First, move the victim out of the sun. Fan the victim while sprinkling him with cool water, or wrap him in wet sheets. If ice is available, place ice packs around the neck, on the stomach, under the arms, and around the groin. Your prompt treatment of heatstroke may very well save a life.

## Preventing Heat-Related Illness

Acclimatization is the key to the prevention of the heat-related illnesses—heat fatigue, cramps, exhaustion, and stroke. To acclimatize, your body needs plenty of time to adjust to being in a warmer climate. Attempting to do too much too soon outdoors in the heat is what usually leads to heat-related problems. To protect yourself, take it easy, and avoid strenuous physical activity during the first few days of your trip. Plan your sightseeing so you will not be out in the midday sun. It takes anywhere from five to ten days for your body to naturally adapt to a warmer climate.

While traveling in the heat, especially early in your journey, replacing the fluids lost through perspiration is essential to staying healthy. Drink fruit juices and plenty of water several times during each day. Don't rely on your thirst to tell you when and how much to drink—it is an insensitive indicator of fluid loss. Instead, drink plenty of fluids even when you're not thirsty.

Salt tablets are no longer recommended for the average traveler. They can actually increase the dangers of heat exposure, especially if they are taken without an adequate amount of water. A safer way to replace needed body nutrients is to rely on eating well-balanced meals. Since fatigue can also make heat-related problems more likely, a good night's sleep each night is also important to staying healthy in the heat. English or not, nobody who is tired and hungry should venture out into the midday sun.

## Prickly Heat

Prickly heat is a common annoyance in hot and humid climates. It is a result of excessive perspiration, which causes the skin to become soggy and its pores to become plugged. Where two parts of the body rub together, redness and irritation result. Keeping your skin cool, clean, and dry is the best prevention. Small amounts of talcum powder applied daily may help. Cotton underwear, because it will keep your skin drier, is recommended in warmer climates.

## Ankle Swelling in the Heat

When traveling in warmer climates you may notice some swelling of your ankles. For people who are otherwise healthy, this is not serious, and the swelling usually disappears in a few days. Heat-related ankle swelling occurs more frequently in women than in men. For people with chronic heart and kidney problems, however, ankle swelling can mean retention of fluids, and an adjustment in medication may be needed.

## THE COLD

Cold weather presents serious health risks for travelers who are unprepared for it or caught unexpectedly in it. Hypothermia and frostbite are the two most dangerous conditions you might encounter while traveling in the cold, and you should know how to prevent both of them before heading out on your own frozen road.

For centuries, alcohol has been touted as a safeguard against the cold. A Saint Bernard bounding through the snow, a brandy flask hanging from its collar, going to the rescue of a stranded traveler is a vivid image to many of us. Unfortunately, the use of spirits in the cold can no longer be recommended. Alcohol is now known to actually make you more susceptible to hypothermia and frostbite because it increases the amount of heat you lose. Save your brandy until you can enjoy it safely next to the warmth of a fire.

### Hypothermia

Hypothermia means low temperature, and it is a dangerous medical condition that occurs when the body temperature falls below normal due to overexposure to the cold. If hypothermia goes untreated and is allowed to progress, it will ultimately be fatal.

Shivering is an early sign of hypothermia, and you should consider it a warning that you need to find shelter from the cold. A more serious sign of impending hypothermia is inappropriate behavior. Victims of overexposure may disregard the cold; they may even say they feel warm and may begin to undress. Later, they may act and appear as though they are intoxicated; slurred speech is soon followed by sleepiness and fatigue. Eventually the victim will be unable to move, and his life will be in extreme danger.

Hypothermia is best treated by preventing it from happening. Make sure you are well prepared to protect yourself before traveling in a cold climate. If you are traveling by motor vehicle, be prepared in case the vehicle breaks down and leaves you stranded.

To protect yourself from the cold, you need the proper clothing. Clothing should be made from dry, lightweight natural fibers. Wool is the best material because it retains much of its insulating ability even when it's wet. All cold weather travelers should pack at least one wool shirt. Clothing made from the newer synthetic materials—such as Thinsulate and Gortex—are also effective. By wearing several layers of clothing, you get the best insulation, and you can add or remove layers as you need them. If clothing becomes wet, it should be changed as soon as possible.

It is important to adequately protect your head and hands from the cold. Approximately one third of your body's heat loss can occur from your head alone. Make sure that you eat properly, and avoid becoming too tired. Both hunger and exhaustion make you more vulnerable to the cold.

Once hypothermia occurs, the treatment is to rewarm the victim, and medical attention should be obtained immediately. Warm the victim by placing him, clothes and all, in a tub of warm water. If you are stranded outdoors, find shelter and protect the victim from the wind. Replace wet clothing with dry. You may save a life by climbing into a sleeping bag with the victim and sharing your body heat. If he is conscious, feed him warm and sweetened drinks (remember, no alcohol!) and keep him as active as possible. The key is to do everything possible to warm the victim as quickly as possible.

## Frostbite

Frostbite occurs when the skin becomes frozen. It is a frequent hazard for travelers in cold climates. Frozen skin turns white and hard, and it feels numb. Areas of the body likely to be affected include the nose, ears, cheeks, fingers, and toes. Preventing frostbite, and knowing how to treat it when it occurs, is important for every traveler who wants to stay healthy in the cold.

It does not have to be intensely cold for frostbite to occur. The combined effect of wind and cold is more dangerous than just cold temperatures alone. People who are wet and exhausted, who are intoxicated with alcohol, or who have previously suffered from frostbite are the most susceptible. Skin can be frozen quickly by contact with cold metal or solvents like gasoline.

To prevent frostbite, you need to keep your entire body warm. Adequate protection for your head, hands, and feet is just as important as a warm parka. Exposed skin should be protected from the wind and from contact with cold objects. Clothing should be kept dry, and it should be loose-fitting. Your hands and feet are more likely to be frostbitten if the circulation to these areas is reduced by tight-fitting clothing. Carry an extra pair of socks and mittens in case the ones you are wearing become wet.

In order to prevent serious and permanent injury, learn to detect frostbite early. Periodically, stop and check yourself and your companions for patches of skin that are turning white. Hands and feet that are beginning to feel numb should be treated immediately, before deep frostbite sets in. Severe frostbite can lead to gangrene and the loss of fingers and toes.

**Treating Frostbite.** The treatment of frostbite consists of rewarming frozen skin. But rewarming should be undertaken cautiously, in order prevent additional damage. Never rub frostbitten patches of skin with your hands or with snow—this causes further damage. Early frostbite, sometimes called frostnip, can be safely treated by applying gentle pressure (not rubbing) with a warm hand to the affected area, or by gently blowing on it through cupped hands. Warming should be continued until the color of the skin returns to normal. Numb hands and feet should be rewarmed before they become frozen. If you are caught outdoors and have no other source of heat available, your hands and feet can be rewarmed by placing them under the parka and against the skin of a companion.

Deep frostbite, where part of the body is entirely frozen, should also be treated cautiously. A cardinal rule of traveling in the cold is: A frozen area should not be thawed if there is any possibility of its being refrozen later. Thawing followed by refreezing can result in much more damage than freezing alone—damage that could result in the loss of a hand or foot. It is safer to leave a finger or foot frozen while you are trying to find shelter.

When shelter has been located, frozen skin should be rewarmed in a bath of lukewarm water. After twenty or thirty minutes, a pink flush should return to the skin, followed by intense pain. Once a frozen part is thawed, it must be protected from the cold, and expert medical attention by a doctor must be provided immediately.

## Chilblains

Chilblains, also called windburn, is a mild cold injury. It is caused when dry skin is exposed to temperatures that can range anywhere from fifty degrees Fahrenheit down to freezing. Skin exposed to the cool air can become red and slightly swollen, and it may burn and itch. The treatment of chilblains is to moisten the involved skin with an ointment like petroleum jelly and protect the area from further exposure to the cold.

## THE ALTITUDE

Traveling in the mountains is exhilarating: crisp, clean air and panoramic vistas no camera can ever capture. You can make the journey from your home to an alpine destination in just a few hours. Such ready access to high-altitude travel does not allow your body time to acclimate itself, and health problems can result.

### Acute Mountain Sickness

Acute mountain sickness, or AMS, is a common hazard for travelers, especially those making a rapid ascent to elevations of 8,000 feet or more. AMS rarely occurs at altitudes below that level. AMS feels much like having the flu. Headache, weakness, nausea, decreased appetite, insomnia, and lack of energy are common. These symptoms are usually mild and pass in a few days. Occasionally, the mountain sickness can be severe enough to be life-threatening, unless precautions are taken.

The most effective way of preventing AMS is to make your ascent to high altitude slowly. Pausing for a couple of days between 5,000 and 7,000 feet will allow time for acclimatization, but pausing for a few days is not always practical for travelers on short vacations. It is interesting to note that physical conditioning will not prevent this problem. In fact, physically fit people are sometimes more susceptible to AMS than their less conditioned counterparts. People who have previously experienced AMS are more likely to experience it again.

To prevent a mild case of AMS from becoming serious, do not ascend higher until the symptoms have entirely passed. Take it easy for the first few days after arriving at your destination. Avoid strenuous exercise. On skiing vacations, don't push yourself early in your trip. Avoid tranquilizing and sedative drugs, as they prolong the period needed for acclimatization.

Acetazolamide (Diamox) is a medicine that is effective in preventing or reducing the symptoms of AMS. Prescribed by a physician, it can be taken once at nighttime, or up to three times a day, depending on the degree of protection required, for the first three days while your body acclimates. This can often be a very effective way of preventing AMS for people who must ascend rapidly.

## HAPE—High Altitude Pulmonary Edema

HAPE is a life-threatening illness that occurs in unacclimatized people making a rapid ascent to altitudes over 8,000 feet. Symptoms usually occur twenty-four to sixty hours after ascent, and they consist of shortness of breath, rapid pulse, confusion, nausea, vomiting, and irrational behavior.

HAPE is caused by the air sacs of the lungs filling with fluid. Treatment requires immediate descent to a lower altitude. Oxygen should be administered if available, and medical attention should be promptly sought. If you are ever in doubt over how severe the symptoms are in yourself, or in a companion, assume the worst and descend.

## Conjunctival Hemorrhage

An alarming but seldom serious problem that occurs at high altitude is the rupture of small blood vessels under the surface of the eyeball. Caused by overexertion in the thin air, the condition results in a flame-shaped hemorrhage across the eyeball. People are often not even aware of it unless someone else notices it. The hemorrhage will fade without treatment. Only if vision begins to blur do you need to seek medical help.

# 13

## Stings and Bites

Travel introduces us to many new and unfamiliar forms of life—in addition to tour operators and customs agents. Most members of the animal kingdom are docile and prefer to be left alone and unbothered. But there are notable exceptions, and it is these exceptions that tend to bite and sting. Knowing what they are and how to avoid them is an important way to stay healthy abroad.

### ALONG THE BEACH

Most stinging injuries that occur along the beach are the result of accidental encounters. Sea creatures prefer not to mix with the tourists. But when an encounter does occur—usually through no fault of their own—nature has endowed several sea creatures with a means of self-defense. They will fight back with a sting if provoked.

### Corals

The enchanting undersea world along a coral reef lures travelers by the score. Many people don't realize that coral is a living organism, ready to defend itself from invading insurance salesmen from Omaha. A frequent result of these close encounters is coral poisoning.

Sea coral has a sharp outer skeleton that can readily cut, and it is able to inject a weak venom into the resulting wound. The injured skin around the wound becomes red and irritated; welts may appear, along with a burning sensation. This is coral poisoning, and it is unwise to ignore even a mild case of it. Without the proper care, the wound can become infected and ulcerated in a short while.

All coral wounds and abrasions should be immediately and thoroughly cleaned with soap and water. After washing, an antibiotic ointment or tincture of iodine should be applied. The itching can be relieved by applying a steroid ointment (all of these medicines should be part of your medical kit). Nurse the wound carefully. If it shows any signs of infection—increased reddening, oozing, or ulceration—antibiotics may be required and medical attention should be obtained.

## Sea Urchins

Sea urchins are small, spiny creatures that are often found washed up onto the beach and are especially common in the Caribbean. They can cause problems for dreamy beachcombers who stop to pick one up. Sharp, brittle spines readily puncture the skin and then just as readily break off, leaving a fragment of the spine buried beneath the skin.

A broken sea urchin spine beneath the skin may take several days to make itself known. The area will slowly become painful and irritated. Removing the fragment of spine is often difficult, and it is often better to leave it in place. You can try to get it to dissolve under the skin by alternately soaking the area in hot and cold water. If it causes great pain, or shows signs of infection, medical attention should be obtained.

## Cone Shells

Cone shells are one of nature's booby traps, and they have taken a lot of unsuspecting beachcombers by surprise. Their attractive, multicolored shells look like great souvenirs, but when they are picked up or stepped on, they suddenly sting and inject a potent venom. If the injured area begins to burn and then turn numb, medical attention should be obtained. Cone shells are found along beaches and in shallow water in Hawaii, Mexico, and California.

## Stinging Tentacles

The Portuguese man-of-war and its close relative, the jellyfish, are notable for their long, filamentous tentacles. The tentacles are notable because they can sting and inject a potent venom. These stings are rarely life-threatening (except for the deadly Chrone jellyfish of Australia), but the pain they cause can be excruciating. Stings usually occur when swimmers inadvertently brush up against the tentacles in the water or beach strollers inadvertently step on tentacles that have been washed ashore.

Immediate treatment of a sting is to remove the tentacles—carefully. Use anything but your hands: a stick, seaweed, or clothing. As soon as possible, rinse the wound with formaldehyde (there is a remote chance a bottle is around), alcohol (undoubtably a bottle is around), vinegar, or ammonia. Do not rinse the wound with fresh water. This may result in the release of even more venom. Medical attention should be obtained for further treatment.

## Stingrays

Called the devilfish and the demon-of-the-sea, stingrays are actually timid creatures that like nothing better than to bury themselves in the sand in the shallow waters along the Pacific, Atlantic, and Gulf coasts. Problems arise when unsuspecting swimmers step on them. In a defensive action, the startled stingray strikes out with its barbed tail and injects a potent venom. The barbed tail is strong enough to inflict a severe wound, and the venom is powerful enough to cause nausea, vomiting, weakness, muscle cramps, and fever.

The first thing to do after a stingray attack is to get back to shore. Irrigate the wound with the coldest water available. If possible, apply a tourniquet above the wound to prevent the spread of venom. If the spine is still present, carefully extract it. After irrigating with cold water and removing the spine, wash the wound with hot water until the pain has stopped. Medical attention should be obtained as soon as possible.

## SPIDERS AND SNAKES

Just thinking about spiders and snakes is enough to keep timid travelers at home. But, in fact, of all the thousands of types of spiders and snakes, very few are dangerous enough to even be considered a risk to your health. Even though they are unloved and generally disdained, spiders and snakes are gentle and docile creatures. And, if you manage to stay out of their way, they will almost certainly stay out of yours.

### Black Widow Spider

The infamous black widow spider can be found worldwide, both in tropical and temperate regions. These spiders prefer dry, dimly lit areas and are often seen hanging around houses and outhouses. They are not hard to recognize, with their shiny black bodies and the famous red hourglass pattern on their undersides.

The black widow spider is a passive creature, and it

will not bite unless it is provoked or disturbed. The bite feels like a pinprick, and it is followed by a dull, cramping pain that begins in about fifteen minutes and later may spread throughout the body. Muscles may go into spasms, and restlessness and anxiety are common reactions. Ice packs placed over the site of the bite will reduce the pain. Although healthy adults will completely recover within a day, it is wise to seek medical attention.

## Brown Recluse Spider

The brown recluse spider is found in Mexico and South America, and it is a well-known inhabitant of the southern United States. It is a small, brown creature with a characteristic black violin marking on its back. It likes to live indoors and is frequently found in laundry and bedding.

This is also a passive and timid spider, and most bites are the result of accidental encounters. Its bite is very mild and may even be overlooked. But, after an hour or two, the skin becomes reddened, and a small bleb, or blister, appears. The bleb slowly enlarges and eventually ruptures, leaving a large and moist crater in the skin referred to as a "volcano lesion." The following day, a mild fever, skin rash, and joint pains may develop. The volcano lesion should be treated by applying an antibiotic ointment, and medical attention should be obtained.

## Scorpion

Scorpions are widespread in warm regions throughout the world. Most North American stings are relatively harmless, but a species of scorpion living in Mexico and the extreme southwestern United States carries a potent venom. Besides causing pain and muscle cramps, this venom can produce a generalized paralysis. An antidote is available in Mexico. Medical attention should be obtained after a sting.

## Tarantula

The much dreaded tarantula is a nocturnal creature that has to be provoked into attacking, and it rarely bites humans. The bite feels like a small pinprick, is usually not toxic, and reactions are rare. There is a Central American species of tarantula that carries a more potent venom, and if it bites, medical attention should be obtained.

## Snakes

In spite of your deepest fears of snakes, they are not hiding along walkways or hanging from trees waiting to ambush you. Regardless of where you travel, the chances are remote that you will even see a snake, much less be bitten by one.

Nonetheless, there are poisonous snakes in the world, and a few precautions are in order. Snakes will strike as a defensive reaction. They are most active at night, and if you are bitten, it is probably because you were walking around in the dark and stepped on one. So the key to avoid snake bites is to watch where you are going, especially at night. Wear high boots, and use a flashlight when walking outdoors in the dark. In the morning, check your clothes and shoes before putting them on, as some snakes have a fondness for camping in them overnight.

If you or a member of your party is bitten by a snake, your first concern should be whether or not the snake was poisonous. Often this is difficult to determine, because the snake may not even have been seen. If the snake is still present, kill it and save it for identification.

After the bite, lay the victim down, and try to keep him as relaxed as possible. The anxiety associated with being bitten can mimic the symptoms of a toxic bite—weakness, sweating, and fainting. Do not try to cut the wound and suck out the venom. Instead, concentrate on locating medical help.

If you plan to visit a rural area where poisonous snakes are known to exist, learn what types are around and how to identify them. Snakebite kits are available, and one should be carried into remote regions with little access to medical care. Specially constructed snake boots are available; they protect against snakebite and should be worn by travelers into remote regions where poisonous snakes abound. But, for most travelers, it is unlikely you will ever be bitten, if you use common sense and watch your step.

## INSECTS

In addition to being a nuisance, insects can transmit serious disease. In tropical regions of the world, mosquitoes transmit diseases such as malaria, yellow fever, dengue fever, and encephalitis. The tsetse fly transmits sleeping sickness, and the reduviid bug can cause Chagas' disease. Knowing how to protect yourself from biting insects will not only make your nights more restful, but help keep you healthy as well. Guidelines on protecting yourself from the mosquito and the reduviid bug are discussed in chapter 9. Though less of a serious health risk, other insects can also be sources of problems for travelers.

### Chiggers

Chiggers are small insects that live in sandy soil all over the world. If a pregnant chigger comes into contact with your skin, it will burrow itself inside to lay its eggs. An irritating rash develops, usually located on the feet. The best prevention is to avoid walking barefoot on sandy soil.

Always use some type of footwear, and always use a blanket or a mat when lying on the beach.

## Bedbugs, Fleas, and Lice

By staying in different rooms night after night, travelers eventually are introduced to bedbugs, fleas, and lice. When you have stayed in the wrong room, it becomes obvious soon enough. Suspect bedbugs or fleas when you awaken in the morning and find yourself covered with small bites. Take a hot shower, wash your clothes, and find a new room. Lice can infect any part of the body, but most commonly are found on the scalp and in the groin area. They make themselves known by the itching they cause, and if you look closely you can identify their crablike shapes or the bundles of eggs, called nits, they leave on shafts of hair. Special lotions and shampoos that are able to take care of this problem are available in drugstores.

## Allergy to Stings

Stings from bees, wasps, and hornets are not only painful; they can cause allergic reactions in many travelers. Stings normally produce pain and redness at the site of the sting; stings in allergic individuals can produce serious and life-threatening reactions.

An allergic reaction to a sting often begins as unusual swelling around the site of the sting—an entire hand, arm, or side of the face can become swollen. Hives often break out over the entire body. Wheezing and progressive difficulty breathing may follow. Severe allergic reactions lead to shock and collapse.

Travelers who are allergic to insect stings should be prepared to treat themselves at all times. There is often little time to find medical help. Special allergy-treatment kits (Ana-Kit and others), which contain antihistamine tablets, injectable epinephrine, and instructions for their use, can be prescribed by your physician. EpiPen, a pen-size epinephrine auto-injecter, also available by prescription, is a convenient way for travelers to carry this life-saving drug.

At the first sign of an allergic reaction, one or two tablets of an antihistamine medication (also a part of your traveler's medical kit) should be taken. If wheezing, difficult breathing, or faintness occur, epinephrine should be injected immediately. Allergic reactions are true emergencies, and medical attention should be obtained as soon as possible.

# IV

# Health Problems
# During Travel

# 14

# Common Health Problems

Your health is the most important asset you bring with you when you leave home. To protect this asset, you need to know how to avoid some of the common hazards travelers encounter abroad as well as take care of the common health problems that might arise.

## ACCIDENTS

Accidents are the leading cause of serious injury and disability among travelers. In foreign surroundings, all types of accidents—fire, electrical, drug, and water—are more likely to occur. By being prepared for them, you can help prevent them.

### Fire Safety

Hotel fires are of significant concern to many travelers. The fire safety regulations currently in effect in the United States do not exist everywhere. In fact, fire safety is an unfamiliar concept in most parts of the world. So you will need to protect yourself with your own fire safety precautions while you are traveling abroad.

When checking into a hotel, ask the desk clerk or the hotel manager about their fire alarm system, and ask them what the alarm sounds like. Their reaction to your request should tell you a lot about the hotel staff's attitude toward fire protection. If you are rebuffed, I would suggest finding another hotel.

After checking into your room, go back into the hall and locate the nearest exit—remember that elevators should not be used during a fire. Make a mental map of the exit route from your room. Inspect the windows and vents in your room to make sure they are functional. Keep your room key in a familiar place, so that you can locate it quickly if you want to leave in a hurry. You want your room key with you, in case your exit route is blocked, and you need to get back into your room.

If the hotel does not have a fire escape, you should question whether or not it is safe to stay there. You can carry your own means of escape by packing a forty-foot length of one-half- to three-quarter-inch hemp rope that is knotted every two feet. Tied to a bed or a radiator, it will provide a means of escape from most third- or fourth-floor rooms.

Smoke detectors have proven to be life-saving, and portable ones are now available for travelers. General Electric's Home and Away Smoke Alarm is battery-operated and designed to be hooked over the door of a hotel room. The Criterion Watch Company makes a battery-operated smoke detector that is built into a travel alarm clock. Both items can be found in department and hardware stores.

Before you leave on your trip, you should brief yourself on what to do if caught in a hotel fire. A free booklet titled, appropriately, "What Do You Do If Caught in a Fire?" is available from the National Fire Prevention Association, Batterymarch Park, Quincy, MA 02269. Write for it—it could save your life.

## Electrical Safety

Another common hazard for travelers is injury from electrical shocks. Check your hotel rooms for faulty electrical cords and exposed wiring. Remember that children may crawl under tables and into areas you can't readily see. So get down on your hands and knees, and look for possible trouble spots.

## Drug Safety

Drug accidents are a surprisingly common cause of injury among travelers. Many potent drugs are available overseas without a physician's prescription, and restrictions on the sale of dangerous drugs often do not exist. Using unfamiliar medicines or combining different medicines can lead to serious drug reactions. An important part of your pre-trip health planning should be determining which medicines you will need, or might need, on your journey. Discuss them with your physician, learn about potential side effects, and bring all the medicine you need with you from home.

The great hazard of buying street drugs should be obvious to everyone. A traveler abroad faces significant health and legal risks when considering the use of illicit drugs. Many street drugs are adulterated with toxic chemicals like strychnine, and they are then sold through the veil of a language barrier to unwary travelers. Travel is challenging and exciting in itself; if you need an artificial high, you are better off staying home.

## Safe Swimming

Every traveler who packs a swim suit should be concerned about water safety. Water accidents and drownings are a greater risk in unfamiliar waters than they are at home. Before swimming on your trip, check into local swimming conditions, and inquire about currents, undertows, and other hazards.

Freshwater swimming in foreign countries carries the risk of waterborne infections. Local sewage control may be poorly managed or nonexistent, and exposure to contaminated water can result in eye, ear, and intestinal infections. Only properly chlorinated pools can ever be assumed to be safe places to swim. Inquire into the safety of all other swimming areas before taking that first plunge.

Tropical freshwater streams, pools, and lakes also carry the risk of schistosomiasis (bilharziasis). Swimming, wading, and washing in infected waters must be avoided. Schistosomiasis is discussed in chapter 9.

Swimming in the sea carries less risk of infection, unless the beach is polluted by local sewage or industrial waste (as some popular Mediterranean beaches are). The beaches at large tourist resort areas usually are clean, but even there you shouldn't take water safety for granted. Find out for yourself by checking into local conditions when you arrive.

## Poisoning

Accidents due to poisoning occur from the ingestion of toxic substances and from overdosing on certain medicines. You can reduce the likelihood of poisoning accidents by keeping all toxic materials and all medicines in their original, labeled containers and by keeping them out of the reach of children. When poisoning occurs, immediate medical attention is necessary. Head for the nearest hospital emergency room, and bring a sample of the poison or its container with you.

When medical help is not immediately available, emergency first aid should be applied. Vomiting should be induced for poisonings that occur with substances other than acids, alkalais, or petroleum products—read the label on the container. Vomiting can be induced by either sticking your finger down the back of the victim's throat (making sure his head is down to prevent choking) or by administering syrup of ipecac—one tablespoon for children, two for adults, followed by several glasses of water. Syrup of ipecac should be part of your medical kit when traveling with children, and its use should be reviewed with your physician.

Vomiting should not be induced following the ingestion of toxic substances that contain either acids, alkalais, or petroleum products, because these caustic agents cause severe internal burning on the way up as well as on the way down. They should be treated instead by having the victim drink milk or water to dilute the poison. Medical attention should be obtained as soon as possible.

## COMMON ILLNESSES

Any health problem that can happen at home can happen abroad. From sore throats to athlete's foot, you can encounter a whole array of common illnesses and injuries. Since you are on your own abroad, knowing how to manage these problems yourself and when to turn for help is an important part of traveling well.

### Colds

Colds are common among travelers because they are exposed to many different strains of the cold virus. The familiar symptoms of headache, nasal congestion, sore throat, cough, and muscle aches usually resolve themselves in three to five days. Antibiotics are not necessary and not recommended for treating the common cold. Treatment should consist of rest, fluids, aspirin or acetaminophen (paracetamol overseas) for pain and fever, and an antihistamine or a decongestant cold preparation.

Complications of colds such as ear pain, worsening cough, shaking chills, or high fever should be medically evaluated. During the first few days of a cold, you should try to postpone air flight, to avoid the problems of barotitis and barosinusitis (discussed in chapter 6).

## Sore Throat

Sore throats are most commonly caused by cold viruses, especially when they are accompanied by a stuffy or runny nose. In this case, the sore throat will resolve as the virus runs its course. In the meantime, cold liquids, aspirin or acetaminophen, and diluted saltwater gargles will help relieve the discomfort. A severe sore throat associated with a fever, especially in children, may indicate a strep throat. The throat should be examined by a physician.

## Fever

Fever is a common problem during travel and is usually due to viral infections associated with colds, flu, sore throats, or earaches. Travelers' diarrhea is also a frequent cause of fever. A fever can also signify a more serious infection, and it is important to know when you should seek a medical evaluation.

A thermometer is essential for diagnosing a fever, and a good medical thermometer in a strong protective case should be part of your medical kit. Normal body temperature is 98.6 degrees Fahrenheit (37 degrees Centigrade), and a mild elevation—99 to 100 degrees—may be a normal temperature elevation in response to a strenuous day of traveling. But it should start you thinking about a fever. A temperature above 100 degrees generally means a fever is present.

Not all fevers have to be treated. Many doctors feel that an elevated temperature is one of several ways the body fights off viral infections, and mild fevers (less than 101 degrees) associated with colds and flu may be best left to run their course. Yet, some fevers, especially in children, may be dangerous, and it is important to know when treatment might be necessary.

Children can develop fevers higher than 101 degrees even with mild viral infections. Temperatures higher than 102 degrees should be lowered by using aspirin, acetaminophen, and cool sponge baths if necessary. Medical attention should be obtained for fevers higher than 101 degrees that are associated with shaking chills or a stiff neck and for fevers that last longer than forty-eight hours.

## Ear Pain

Earaches are caused by a variety of ear problems. If the ear canal becomes inflamed, which can occur after swimming, it is called external otitis. There may be a small amount of discharge, and the outside of the ear becomes tender to the touch. Eardrops containing a combination of antibiotic and steroid is the usual treatment.

When ear pain is associated with dulled hearing and a sensation of fullness, a middle-ear infection, called otitis media, may be present. Otitis media is common in children and often follows a sore throat or a cold. When these symptoms occur, a physician should be consulted, because oral antibiotics may be necessary.

Ear pain can occur during air flight and is called barotitis media. It is the result of the change in air pressure as the plane descends for a landing, and it occurs when the Eustachian tube leading from the middle ear is blocked during colds, allergies, or sinus infections. Treatment of barotitis media is discussed in chapter 6.

Discharge from the ear, with or without ear pain, can also be the result of a variety of ear problems. Often it is due to a buildup of earwax and can be remedied by gentle irrigation with lukewarm water. Discharge from the ear may also be due to a condition called swimmer's ear, which is a form of external otitis resulting from swimming in contaminated water. A thick white or yellow discharge may be a sign of a ruptured eardrum, caused by an advanced middle-ear infection. Medical attention should be obtained whenever a discharge from the ear occurs.

## Cough

A persistent cough can be a troublesome and annoying symptom, especially when traveling away from home. Most coughs are due to viral infections, such as colds and flu, or to cigarette smoking. Viral infections will run their course, and the cough will resolve. Nobody who wants to stay healthy should smoke cigarettes, coughing or not.

Coughing is best treated by keeping the throat moist. This can be accomplished by frequent sips of liquids, cough lozenges, and room vaporizers. Cough medicines made with dextromethorphan, glycerol guaiacolate, and codeine are effective in suppressing a cough. Antihistamines, which are used in cold preparations to open nasal air passages, may actually make a cough worse by drying the throat.

Croup is a distinctive high-pitched cough that occurs in children. It is caused by a buildup of thick secretions in the throat during a viral infection. Breathing difficulty can develop. Mist is often an effective treatment, and placing your child in a bathroom while running a hot shower may relieve a croupy cough. But, if there is no improvement after twenty minutes of mist treatment, medical attention should be obtained.

## Headaches

The stress of traveling from one place to another is a common cause of headaches among travelers. A typical stress—or tension—headache is felt as a dull, steady pain over the eyes and at the back of the head and neck. Treatment is to slow down, rest, and try to relax. A long, hot shower and aspirin or acetaminophen will help.

A persistent or unusually severe headache, especially if it is associated with weakness or changes in vision, should receive a prompt evaluation by a physician.

## Nosebleeds

Nosebleeds can be caused by injury, vigorous nose-blowing, viruses, dry air, and nose-picking. They often can be treated by simply squeezing the nose between the thumb and forefinger below the hard bony ridge for ten minutes or more. While squeezing the nose in this fashion, it is better to lean forward with the head down, to prevent the blood from draining down the back of the throat. If several attempts at prolonged nose-squeezing do not control the bleeding, medical attention should be sought.

## Constipation

The disruption travel produces in our daily routine is a common cause of constipation among travelers. If you are prepared, constipation should not interfere with a single day of your travels. Bring along a laxative that you are familiar with—milk of magnesia or some other stimulant. If you chronically suffer from constipation, ask your physician for recommendations on how to treat yourself during your travels.

## Vaginal Discharge

This is a frequent problem among overseas travelers—especially among those taking antibiotics, like tetracycline, which can lead to a vaginal yeast infection. But a vaginal discharge may also represent venereal disease. It is more difficult to be evaluated overseas and often embarrassing, but it cannot wait.

# COMMON INJURIES

## Cuts

Knowing when a cut is serious enough to warrant medical attention is often difficult. You should immediately see a physician when

- a wound is obviously deep and the edges are gaping open. Proper healing will most likely require stitches, and foregoing medical attention will likely mean prolonged and delayed healing—if it heals at all—and scarring.
- bleeding from a wound cannot be stopped by applying firm and direct pressure for at least fifteen minutes.
- numbness occurs in the skin beyond the site of the wound; this may signify nerve injury.
- the victim is unable to move the fingers or toes of the limb that has been cut. This may signify nerve or ligament injury.
- there are signs of infection in a wound: pus, fever, or redness.
- you are unsure how serious a cut really is.

Minor cuts and scrapes should be treated by a thorough cleansing with soap and water. The edges of a minor cut can be pulled together with Steri-Strips—thin adhesive bandages that can be applied across the wound to hold the edges together.

## Punctures

Puncture wounds are produced by nails and other sharp pointed objects. They are a special problem because they are likely to become infected. The most important treatment is preventive: make sure that your tetanus vaccination is up-to-date. But on-the-spot treatment is also important if infections are to be prevented.

- Examine the wound carefully, to make sure nothing is left under the skin—splinters of wood or glass, for example. If you can remove remaining fragments easily, do so. Otherwise, get medical help.
- Allow puncture wounds to bleed. Do not apply pressure to stop bleeding unless the wound is pumping blood (a sign that an artery has been damaged). A slow, steady oozing of the blood will help cleanse the wound and prevent infection.
- Soak puncture wounds in warm water several times a day.
- Watch carefully for signs of infection: discharge of pus, redness around the wound, swelling, or fever. If an infection develops, medical attention should be sought immediately.
- Puncture wounds located on the hands are especially dangerous because a serious infection can readily develop among the intricate structures that make up the hand. To be safe, medical attention should be obtained.

## Burns

A superficial burn that produces redness (like a sunburn) is a first-degree burn. A burn that produces blistering is a second-degree burn. A burn that destroys several layers of skin is a third-degree burn.

All burns should be treated with cold water and ice to prevent further injury. First-degree burns are usually not dangerous, and aspirin to reduce the pain is the only treatment necessary. Large second-degree and all third-degree burns should be evaluated by a physician immediately.

## Animal Bites

Animal bites present two problems: puncture wounds and a concern about rabies. Puncture wounds from bites should be thoroughly cleaned and treated as indicated above. Animals that may be infected by rabies are skunks, foxes, raccoons, opossums, dogs, and cats. Rabies is unlikely in squirrels, chipmunks, rats, and mice. An unprovoked attack by an animal is an indication that it may harbor rabies and raises the question of whether rabies treatment should be instituted. Authorities should be notified, and the animal should be captured. Medical attention should be obtained.

## Ankle Injuries

Abruptly twisting or turning the foot can cause injury to the ligaments in the ankle. A strain occurs when these ligaments are stretched; a sprain occurs when the ligament is partially torn and the ankle swells. Fractures in the ankle are uncommon in walking or running injuries.

Pain in the ankle following an injury should guide your behavior. If it hurts, do not walk on it. Walking on an injured ankle will not only delay healing, it can also increase the size of a tear in the ligament. During the first twenty-four to forty-eight hours, pack the ankle in ice, and keep it elevated. This will reduce the swelling. After two or three days, if the pain is decreased, cautiously try walking again. If the pain returns, stop walking, and seek medical help.

## Knee Injuries

Knee sprains are produced by sudden twisting or bending and result in tenderness and swelling in the joint. Severe trauma to the knee may tear an internal ligament or cartilage. Such injuries produce marked swelling, and "joint-locking" may occur. If the integrity of the joint is disrupted, the knee may suddenly give way while walking.

Knee injuries are treated by weight-bearing restrictions. Only absolutely necessary walking is allowed. Kneeling, squatting, and climbing stairs should be entirely avoided. Aspirin can be very helpful in reducing pain and swelling, and it should be taken regularly every four to six hours. If the pain and swelling subside after a few days of rest, cautious weight-bearing should be tried. If pain returns, or the joint locks or gives way, prompt medical attention should be obtained.

## SKIN PROBLEMS

### Poison Ivy and Poison Oak

The rash caused by contact with poison ivy or poison oak is a familiar problem to anyone who spends time outdoors. These plants contain a resin that produces a dermatitis characterized by burning, itching, redness, and blistering. The resin is easily spread to other parts of the body by your hands. The best prevention is to learn how to recognize the plants and then avoid them—leaves of three, let it be.

Treatment of the dermatitis caused by poison ivy or poison oak starts with a thorough washing with soap and water to remove the resin. A hot bath or shower will bring temporary relief from the burning and itching. Additional effective treatments are:

- aspirin, which is effective in reducing the burning and itching.
- cool, moist compresses applied to blistered areas of skin. If the rash is widespread, an oatmeal bath (one cup of oatmeal to a full tub of water) will relieve burning and itching.
- steroid creams, which are effective in treating dermatitis. They take several hours to work, but they can dramatically hasten recovery.
- antihistamine drugs to relieve itching. They are a useful way to get a good night's sleep when you are being tortured by itching.

If the rash involves over half of the body, or is dangerously close to the eyes, medical attention should be obtained.

## Boils

Boils are localized skin infections caused by *Staphylococcus* bacteria. They may be single or multiple, pea-sized or golfball-sized. They begin as an area of red and tender skin, and they slowly enlarge until they begin to "point." They eventually rupture and drain. No boil should be squeezed before its time or the infection may be spread to surrounding tissue. Instead, warm, moist compresses should be applied several times a day, until the boil ruptures on its own. If it is extremely painful, or the surrounding skin is becoming red and inflamed, medical attention should be obtained.

## Athlete's Foot

Athlete's foot is a fungal infection of the feet and toenails that is difficult to cure. Flare-ups of athlete's foot occur frequently in travelers who wear the same pair of shoes day after day. The best treatment is good foot hygiene. Wash your feet daily with soap and water; dry carefully; use foot powder to keep your feet dry; and use fresh socks. Antifungal ointments and sprays are available in drugstores and may help quiet a flare-up, but they are unlikely to produce a permanent cure.

## Jock Itch

Jock itch is fungal infection that affects the skin in the groin. It is caused by moisture and friction on the skin, and it commonly occurs in active travelers in warm climates. Treatment is to relieve the friction and moisture. Loose-fitting undergarments should be worn, and powder should be applied to the groin after bathing. It may take as long as two weeks to clear.

## Scabies

Scabies is a contagious infection caused by a tiny mite that is widespread throughout the world. It commonly affects travelers who have stayed in inexpensive lodgings, but infections can be picked up almost anywhere. The rash begins as an itching eruption that usually involves the skin between the fingers, on the wrists, armpits, waist, and buttocks. Several antiscabies preparations are available in drugstores, and clothes and bedding should be washed when treatment is applied.

## EYE PROBLEMS

### Pink Eye (Conjunctivitis)

Irritation and redness of the eyes can occur from many causes—colds and flu, swimming, allergies, sun glare, or smoke irritation. However, if a red and irritated eye is associated with a thick, sticky discharge, an eye infection is probably present, and a doctor should be consulted.

### Sty

A sty is an infection in a small gland along the eyelid. A small and painful pimple is usually evident along the inside of the lid. Treatment consists of frequent warm, moist compresses applied to the lid. An antibiotic eye solution may also be helpful.

### Foreign Object in the Eye

Foreign objects, called foreign bodies, in the eye are common and sometimes serious problems. If something lands in the eye, rinse it out with clean water. Inspect the eye carefully. If the object is still visible, see a doctor to have it removed. Even if a foreign body is removed from the eye, it will likely cause an abrasion, which itself produces a sensation of scratchiness. If no foreign body can be seen, apply an eyepatch. If after twenty-four hours the irritation and pain persist, seek medical attention.

# 15

# Disabled Travelers

The United Nations declared 1981 the International Year of Disabled Persons, and the world is now awakening to the special needs of some 450 million disabled persons. The travel industry has been exceptionally responsive, and disabled persons are now able to travel more than ever before.

## ACCESSIBILITY

Access is the key to successful travel for the disabled. Without it, there can be no travel. Access is needed to hotels, restaurants, museums, rest rooms, buses, trains, and planes. Accessibility is steadily improving worldwide, but wide variations still exist. Western Europe has generally good access, while the Soviet Union and developing countries lag far behind.

Information concerning access abroad can be obtained by contacting RIUSA (Rehabilitation International, USA), which distributes an international directory of access guides. Access guides, prepared by communities throughout the world, are handbooks that describe local hotels, theaters, churches, museums, etcetera, in terms of their physical accessibility to mobility-impaired travelers. The current RIUSA directory lists 458 access guides for as many communities around the world. Donations are requested, and directories can be obtained by writing to:

— RIUSA
  20 West 40th Street
  New York, NY 10018

Another source of information about accessibility is the Travel Information Center of Ross Rehabilitation Hospital. If you send the center a list of the countries and cities you would like to visit, your travel interests, and your level of disability, they will provide information about accessibility in that area. The center will also let you know how to get in touch with groups with similar interests. Write to:

— Travel Information Center
  Ross Rehabilitation Hospital
  12th Street and Tabor Road
  Philadelphia, PA 19141


## AIR TRAVEL FOR THE DISABLED

Recent developments have made air travel easier for wheelchair-bound travelers. The introduction of the portable dry-cell battery now allows the transportation of electric wheelchairs aboard commercial aircraft (older wet-cell batteries were not allowed on board). And the development of portable push-style wheelchairs designed to fold and fit under a standard airline seat allows easier boarding and deplaning. In addition, Boeing has recently introduced a special version of the 767 that has been designed to accommodate the disabled traveler. The new plane has wider aisles, liftable armrests, an on-board wheelchair, and specially designed lavatories.

When making your flight reservation, let the airline know of your disability. When notified in advance, airline personnel will be able to provide you with boarding privileges and seating priority. In general, wheelchair passengers are able to fly alone if they are able to accomplish a transfer from seat to chair without requiring the assistance of flight crew members. Otherwise, arrangements for an attendant should be made in advance.

An access guide to airport facilities, which describes the special features and services at various airports that could help a disabled traveler, is available by writing to:

— "Access Travel: A Guide to Accessibility
of Airport Terminals"
Airport Operators Council International, Inc.
1700 K Street N.W.
Washington, DC 20006

## ORGANIZATIONS TO ASSIST THE DISABLED TRAVELER

THETA Association, Inc. provides a wide range of travel services and special tour programs for disabled travelers. THETA's stated purpose is to "develop, implement, operate, and coordinate worldwide travel services for the benefit of the mobility impaired and those who require special attention." That is quite a mission, but it is working, and their membership is growing rapidly. An annual membership, which is currently $35, will provide you with special trip-planning services, access information, airport assistance, personal escorts (for an additional fee), and a newsletter. Medical insurance programs are also available. Membership information can be obtained at most airports and travel agencies, or by writing to:

— THETA Association, Inc.
1058 Shell Boulevard
Bldg. #1, P.O. Box 4850
Foster City, CA 94404
415-573-9701

## SPECIAL TOURS AND TRIP OPERATORS

Your travel agent can be a valuable source of information about special tours and trips for disabled travelers. A few agencies that specialize in services for the handicapped traveler include:

— Flying Wheels Tours
143 West Bridge Street, Box 382
Owatonna, MN 55060
507-451-5005

Flying Wheels Tours operates several group tours, and they are knowledgeable in the special needs of disabled travelers.

— Wings on Wheels
Evergreen Travel Service
19505 L 44th Avenue West
Lynwood, WA 98036
206-776-1184

Wings on Wheels specializes in glamour trips—like around the world in twenty-one days—for blind, deaf, and physically disabled travelers.

— Rambling Tours, Inc.
Box 1304
Hallendale, FL 33009
305-456-2161

Rambling Tours specializes in international group tours for disabled travelers, including quadraplegic, paraplegic, deaf, blind, and chronically ill persons.

— Handy-Cap Horizons
   3250 East Loretta Drive
   Indianapolis, IN 46227
   317-784-5777

Handy-Cap Horizons is an international membership organization that conducts tours all over the world for physically disabled travelers.

## ORGANIZATIONS TO ASSIST NONHEARING TRAVELERS

An organization named Signed Seekers has recently been formed to cater to the travel needs of the deaf and hearing impaired. Signed Seekers plans to organize and conduct international sign-language tours to wherever its clients would like to go. For more information, contact:

— Signed Seekers
   Box 53354
   Washington, DC 20009
   202-265-5451
   (Voice/TTY, a teletype service for the deaf, is available to phone callers.)

Another agency that conducts tours for the deaf is Ruth Skinner's Interpret Tours. Her tours include an interpreter who also acts as a tour guide. For additional information, contact:

— Ruth Skinner's Interpret Tours
   Encino Travel Service, Inc.
   16660 Ventura Boulevard
   Encino, CA 91436

Additional information about traveling with disability can be found in *Access to the World* by Louis Weiss (New York: Chatham Square Press, 1977). This book offers advice on air, train, ship, bus, and automobile travel for disabled travelers. It also tells you where to write for access guides in all fifty states and provides access information on hotels and motels located all over the world.

# 16

## Traveling with Special Health Problems

Thanks to modern transportation, concerned organizations, and the desire to get out and see the world, travel is possible for nearly everyone, regardless of health or disability. In order to make your next trip as safe and enjoyable as possible, be well prepared before you leave.

### SPECIAL HEALTH PREPARATIONS

Traveling with a health problem requires some additional preparations, preparations that need to be tailored to your own special health needs. Begin by setting realistic goals.

#### Setting Your Goals

Although there are countless interesting and exciting places to visit, no place will be enjoyable if it is too physically demanding or causes you to worry about your health. Avoid being disappointed or frustrated abroad. Be realistic about your travel goals. Set your sights on places that you will be comfortable visiting and on places you can fully enjoy.

## Consult Your Physician

The physician who has been attending to your current health problem is the person who can best advise you on the safety of your proposed travel plans and on the preparations you should make before you leave. At least two months before your departure, make an appointment for a complete medical checkup. Discuss your itinerary with your physician, and inquire about the potential health risks you should be concerned with. How will your medical condition be affected by exposure to heat or altitude; by air or sea travel; by exposure to travelers' diarrhea or tropical disease? Some places may be healthier to visit than others.

Ask your physician to provide you with a typed medical summary that explains in detail any treatment you are currently undergoing. If it is possible that you will need the attention of a specialist overseas, ask your doctor for a letter of introduction. Even if the letter is addressed to "To Whom It May Concern" or "Dear Doctor," it helps get you the services you need.

## A Traveling Companion

A knowledgeable traveling companion can be a great asset to travelers with health problems and disabilities. Your companion should be aware of your current health problems, the medications you are taking, and whom to contact if an urgent problem should arise.

## Special Diets

Travelers with special health problems often need to follow certain dietary guidelines. Airlines and cruise ships can accommodate most special diets if given enough advance notice. Usually twenty-four hours is required, but the optimum time to order a special diet is when you book your fare. Airlines are able to provide the following diets.

- diabetic
- salt-free
- low-fat, low-cholesterol
- bland
- gluten-free
- vegetarian
- kosher
- baby food

However, adhering to a special diet while traveling in foreign cities is often a challenge. The best advice is to become as familiar as you can with your own dietary needs and the composition of basic food groups. Meeting with a dietician before you leave can be very helpful. For travelers with special dietary requirements planning to travel to Europe, the following guide provides information and the translations necessary for ordering low-salt, diabetic, bland, and other diets in Spanish, German, French, and Italian: *The Special Diet Foreign Phrase Book* by Helen Jacobson (Emmaus, PA: Rodale Press, 1982).

## Can You Ask For Help?

It is a good idea for travelers, especially travelers with health problems, to be able to ask for help in the language of the country they will be visiting. A list of foreign phrases that may be useful is provided in appendix E. Additional phrases can often be found in pocket language guides.

## National Organizations

Many medical illnesses are represented by national organizations such as the American Diabetes Association, American Heart Association, and Kidney Foundation. These organizations can provide information and recommendations about overseas travel. Often, special tours are organized through these organizations that can help solve problems with special transportation needs, health care, and dietary requirements.

## FLYING WITH HEALTH PROBLEMS

Since air travel is the easiest and least strenuous mode of transportation, most people with health problems have little difficulty flying. Given at least twenty-four hours notice, most airlines will try to accommodate travelers with special health problems. Special diets, wheelchair services, and oxygen are available for passengers—but only if the airlines are notified in advance.

The use of oxygen on board is subject to FAA regulations. You may bring your own oxygen into the cabin only if it has been properly supplied and packaged. Air Medic is a private company that offers medical services to air travelers. The company can arrange air ambulance services, nursing care, respiratory therapists, and physician services for travelers with special health needs. They can also supply oxygen for use in flight or as cargo for use after you land. Air Medic can be contacted at:

— Air Medic
  12517 Chandler Boulevard
  North Hollywood, CA 91607
  800-423-2667 (in California 213-985-2020)

If you can get around without difficulty or restriction, air travel should pose no problems. Your physician, however, is the person who can best advise you on the safety of air flight. Some medical reasons to avoid or postpone air travel are as follows.

- Women in their ninth month of pregnancy should not fly.
- Travelers with severe heart or lung disease should receive clearance from their physicians.
- Following a heart attack, you should postpone air travel for three to six weeks (and obtain clearance from your physician).
- Following intestinal or urologic surgery, you should postpone travel for at least two weeks.
- Travelers with sickle cell disease may require oxygen during flight; air travel, however, poses no risk for travelers with sickle cell trait.
- People with a wired jaw (for treatment of a fracture) should not fly.
- People with recent onsets of colds, hay fever, or sinus infections should postpone air travel, or they should take steps to prevent barotitis and barosinusitis as outlined in chapter 6.

## TRAVEL DURING PREGNANCY

Confinement during pregnancy is over. Healthy women with normal pregnancies are traveling more frequently today than ever before. If you are pregnant or plan to become pregnant soon and are planning to travel abroad, the same general health measures apply to you as to any other traveler—with a few added precautions.

Travel during the second trimester—months four through six—is less risky than it is during either the first or last three months, when complications are more likely to arise. For obvious reasons (unless you prefer to have your child born abroad), it is generally agreed that travel should be avoided during the ninth month. Since it is possible for medical problems to arise anytime during pregnancy, make sure you are covered by medical insurance and know where to turn for medical help if it is needed (see chapter 8).

## Consult Your Physician

The first step to take in preparing to travel during pregnancy is to consult with your personal physician or obstetrician. Your doctor can advise you on the safety of travel and can provide you with a written medical summary that should include your expected delivery date. If there are any potential complications associated with your pregnancy, you will almost certainly be advised to stay home. Most airlines require written permission from your physician to allow you to fly during the ninth month of pregnancy.

## Vaccinations During Pregnancy

In general, live-virus vaccines—particularly mumps, measles, and rubella—should not be given during pregnancy, or to persons who are likely to become pregnant within three months after receiving the vaccine. In certain instances, however, the risk of acquiring a serious infection outweighs the risk from vaccine. This caveat applies to the oral polio vaccine: When there is a substantial risk of acquiring polio abroad, the vaccine should be given, even during pregnancy.

Yellow fever vaccine is another live-virus vaccine that, if possible, should be avoided during pregnancy. In cases where travel to an actively infected region is absolutely necessary, however, the vaccine is recommended during pregnancy, because the health risks are far greater from the disease than from the vaccine. The safest route to follow is to avoid traveling to areas where the risks of infection are high until your pregnancy is over. Both the polio and yellow fever vaccines should be thoroughly discussed with your attending physician before you receive either of them.

The currently available cholera vaccine provides poor protection against the disease, and it should be avoided during pregnancy, even though harmful effects from the vaccine have never been proven. It is simply not worth the risk, because there is little health benefit from the vaccination. A letter from your physician may be sufficient to waive the cholera vaccination requirement to gain entry into countries that impose it. The typhoid vaccine has not been proven safe during pregnancy and should be avoided. Hepatitis immune globulin, however, is considered to be safe during pregnancy and should be administered as recommended in chapter 3 if the risk of acquiring hepatitis is high.

## Traveling in the Tropics While Pregnant

When traveling to the tropics, all travelers will encounter a variety of health risks that do not exist in other parts of the world. When you are pregnant, these risks become doubly important. Preventing health hazards often requires medications and additional vaccinations, and during pregnancy, these present hazards in themselves. Travel to the tropics can be undertaken during pregnancy, but you have to be aware of the health risks you will encounter and the potential side effects of all medicines and vaccinations that you will receive—side effects that can affect you and your unborn child. One such example is malaria prevention.

The antimalarial drug chloroquine has been used for many years, and it is considered to be safe during pregnancy—certainly much safer than a malaria infection. So chloroquine is recommended during pregnancy when travel to a malarious region is necessary. However, resistance to chloroquine is spreading, and the antimalarial Fansidar has not been proven safe during pregnancy. In fact, some of its ingredients have been shown to be actually harmful to the fetus. Fansidar should not be taken during pregnancy, and pregnant travelers are advised to avoid areas where chloroquine-resistant malaria has been reported (see chapter 9). If you must travel to such a region, thoroughly review the precautions you should take with your physician.

The most important precaution pregnant travelers can take is to discuss the safety of all medications and vaccinations with their physician before they leave home. Using an unfamiliar medicine or receiving an unfamiliar vaccination while abroad may not only pose a serious health risk to yourself, but also to your unborn child.

## TRAVELING WITH DIABETES

For most diabetics, traveling is not difficult. As for all travelers, however, preventive health planning is important. Diabetics should be especially attuned to preventing some of the common travel-related health problems—motion sickness, heat exhaustion, traveler's diarrhea—because these temporary maladies can cause an otherwise well-controlled diabetic to become poorly controlled. A few additional considerations apply specifically to diabetic travelers.

### Diabetic Medications

Not all diabetics need to take medications. And for those who don't, maintaining your diet and weight while abroad—with periodic urine checks for sugar—may be all that is required for a safe and healthy trip.

If you are a diabetic taking a hypoglycemic medication, make sure you bring along a sufficient supply to last the entire trip. All diabetic medicines are available overseas, but it is safer to stick to the brand you are used to taking.

Insulin travels well, and it maintains its potency for at least three months. Although insulin does not require refrigeration, it should not be exposed to extreme heat. Disposable syringes are much more convenient to use while traveling than are glass syringes. Always carry at least a week's supply of insulin and syringes on your person in case your luggage is lost.

Customs officials are sometimes wary of persons carrying syringes. So be sure you can produce a letter from your physician, written on office letterhead, that describes your diabetic condition and why you are carrying insulin and syringes.

Diabetic testing is important while you are traveling because changes in your normal routine—time-zone changes, dietary changes, and activity changes—can readily alter the control of your diabetes. Carry enough testing materials to last your entire trip. These materials should also be carried in your hand luggage with the rest of your medicine.

## Diabetic Diet

While diet is a fundamental way of controlling diabetes, culinary adventures are often a fundamental part of travel to foreign lands. Brush up on your food exchanges before you leave: bread is bread; meat is meat; and so forth. Use discretion, but don't be afraid to sample the local dishes.

## Diabetic Foot Care

Since skin and foot problems are common with diabetes, you must take very good care of your feet while traveling. Bring along two pairs of well-fitting, broken-in shoes.

In warm and humid climates, daily foot soaks, followed by careful drying and foot powder, are recommended. Foot care is further discussed in chapter 7.

## Jet Lag and Insulin

Flying across several time zones will throw your meal times and your insulin times off their usual schedule, and adjustments have to be made. Before you leave, ask your physician how to adjust the timing and dose of your insulin injections to compensate for time-zone changes. Some general recommendations are:

1. While flying, keep your watch set to "home" time and try to follow your normal eating and insulin schedule. If arranged in advance, airlines will be able to serve your meal to meet your schedule.
2. When you arrive at your destination, adjust your next dose of insulin to compensate for the time-zone change. If you have flown east, the day will have been shortened, and your next insulin dose should be reduced slightly. If you have flown west, the day will have been lengthened, and your next insulin dose should be increased slightly. Obviously, northward or southward travel would not affect your insulin schedule or dose.

## Services for Diabetic Travelers

The Diabetes Travel Service Club (DTS) was formed specifically for diabetics who want to enjoy travel but are concerned about their health and well-being while abroad. The club provides information about diets and calories and about foot care and exercise while traveling. In addition, the club publishes a monthly newsletter with information on new books, meetings, and special tours. Membership is about $15 a year, and it entitles you to use a private

DTS hotline telephone number for emergency assistance while traveling. For more information contact:

— Diabetic Travel Services, Inc.
349 East 52nd Street
New York, NY 10016

An informative booklet titled "Traveling With Diabetes, Not From Diabetes" is available free of charge from:

— American Diabetes Association
500 Fifth Avenue
New York, NY 10029

## TRAVELING WITH HEART DISEASE

Having heart disease no longer means staying at home. Cardiac patients are getting out and seeing the world firsthand more than ever. But, if you have a heart problem, getting out and seeing the world safely requires a few health considerations in addition to the special preparations outlined earlier.

Your functional ability—the measure of how much a person with a heart condition can exert himself without developing chest pain, shortness of breath, or weakness—will determine how you should plan for your trip. Travelers with low functional ability should plan trips that will be the least stressful. They should allow themselves plenty of time to make travel connections (no last-minute rushing around to get to the airport) and should plan trips to areas where they will be comfortable, avoiding extremes in climate or altitude that could strain the heart. Your physician can help you plan a trip that will be interesting and enjoyable, while avoiding an unnecessary risk to your health.

## Medical Information to Carry

Travelers with heart problems should carry, in addition to their written medical history, a copy of a recent electrocardiogram. If you have a pacemaker, your records should list the manufacturer of the pacemaker, the type of electrode, and the date of implantation. A wallet-sized card is available for travelers with cardiac disease that provides a recent electrocardiogram tracing, a list of the medicines you are taking, and information about your health history and pacemaker. The card is available by writing to:

— The Heart Chart
P.O. Box 221
New Rochelle, NY
914-632-3388

## Pacemakers

Traveling with a pacemaker generally presents no special problems. Airport security devices are not hazardous to pacemakers. If it has been several years since the pacemaker was implanted, make sure that the life of the battery is still good. And remember that you can have your pacemaker monitored from any place in the world by calling your monitoring center.

## Flying With Heart Disease

Flying is often the safest way to travel for people with heart disease, because it is the least stressful. The reduced oxygen content during flight, however, can cause difficulty for some travelers with severe heart problems. A time-honored dictum is that if you can walk 100 yards or climb a flight of twelve stairs without difficulty, you should have no difficulty flying. If oxygen is needed during flight, it can be provided if it is arranged for in advance. Ask your physician about the safety of air travel with your particular heart condition.

## TRAVELING WITH KIDNEY DISEASE

One of the benefits of kidney transplantation is it has allowed thousands of recipients to travel. Kidney patients on hemodialysis, with their physician's approval, are also able to travel abroad and continue their dialysis routines at hospitals and renal centers that have guest dialysis services available. If you are planning a trip abroad, your local chapter of the Kidney Foundation should have information about dialysis centers overseas that are willing and able to treat the traveling patient. An invaluable guide titled *Dialysis World-Wide for the Traveling Patient* is published by the National Association of Patients on Hemodialysis and Transplantation. The guide contains information about U.S. and foreign dialysis centers and is available by writing to:

— NAPHT
    156 William Street
    New York, NY 10038
    212-619-2727

Cruises for dialysis patients are arranged by:

— Brenden Cruise Tours
    510 West Sixth Street
    Los Angeles, CA 90014
    213-629-9040

## CANCER CHEMOTHERAPY

It is possible to continue your schedule of chemotherapy treatments while traveling in most foreign countries.

However, careful planning and detailed arrangements will be necessary.

Discuss your travel plans and itinerary with your attending physician. Thoroughly understand the dosage, frequency, and side effects of all the drugs prescribed. If laboratory tests will be required en route, develop a schedule to have these tests performed when you will be in cities with large medical centers.

If you require chemotherapy injections or infusions, your doctor should personally contact a medical specialist abroad and provide you with a letter of introduction. You should also carry a full supply of all the drugs you are taking. Do not rely on being able to obtain them overseas.

Carry a detailed medical summary of your cancer treatment. Chemotherapy regimens vary from country to country, so it is essential to have your regimen outlined in detail. Also carry your personal physician's office and home phone numbers with you at all times. If a complication arises, the foreign doctor taking care of you will want to talk directly with your physician at home.

## TRAVELING WITH COLOSTOMIES

Traveling with a colostomy is generally not difficult, provided you carry all the necessary equipment and supplies you will need. The problems that do arise usually involve difficulty obtaining supplies abroad—especially at night, on weekends, and holidays. Atmospheric pressure changes can cause the gases inside colostomy bags to expand during air flight. To allow for expansion, wear a larger size bag while flying.

## TRAVELING WITH LUNG PROBLEMS

If you have asthma, bronchitis, or emphysema, be sure to follow the special precautions discussed earlier in this chapter. If your lung problem is severe, ask your physician if you will encounter difficulty from the reduced oxygen during air flight. As noted earlier, oxygen can be arranged if it is needed.

People with lung problems who plan to travel to areas where medical services may not be readily available should discuss with their physicians what they should do if their problems suddenly become worse. Medicines can be prescribed to treat flare-ups of asthma, emphysema, or bronchitis. When and how to take these medicines should be thoroughly reviewed by your physician.

# APPENDIX A

# Vaccination and Health Risk Guide

This guide presents information on vaccinations, malaria and tropical disease risks, and water and food safety for individual countries throughout the world. This information is presented to assist you in your preparations for traveling well. Since health information can change virtually overnight—as quickly as a new outbreak of disease can be discovered and reported—you should understand that the health conditions you encounter in individual countries may differ from the conditions described below. Do not be surprised if the vaccination requirements for a country on your itinerary have changed. Be alert for new outbreaks of malaria or other tropical disease. And be cautious of the safety of food and water no matter where you travel.

### DETERMINING INTERNATIONAL VACCINATION REQUIREMENTS

Once your itinerary is established, you will need to determine if a cholera or a yellow fever vaccination will be required to gain entry into individual countries. The following steps will enable you to do so.

1. From this guide, determine the current vaccination regulations for each country on your itinerary.
2. Call your local health department (or other source of health information) to:
   a. confirm existing vaccination regulations, and
   b. find out if any countries on your itinerary are reported to be infected with either cholera or yellow fever.

3. Check the yellow fever endemic zone illustrated in appendix C to determine if any countries on your itinerary are within this zone.

With the above information, you can determine which vaccinations, if any, are required for your itinerary.

- All travelers, regardless of destination, should have their routine series of vaccinations up-to-date.
- If no vaccination requirements are listed by a country, no vaccinations are required in order to gain entry.
- If a country requires a cholera or a yellow fever vaccination of all travelers, you will need to be vaccinated regardless of where you have traveled.
- If a country requires a cholera or a yellow fever vaccination only of travelers arriving from an infected country, you will need to be vaccinated only if you have previously traveled in a country reported to be infected with either cholera or yellow fever.
- If a country requires a yellow fever vaccination only of travelers arriving from countries within the yellow fever endemic zone, you will need to be vaccinated only if you have previously traveled through this region.
- No vaccinations are required for reentry into the United States, regardless of where you have traveled.

## DETERMINING MALARIA RISK

Once your itinerary is established, determine the risk of malaria in the countries you will be visiting. If there is a risk, find out if you will be exposed to the chloroquine-resistant strain of malaria, so that you can protect yourself with the appropriate medications. Your personal physician or state department of health can provide you with up-to-date information.

## SOURCES OF INFORMATION

The information on vaccination certificate requirements and malaria risk in countries is drawn, with the permission of the World Health

Organization, from their publication *Vaccination Certificate Requirements for International Travel and Health Advice to Travellers, 1984*. A new edition of this book, giving the situation as of January 1 of each year, is published annually by the World Health Organization (WHO). The information is kept up-to-date during the year by amendments published by WHO in the *Weekly Epidemiological Record*, in which there is from time to time a special section titled "Information on Malaria Risk for International Travelers." Information on vaccination certificate requirements and on malaria risk in countries is also drawn from the U.S. Department of Health and Human Services publication *Health Information for International Travel 1984*, which is available through the U. S. Government Printing Offices. Information on other tropical disease risks and on water and food safety was drawn, with permission, from information provided by the International Association for Medical Assistance to Travelers (IAMAT), 736 Center Street, Lewiston, NY 14092.

## DIRECTORY OF COUNTRIES

### Afghanistan
**Vaccinations**
— *Yellow fever:* A yellow fever vaccination certificate is required from travelers arriving from infected areas.
— *Hepatitis and typhoid:* Immune globulin and typhoid vaccination are recommended for travelers' protection when visiting rural regions off the usual tourist itinerary.

**Malaria and Tropical Disease Risk**
Malaria risk exists from May through November below 2,000 meters, urban areas included.
— *Other tropical disease:* No known risk.

**Water and Food Safety**
All local water should be considered contaminated, and all water used for drinking, brushing teeth, and making ice cubes should be boiled for ten minutes. Bottled water is recommended.

Dairy products should not be considered safe. All meat, seafood, poultry, and vegetables must be well cooked and served hot. Salads and cold buffets should be avoided.

### Albania
**Vaccinations**
— *Cholera:* A cholera vaccination certificate is required from travelers over six months of age coming from infected areas.
— *Yellow fever:* A yellow fever vaccination certificate is required from

travelers over one year of age coming from infected areas.

— *Hepatitis and typhoid:* Immune globulin and typhoid vaccination are recommended for travelers' protection when visiting rural regions off the usual tourist itinerary.

## Malaria and Tropical Disease Risk

No known malaria risk.

— *Other tropical disease:* No known risk.

## Water and Food Safety

Drinking water is chlorinated and generally safe to drink, but variations in local bacterial flora may cause diarrhea in some travelers. Bottled water is recommended for the first few weeks. Dairy products, meat, poultry, seafood, vegetables, and fruits are safe to eat.

## Algeria

### Vaccinations

— *Yellow fever:* A yellow fever vaccination certificate is required from travelers over one year of age coming from infected areas.

— *Hepatitis and typhoid:* Immune globulin and typhoid vaccination are recommended for travelers' protection when visiting rural regions off the usual tourist itinerary.

### Malaria and Tropical Disease Risk

Malaria risk cannot be excluded from May through October in some rural areas of the Metidja plain and from November through March in the departments in the Sahara region. No reported risk in urban areas.

— *Other tropical disease:* Schistosomiasis risk is present only in restricted areas; most of the country is free of infection. Infection is present in the area of Biskra; along the river (Oued) Djidioua and in Khemis el Khechna in Northern Algeria; in the oasis of Djanet (Forth Charlet) near the border with Libya; and in the area of Beni-Abbes in the western part of the country near the border with Morocco.

### Water and Food Safety

All local water should be considered contaminated, and all water used for drinking, brushing teeth, and making ice cubes should be boiled for ten minutes. Bottled water is recommended.

Dairy products should not be considered safe. All meat, seafood, poultry, and vegetables must be well cooked and served hot. Salads and cold buffets should be avoided.

In Alger (Algiers), Annaba, Constantine, and Oran, drinking water is chlorinated and generally safe to drink, but variations in local bacterial flora may cause diarrhea in some travelers. Bottled water is recommended for the first few weeks.

## American Samoa
### Vaccinations
— *Yellow fever:* A yellow fever vaccination certificate is required from travelers over one year of age coming from infected areas.
— *Hepatitis and typhoid:* Immune globulin and typhoid vaccination are recommended for travelers' protection when visiting rural regions off the usual tourist itinerary.
### Malaria and Tropical Disease Risk
No known malaria risk.
— *Other tropical disease:* No known risk.
### Water and Food Safety
Drinking water is chlorinated and generally safe to drink, but variations in local bacterial flora may cause diarrhea in some travelers. Bottled water is recommended for the first few weeks. Dairy products, meat, poultry, seafood, vegetables, and fruits are safe to eat.

## Angola
### Vaccinations
— *Cholera:* A cholera vaccination certificate is required from travelers coming from infected areas.
— *Hepatitis and typhoid:* Immune globulin and typhoid vaccination are recommended for travelers' protection when visiting rural regions off the usual tourist itinerary.
### Malaria and Tropical Disease Risk
Malaria risk exists throughout the year in the whole country, urban areas included.
— *Other tropical disease:* Schistosomiasis risk present in most of the country, except for the Districts of Cabinda, Zaire, and Uige in northwestern part of country. Dengue fever risk present in entire country, excluding urban areas.
### Water and Food Safety
All local water should be considered contaminated, and all water used for drinking, brushing teeth, and making ice cubes should be boiled for ten minutes. Bottled water is recommended.

Dairy products should not be considered safe. All meat, seafood, poultry, and vegetables must be well cooked and served hot. Salads and cold buffets should be avoided.

## Antigua and Barbuda
### Vaccinations
— *Yellow fever:* A yellow fever vaccination certificate is required from travelers over one year of age coming from infected areas.
### Malaria and Tropical Disease Risk
No known malaria risk.

— *Other tropical disease:* Schistosomiasis risk present in entire country, including urban areas. Dengue fever risk present.

**Water and Food Safety**
Local water is safe to drink. Dairy products, meat, poultry, seafood, vegetables, and fruits are safe to eat.

## Argentina
**Vaccinations**
No vaccination requirements for any international traveler.

— *Hepatitis and typhoid:* Immune globulin and typhoid vaccination are recommended for travelers' protection when visiting rural regions off the usual tourist itinerary.

**Malaria and Tropical Disease Risk**
Malaria risk exists from October through May below 1,200 meters in rural areas of Iruya, Orán, San Martin, Santa Victoria Dep. (Salta Prov.) and Ledesma Dep. (Jujuy Prov.), and a small area near the border with Bolivia.

— *Other tropical disease:* Chagas' disease risk present.

**Water and Food Safety**
Local water is safe to drink. Dairy products, meat, poultry, seafood, vegetables, and fruits are safe to eat.

In smaller communities, drinking water is chlorinated and generally safe to drink, but variations in local bacterial flora may cause diarrhea in some travelers. Bottled water is recommended for the first few weeks.

## Australia
**Vaccinations**
— *Yellow fever:* A yellow fever vaccination certificate is required from travelers over one year of age coming from infected areas. The countries and areas included in the endemic zone (appendix C) are considered by Australia as infected areas.

**Malaria and Tropical Disease Risk**
No known malaria risk.

— *Other tropical disease:* Dengue fever risk present.

**Water and Food Safety**
Local water is safe to drink. Dairy products, meat, poultry, seafood, vegetables, and fruits are safe to eat.

## Austria
**Vaccinations**
No vaccination requirements for any international traveler.

**Malaria and Tropical Disease Risk**
No known malaria risk.

— *Other tropical disease:* No known risk.

**Water and Food Safety**

Local water is safe to drink. Dairy products, meat, poultry, seafood, vegetables, and fruits are safe to eat. In Vienna drinking water is chlorinated and generally safe to drink, but variations in local bacterial flora may cause diarrhea in some travelers. Bottled water is recommended for the first few weeks.

## Bahamas

**Vaccinations**

— *Yellow fever:* A yellow fever vaccination certificate is required from travelers over one year of age coming from infected areas.

**Malaria and Tropical Disease Risk**

No known malaria risk.

— *Other tropical disease:* Dengue fever risk present.

**Water and Food Safety**

All local water should be considered contaminated, and all water used for drinking, brushing teeth, and making ice cubes should be boiled for ten minutes. Bottled water is recommended.

Dairy products should not be considered safe. All meat, seafood, poultry, and vegetables must be well cooked and served hot. Salads and cold buffets should be avoided.

In Freeport, drinking water is chlorinated and generally safe to drink, but variations in local bacterial flora may cause diarrhea in some travelers. Bottled water is recommended for the first few weeks.

## Bahrain

**Vaccinations**

— *Yellow fever:* A yellow fever vaccination certificate is required from travelers over one year of age coming from infected areas.

— *Hepatitis and typhoid:* Immune globulin and typhoid vaccination are recommended for travelers' protection when visiting rural regions off the usual tourist itinerary.

**Malaria and Tropical Disease Risk**

No known malaria risk.

— *Other tropical disease:* No known risk.

**Water and Food Safety**

All local water should be considered contaminated, and all water used for drinking, brushing teeth, and making ice cubes should be boiled for ten minutes. Bottled water is recommended.

Dairy products should not be considered safe. All meat, seafood, poultry, and vegetables must be well cooked and served hot. Salads and cold buffets should be avoided.

## Bangladesh

**Vaccinations**

— *Yellow fever:* A yellow fever vaccination certificate is required from travelers who have left an infected area within the preceding six days. The countries and areas in the endemic zone (appendix C) are considered to be infected.

— *Hepatitis and typhoid:* Immune globulin and typhoid vaccination are recommended for travelers' protection when visiting rural regions off the usual tourist itinerary.

**Malaria and Tropical Disease Risk**

Malaria risk throughout the year in the whole country, excluding Dhaka City. Resistance to chloroquine reported in areas bordering States of Assam, Meghalaya, Tripura, Mizoram, India, and Burma.

— *Other tropical disease:* Dengue fever risk present.

**Water and Food Safety**

All local water should be considered contaminated, and all water used for drinking, brushing teeth, and making ice cubes should be boiled for ten minutes. Bottled water is recommended.

Dairy products should not be considered safe. All meat, seafood, poultry, and vegetables must be well cooked and served hot. Salads and cold buffets should be avoided.

**Barbados**

**Vaccinations**

— *Yellow fever:* A yellow fever vaccination certificate is required from travelers over one year of age coming from countries with infected areas as well as from the following:

— *Africa:* Angola, Benin, Burundi, Central African Republic, Chad, Congo, Djibouti, Equatorial Guinea, Ethiopia, Gabon, Gambia, Ghana, Guinea, Guinea-Bissau, Ivory Coast, Kenya, Liberia, Mali, Niger, Nigeria, Rwanda, Sao Tome and Principe, Senegal, Sierra Leone, Somalia, Sudan, Togo, Uganda, United Republic of Cameroon, United Republic of Tanzania, Upper Volta, Zaire.

— *America:* Bolivia, Brazil, Colombia, Ecuador, French Guiana, Guyana, Panama, Peru, Surinam, Venezuela.

**Malaria and Tropical Disease Risk**

No known malaria risk.

— *Other tropical disease:* Dengue fever risk present.

**Water and Food Safety**

Local water is safe to drink. Dairy products, meat, poultry, seafood, vegetables, and fruits are safe to eat.

**Belgium**

**Vaccinations**

No vaccination requirements for any international traveler.

**Malaria and Tropical Disease Risk**

No known malaria risk.

— *Other tropical disease:* No known risk.

**Water and Food Safety**
Local water is safe to drink. Dairy products, meat, poultry, seafood, vegetables, and fruits are safe to eat.

## Belize

**Vaccinations**
— *Yellow fever:* A yellow fever vaccination certificate is required from travelers coming from infected areas.
— *Hepatitis and typhoid:* Immune globulin and typhoid vaccination are recommended for travelers' protection when visiting rural regions off the usual tourist itinerary.

**Malaria and Tropical Disease Risk**
Malaria risk exists throughout the year, excluding Belize Dist. and urban areas.
— *Other tropical disease:* Chagas' disease risk present.

**Water and Food Safety**
All local water should be considered contaminated, and all water used for drinking, brushing teeth, and making ice cubes should be boiled for ten minutes. Bottled water is recommended.

Dairy products should not be considered safe. All meat, seafood, poultry, and vegetables must be well cooked and served hot. Salads and cold buffets should be avoided.

## Benin

**Vaccinations**
— *Yellow fever:* A yellow fever vaccination certificate is required from travelers over one year of age coming from all countries.
— *Hepatitis and typhoid:* Immune globulin and typhoid vaccination are recommended for travelers' protection when visiting rural regions off the usual tourist itinerary.

**Malaria and Tropical Disease Risk**
Malaria risk exists throughout the year in the whole country.
— *Other tropical disease:* Schistosomiasis risk present in entire country, including urban areas.

**Water and Food Safety**
All local water should be considered contaminated, and all water used for drinking, brushing teeth, and making ice cubes should be boiled for ten minutes. Bottled water is recommended.

Dairy products should not be considered safe. All meat, seafood, poultry, and vegetables must be well cooked and served hot. Salads and cold buffets should be avoided.

## Bermuda

**Vaccinations**
No vaccination requirements for any international traveler.

**Malaria and Tropical Disease Risk**
No known malaria risk.
— *Other tropical disease:* No known risk.

#### Water and Food Safety

Local water is safe to drink. Dairy products, meat, poultry, seafood, vegetables, and fruits are safe to eat.

### Bhutan

#### Vaccinations

No vaccination requirements for any international traveler.

— *Yellow fever:* A yellow fever vaccination certificate is required from travelers coming from infected areas.

— *Hepatitis and typhoid:* Immune globulin and typhoid vaccination are recommended for travelers' protection when visiting rural regions off the usual tourist itinerary.

#### Malaria and Tropical Disease Risk

Malaria risk exists throughout the year in the southern belt of five districts: Chirang, Gaylegphug, Samchi, Samdrupjongkhar, and Shemgang.

— *Other tropical disease:* No known risk.

#### Water and Food Safety

All local water should be considered contaminated, and all water used for drinking, brushing teeth, and making ice cubes should be boiled for ten minutes. Bottled water is recommended.

Dairy products should not be considered safe. All meat, seafood, poultry, and vegetables must be well cooked and served hot. Salads and cold buffets should be avoided.

### Bolivia

#### Vaccinations

— *Yellow fever:* A yellow fever vaccination certificate is required from persons traveling to countries with infected areas and from persons traveling from such countries. All travelers going to Santa Cruz de la Sierra, Bolivia, must be in possession of a valid yellow fever certificate. A yellow fever vaccination is recommended for all travelers' protection.

— *Hepatitis and typhoid:* Immune globulin and typhoid vaccination are recommended for travelers' protection when visiting rural regions off the usual tourist itinerary.

#### Malaria and Tropical Disease Risk

Malaria risk exists throughout the year below 2,500 meters, excluding urban areas and excluding Oruo Dept., the provinces of Ingavi, Los Andes, Omasuyos, and Pacajes (La Paz Dept.), and Southern and Central Potosi Dept. Resistance to chloroquine reported.

— *Other tropical disease:* Chagas' disease risk present.

#### Water and Food Safety

All local water should be considered contaminated, and all water used for drinking, brushing teeth, and making ice cubes should

be boiled for ten minutes. Bottled water is recommended.

Dairy products should not be considered safe. All meat, seafood, poultry, and vegetables must be well cooked and served hot. Salads and cold buffets should be avoided.

## Botswana

### Vaccinations

No vaccination requirements for any international traveler.

— *Hepatitis and typhoid:* Immune globulin and typhoid vaccination are recommended for travelers' protection when visiting rural regions off the usual tourist itinerary.

### Malaria and Tropical Disease Risk

Malaria risk exists from November through May in the northern part of the country (north of 21° S).

— *Other tropical disease:* Schistosomiasis risk present in the country, extent of infection not determined. Known endemic areas of infection are present in the area of Maun, along the Okavango River in the north of the country.

### Water and Food Safety

All local water should be considered contaminated, and all water used for drinking, brushing teeth, and making ice cubes should be boiled for ten minutes. Bottled water is recommended.

Dairy products should not be considered safe. All meat, seafood, poultry, and vegetables must be well cooked and served hot. Salads and cold buffets should be avoided.

## Brazil

### Vaccinations

— *Yellow fever:* A yellow fever vaccination certificate is required from travelers over six months of age coming from infected areas. Vaccination is recommended for travelers visiting rural areas off of the usual tourist itinerary.

— *Hepatitis and typhoid:* Immune globulin and typhoid vaccination are recommended for travelers' protection when visiting rural regions off the usual tourist itinerary.

### Malaria and Tropical Disease Risk

Malaria risk exists throughout the year below 900 meters in Acre State, Terr. of Amapa, Rondônia, Roraima, and in part of rural areas of Amazonas, Goias, Maranhao, Mato Grosso, Para State.

Resistance to chloroquine reported in states in interior of country and Espirito Santo State, the coastal area north of Rio de Janeiro.

— *Other tropical disease:* Schistosomiasis risk is present in the country. Infection occurs in the following areas.

• The Federal District including Brasilia is infected.

- Scattered areas of infection are present in the southern part of Goiás.

- In the north of Brazil, isolated areas of infection are present in the state of Pará: in the area of Fordlândia at the mouth of the Tapajós River; west of Santarêm; and in the coastal region of Bragança.

- To the east, in the state Maranhño, numerous areas of infection are present in the coastal region extending from the border with the state of Pará to the bay of São Marcos, including the island of São Luís.

- Further to the east, numerous areas of infection are scattered over the state of Ceará.

- The eastern states of Rio Grande do Norte, Paraíba, Pernambuco, Alagoas, and Sergipe are highly infected.

- The state of Bahia is heavily infected in the eastern part, including the basin of the Sao Francisco River.

- The whole state of Espírito Santo is infected.

- The state of Minas Gerais is highly infected, except for the extreme western part.

- In the state of Rio de Janeiro, the infection is scattered, therefore the whole state should be considered infected.

- In the state of São Paulo, the infection is widely spread in the northern part, including the city of Santos.

- Areas of infection are scattered throughout the state of Paraná.

Chagas' disease risk present.

**Water and Food Safety**

All local water should be considered contaminated, and all water used for drinking, brushing teeth, and making ice cubes should be boiled for ten minutes. Bottled water is recommended.

Dairy products should not be considered safe. All meat, seafood, poultry, and vegetables must be well cooked and served hot. Salads and cold buffets should be avoided.

**British Virgin Islands**

**Vaccinations**

No vaccination requirements for any international traveler.

**Malaria and Tropical Disease Risk**

No known malaria risk.

— *Other tropical disease:* Dengue fever risk present.

**Water and Food Safety**

Drinking water is chlorinated and generally safe to drink, but

variations in local bacterial flora may cause diarrhea in some travelers. Bottled water is recommended for the first few weeks. Dairy products, meat, poultry, seafood, vegetables, and fruits are safe to eat.

## Brunei
### Vaccinations
— *Yellow fever:* A yellow fever vaccination certificate is required from travelers over one year of age coming from infected areas.

— *Hepatitis and typhoid:* Immune globulin and typhoid vaccination are recommended for travelers' protection when visiting rural regions off the usual tourist itinerary.

### Malaria and Tropical Disease Risk
No known malaria risk.

— *Other tropical disease:* Dengue fever risk present.

### Water and Food Safety
All local water should be considered contaminated, and all water used for drinking, brushing teeth, and making ice cubes should be boiled for ten minutes. Bottled water is recommended.

Dairy products should not be considered safe. All meat, seafood, poultry, and vegetables must be well cooked and served hot. Salads and cold buffets should be avoided.

## Bulgaria
### Vaccinations
No vaccination requirements for any international traveler.

### Malaria and Tropical Disease Risk
No known malaria risk.

— *Other tropical disease:* No known risk.

### Water and Food Safety
Drinking water is chlorinated and generally safe to drink, but variations in local bacterial flora may cause diarrhea in some travelers. Bottled water is recommended for the first few weeks. Dairy products, meat, poultry, seafood, vegetables, and fruits are safe to eat.

## Burma
### Vaccinations
— *Yellow fever:* A yellow fever vaccination certificate is required from travelers over one year of age coming from infected areas. Countries and areas in the endemic zone (appendix C) are regarded as infected.

— *Hepatitis and typhoid:* Immune globulin and typhoid vaccination are recommended for travelers' protection when visiting rural regions off the usual tourist itinerary.

### Malaria and Tropical Disease Risk
Malaria risk exists (a) from April through December in rural areas

(part) of Tenasserim Div.; (b) from May through December in Ir-
rawaddy Div. (part) and rural areas (part) of Mandalay Div.; (c)
from June through December in rural areas (part) of Pegu and
Rangoon Div. and in rural areas of Arakan, Chin, Kachin, Karen,
Kayah, Mon, and Shan States; (d) from June through October in
rural areas (part) of Magwe Div. and in Sagaing Div. (part). Resistance to chloroquine reported.
— *Other tropical disease:* Dengue fever risk present.

**Water and Food Safety**

All local water should be considered contaminated, and all water
used for drinking, brushing teeth, and making ice cubes should
be boiled for ten minutes. Bottled water is recommended.

Dairy products should not be considered safe. All meat, seafood, poultry, and vegetables must be well cooked and served
hot. Salads and cold buffets should be avoided.

## Burundi

**Vaccinations**

— *Yellow fever:* A yellow fever vaccination certificate is required from
travelers over one year of age coming from infected areas.
— *Hepatitis and typhoid:* Immune globulin and typhoid vaccination
are recommended for travelers' protection when visiting rural regions off the usual tourist itinerary.

**Malaria and Tropical Disease Risk**

Malaria risk exists throughout the year in the whole country.
— *Other tropical disease:* Schistosomiasis risk present in the country;
extent of infection not determined.

**Water and Food Safety**

All local water should be considered contaminated, and all water
used for drinking, brushing teeth, and making ice cubes should
be boiled for ten minutes. Bottled water is recommended.

Dairy products should not be considered safe. All meat, seafood, poultry, and vegetables must be well cooked and served
hot. Salads and cold buffets should be avoided.

## Cambodia (see Democratic Kampuchea)

## Cameroon, United Republic of

**Vaccinations**

— *Yellow fever:* A yellow fever vaccination certificate is required from
travelers over one year of age coming from infected areas.
— *Hepatitis and typhoid:* Immune globulin and typhoid vaccination
are recommended for travelers' protection when visiting rural regions off the usual tourist itinerary.

**Malaria and Tropical Disease Risk**

Malaria risk exists throughout the year in the whole country.

— *Other tropical disease:* Schistosomiasis risk present in entire country, including urban areas.

**Water and Food Safety**

All local water should be considered contaminated, and all water used for drinking, brushing teeth, and making ice cubes should be boiled for ten minutes. Bottled water is recommended.

Dairy products should not be considered safe. All meat, seafood, poultry, and vegetables must be well cooked and served hot. Salads and cold buffets should be avoided.

## Canada

**Vaccinations**

No vaccination requirements for any international traveler.

**Malaria and Tropical Disease Risk**

No known malaria risk.

— *Other tropical disease:* No known risk.

**Water and Food Safety**

Local water is safe to drink. Dairy products, meat, poultry, seafood, vegetables, and fruits are safe to eat.

## Canary Islands

**Vaccinations**

No vaccination requirements for any international traveler.

**Malaria and Tropical Disease Risk**

No known malaria risk.

**Water and Food Safety**

Drinking water is chlorinated and generally safe to drink, but variations in local bacterial flora may cause diarrhea in some travelers. Bottled water is recommended for the first few weeks. Dairy products, meat, poultry, seafood, vegetables, and fruits are safe to eat.

## Cape Verde

**Vaccinations**

— *Cholera:* A cholera vaccination certificate is required from travelers coming from infected countries.

— *Yellow fever:* A yellow fever vaccination certificate is required from travelers over one year of age coming from infected areas. The requirement does not apply to travelers arriving in São Vicente, Sal, Maio, Boa Vista, and Santiago.

— *Hepatitis and typhoid:* Immune globulin and typhoid vaccination are recommended for travelers' protection when visiting rural regions off the usual tourist itinerary.

**Malaria and Tropical Disease Risk**

Malaria risk exists throughout the year only in some rural parts of Concelho de Santa Cruz (São Tiago Island).

— *Other tropical disease:* No known risk.

**Water and Food Safety**

All local water should be considered contaminated, and all water used for drinking, brushing teeth, and making ice cubes should be boiled for ten minutes. Bottled water is recommended.

Dairy products should not be considered safe. All meat, seafood, poultry, and vegetables must be well cooked and served hot. Salads and cold buffets should be avoided.

## Cayman Islands

**Vaccinations**

No vaccination requirements for any international traveler.

**Malaria and Tropical Disease Risk**

No known malaria risk.

— *Other tropical disease:* No known risk.

**Water and Food Safety**

All local water should be considered contaminated, and all water used for drinking, brushing teeth, and making ice cubes should be boiled for ten minutes. Bottled water is recommended.

Dairy products should not be considered safe. All meat, seafood, poultry, and vegetables must be well cooked and served hot. Salads and cold buffets should be avoided.

## Central African Republic

**Vaccinations**

— *Yellow fever:* A yellow fever vaccination certificate is required from travelers over one year of age coming from infected areas.

— *Hepatitis and typhoid:* Immune globulin and typhoid vaccination are recommended for travelers' protection when visiting rural regions off the usual tourist itinerary.

**Malaria and Tropical Disease Risk**

Malaria risk exists throughout the year in the whole country.

— *Other tropical disease:* Schistosomiasis risk present in the country; extent of infection not determined.

**Water and Food Safety**

All local water should be considered contaminated, and all water used for drinking, brushing teeth, and making ice cubes should be boiled for ten minutes. Bottled water is recommended.

Dairy products should not be considered safe. All meat, seafood, poultry, and vegetables must be well cooked and served hot. Salads and cold buffets should be avoided.

## Chad

**Vaccinations**

No vaccinations are required from any international travelers, but the government of Chad recommends a cholera vaccination for travelers coming from infected areas and a yellow fever vaccination for all travelers over the age of one.

— *Hepatitis and typhoid:* Immune globulin and typhoid vaccination are recommended for travelers' protection when visiting rural regions off the usual tourist itinerary.

**Malaria and Tropical Disease Risk**

Malaria risk exists throughout the year in the whole country.

— *Other tropical disease:* Schistosomiasis risk present in the country; extent of infection not determined.

**Water and Food Safety**

All local water should be considered contaminated, and all water used for drinking, brushing teeth, and making ice cubes should be boiled for ten minutes. Bottled water is recommended.

Dairy products should not be considered safe. All meat, seafood, poultry, and vegetables must be well cooked and served hot. Salads and cold buffets should be avoided.

## Chile

**Vaccinations**

No vaccination requirements for any international traveler.

— *Hepatitis and typhoid:* Immune globulin and typhoid vaccination are recommended for travelers' protection when visiting rural regions off the usual tourist itinerary.

**Malaria and Tropical Disease Risk**

No known malaria risk

— *Other tropical disease:* Chagas' disease risk present.

**Water and Food Safety**

All local water should be considered contaminated, and all water used for drinking, brushing teeth, and making ice cubes should be boiled for ten minutes. Bottled water is recommended.

Dairy products should not be considered safe. All meat, seafood, poultry, and vegetables must be well cooked and served hot. Salads and cold buffets should be avoided.

In Santiago, Valdivia, Valparaiso, and Antofagasta, drinking water is chlorinated and generally safe to drink, but variations in local bacterial flora may cause diarrhea in some travelers. Bottled water is recommended for the first few weeks.

## China, People's Republic of

**Vaccinations**

— *Yellow fever:* A yellow fever vaccination certificate is required from travelers coming from infected areas.

— *Hepatitis and typhoid:* Immune globulin and typhoid vaccination are recommended for travelers' protection when visiting rural regions off the usual tourist itinerary.

**Malaria and Tropical Disease Risk**

Malaria risk exists throughout the country below 1,500 meters, except in Heilong Jiang, Jilin, Nei Monggol, Gansu, Beijing, Shanxi, Ningxia, Quinghai, Xinjiang (except along the valley of the Yili River), and Xizang (except along the valley of the Zangbo River in the extreme southeast). North of 33°N latitude transmission occurs from July to November, between 33°N and 25°N, from May to December and south to 25°N latitude, throughout the year. Resistance to chloroquine reported.

— *Other tropical disease:* Schistosomiasis risk present in entire country. The major endemic area is located in the central and lower Chang Jiang (Yangtze River) valley, including its tributaries and adjacent lakes. The area extends from the western city of Yichang (Ich'ang) in Hubei (Hupeh) Province to and including the suburbs of Shanghai in the east on the mouth of the river. In the north, the area is limited by the cities of Tianmen (T'ien-men) on the Han River, Zaoshi (Tsaoshih) and the surrounding lake areas (Hubei Province), the area of Hufei (Hofei) in Anhui (Anhwei) Province, and the area of Yangzhou (Yangchou) in central Jiangsu (Kiangsu) Province. To the south of the Chang Jiang, the risk extends to the lake area of Dongting (Tungt'ing) and the areas of the cities of Changde (Ch'angte) on the Yuan River, Xiangtan (Hsiangt'an) on the Xiang Jiang (Hsiang) River, and Pingjiang (P'ingchiang) to the east of the lake (Hunan Province). In the province of Zhejian (Chekiang), the risk extends from the Tai Lake area to the delta of the Fuchun River and the coastal areas of Hangzhou (Hangchou) Bay. A restricted focus of infection is present in Fujian (Fukien) Province: the area of Changle (Ch'anglo) on the Min River delta, south of Fuzhou (Fuchou). In southern China, two restricted areas of infection are present: one on the Han River north of Shantou in Guangdong (Kwangtung) Province, and other in the area of Binyang (Pinyang) north of Nanning in Guangxi (Kwangsi) Province. A restricted focus is present in western China, in the Province of Sichuan (Szechuan), south of Chengdu (Cheng'tu), in the villages of Renshou (Jenshowsien) and Rongxian (Junghsien).

**Water and Food Safety**

All local water should be considered contaminated, and all water used for drinking, brushing teeth, and making ice cubes should be boiled for ten minutes. Bottled water is recommended.

Dairy products should not be considered safe. All meat, seafood, poultry, and vegetables must be well cooked and served hot. Salads and cold buffets should be avoided.

**China, Republic of (Taiwan)**
**Vaccinations**
— *Hepatitis and typhoid:* Immune globulin and typhoid vaccination are recommended for travelers' protection when visiting rural regions off the usual tourist itinerary.
**Malaria and Tropical Disease Risk**
No known malaria risk.
— *Other tropical disease:* No known risk.
**Water and Food Safety**
All local water should be considered contaminated, and all water used for drinking, brushing teeth, and making ice cubes should be boiled for ten minutes. Bottled water is recommended.

Dairy products should not be considered safe. All meat, seafood, poultry, and vegetables must be well cooked and served hot. Salads and cold buffets should be avoided.

**Christmas Island (Indian Ocean)**
**Vaccinations**
— *Yellow fever:* A yellow fever vaccination certificate is required from travelers coming from infected areas.
**Malaria and Tropical Disease Risk**
No known malaria risk.
— *Other tropical disease:* No known risk.
**Water and Food Safety**
Unknown. Precautions are recommended.

**Colombia**
**Vaccinations**
No vaccination requirements for any international traveler.
— *Yellow fever:* It is recommended that travelers who plan to visit rural regions off of the usual tourist itinerary be vaccinated against yellow fever.
— *Hepatitis and typhoid:* Immune globulin and typhoid vaccination are recommended for travelers' protection when visiting rural regions off the usual tourist itinerary.
**Malaria and Tropical Disease Risk**
Malaria risk exists throughout the year in rural areas below 800 meters of Uraba (Antioquia Dep.), Bajo Cauca-Nechi (Cauca and Antioquia Dep.), Magdalena Medio, Caquetá (Caquetá Intendencia), Sarare (Arauca Intendencia), Catatumbo (Norte de Santander Dept.), Pacifico Central and Sur, Putumayo (Putumayo Intendencia), Ariari (Meta Dep.), Alto Vaupes (Vaupes Comisaria) and Amazonas. Resistance to chloroquine reported.
— *Other tropical disease:* Dengue fever risk present. Chagas' disease risk present.

### Water and Food Safety

All local water should be considered contaminated, and all water used for drinking, brushing teeth, and making ice cubes should be boiled for ten minutes. Bottled water is recommended.

Dairy products should not be considered safe. All meat, seafood, poultry, and vegetables must we well cooked and served hot. Salads and cold buffets should be avoided.

## Comoros

### Vaccinations

No vaccination requirements for any international traveler.

— *Hepatitis and typhoid:* Immune globulin and typhoid vaccination are recommended for travelers' protection when visiting rural regions off the usual tourist itinerary.

### Malaria and Tropical Disease Risk

Malaria risk exists throughout the year in the whole country. Resistance to chloroquine reported in all malarious areas.

— *Other tropical disease:* No known risk.

### Water and Food Safety

All local water should be considered contaminated, and all water used for drinking, brushing teeth, and making ice cubes should be boiled for ten minutes. Bottled water is recommended.

Dairy products should not be considered safe. All meat, seafood, poultry, and vegetables must be well cooked and served hot. Salads and cold buffets should be avoided.

## Congo

### Vaccinations

— *Yellow fever:* A yellow fever vaccination certificate is required from all travelers over one year of age, except those arriving from a noninfected country and staying less than two weeks in the country.

— *Hepatitis and typhoid:* Immune globulin and typhoid vaccination are recommended for travelers' protection when visiting rural regions off the usual tourist itinerary.

### Malaria and Tropical Disease Risk

Malaria risk exists throughout the year in the whole country.

— *Other tropical disease:* Schistosomiasis risk present in the country; extent of infection not determined.

### Water and Food Safety

All local water should be considered contaminated, and all water used for drinking, brushing teeth, and making ice cubes should be boiled for ten minutes. Bottled water is recommended.

Dairy products should not be considered safe. All meat, seafood, poultry, and vegetables must be well cooked and served hot. Salads and cold buffets should be avoided.

## Cook Islands
### Vaccinations
No vaccination requirements for any international traveler.
### Malaria and Tropical Disease Risk
No known malaria risk.
— *Other tropical disease:* No known risk.
### Water and Food Safety
Drinking water is chlorinated and generally safe to drink, but variations in local bacterial flora may cause diarrhea in some travelers. Bottled water is recommended for the first few weeks. Dairy products, meat, poultry, seafood, vegetables, and fruits are safe to eat.

## Costa Rica
### Vaccinations
No vaccination requirements for any international travelers.
— *Hepatitis and typhoid:* Immune globulin and typhoid vaccination are recommended for travelers' protection when visiting rural regions off the usual tourist itinerary.
### Malaria and Tropical Disease Risk
Malaria risk exists throughout the year in the rural areas below 500 meters of Alajuela, Guanacaste, Limón and Puntarenas Prov.
— *Other tropical disease:* Chagas' disease risk present.
### Water and Food Safety
All local water should be considered contaminated, and all water used for drinking, brushing teeth, and making ice cubes should be boiled for ten minutes. Bottled water is recommended.
Dairy products should not be considered safe. All meat, seafood, poultry, and vegetables must be well cooked and served hot. Salads and cold buffets should be avoided.

## Cuba
### Vaccinations
— *Yellow fever:* A yellow fever vaccination certificate is required from travelers over one year of age coming from infected areas.
— *Hepatitis and typhoid:* Immune globulin and typhoid vaccination are recommended for travelers' protection when visiting rural regions off the usual tourist itinerary.
### Malaria and Tropical Disease Risk
No known malaria risk.
— *Other tropical disease:* No known risk.
### Water and Food Safety
All local water should be considered contaminated, and all water used for drinking, brushing teeth, and making ice cubes should be boiled for ten minutes. Bottled water is recommended.
Dairy products should not be considered safe. All meat, sea-

food, poultry, and vegetables must be well cooked and served hot. Salads and cold buffets should be avoided.

## Cyprus

### Vaccinations

No vaccination requirements for any international traveler.

— *Hepatitis and typhoid:* Immune globulin and typhoid vaccination are recommended for travelers' protection when visiting rural regions off the usual tourist itinerary.

### Malaria and Tropical Disease Risk

No known malaria risk.

— *Other tropical disease:* No known risk.

### Water and Food Safety

Drinking water is chlorinated and generally safe to drink, but variations in local bacterial flora may cause diarrhea in some travelers. Bottled water is recommended for the first few weeks. Dairy products, meats, poultry, seafood, vegetables, and fruits are safe to eat.

## Czechoslovakia

### Vaccinations

No vaccination requirements for any international traveler.

### Malaria and Tropical Disease Risk

No known malaria risk.

— *Other tropical disease:* No known risk.

### Water and Food Safety

Drinking water is chlorinated and generally safe to drink, but variations in local bacterial flora may cause diarrhea in some travelers. Bottled water is recommended for the first few weeks. Dairy products, meats, poultry, seafood, vegetables, and fruits are safe to eat.

## Democratic Kampuchea (formerly Cambodia)

### Vaccinations

— *Yellow fever:* A yellow fever vaccination certificate is required from travelers coming from infected areas.

— *Hepatitis and typhoid:* Immune globulin and typhoid vaccination are recommended for travelers' protection when visiting rural regions off the usual tourist itinerary.

### Malaria and Tropical Disease Risk

Malaria risk exists throughout the year in the whole country. Resistance to chloroquine reported.

— *Other tropical disease:* Schistosomiasis risk present in restricted areas; most of the country is free of infection.

### Water and Food Safety

All local water should be considered contaminated, and all water used for drinking, brushing teeth, and making ice cubes should

be boiled for ten minutes. Bottled water is recommended.

Dairy products should not be considered safe. All meats, seafood, poultry, and vegetables must be well cooked and served hot. Salads and cold buffets should be avoided.

## Denmark

### Vaccinations

No vaccination requirements for any international traveler.

### Malaria and Tropical Disease Risk

No known malaria risk.

— *Other tropical disease:* No known risk.

### Water and Food Safety

Local water is safe to drink. Dairy products, meats, poultry, seafood, vegetables, and fruits are safe to eat.

## Djibouti

### Vaccinations

— *Yellow fever:* A yellow fever vaccination certificate is required from travelers over one year of age coming from infected countries.

— *Hepatitis and typhoid:* Immune globulin and typhoid vaccination are recommended for travelers' protection when visiting rural regions off the usual tourist itinerary.

### Malaria and Tropical Disease Risk

Malaria risk exists throughout the year in the whole country.

— *Other tropical disease:* No known risk.

### Water and Food Safety

In the city of Djibouti, drinking water is chlorinated and generally safe to drink, but variations in local bacterial flora may cause diarrhea in some travelers. Bottled water is recommended for the first few weeks.

## Dominica

### Vaccinations

— *Yellow fever:* A yellow fever vaccination certificate is required from travelers over one year of age coming from infected areas.

— *Hepatitis and typhoid:* Immune globulin and typhoid vaccination are recommended for travelers' protection when visiting rural regions off the usual tourist itinerary.

### Malaria and Tropical Disease Risk

No known malaria risk.

— *Other tropical disease:* Dengue fever risk present.

### Water and Food Safety

Drinking water is chlorinated and generally safe to drink, but variations in local bacterial flora may cause diarrhea in some travelers. Bottled water is recommended for the first few weeks. Dairy products, meat, poultry, seafood, vegetables, and fruits are safe to eat.

## Dominican Republic
### Vaccinations
No vaccination requirements for any international traveler.

— *Hepatitis and typhoid:* Immune globulin and typhoid vaccination are recommended for travelers' protection when visiting rural regions off the usual tourist itinerary.

### Malaria and Tropical Disease Risk
Malaria risk exists throughout the year in rural areas of Pedernales Municipio (Pedernales Prov.); Elias Pina, El Llano, Banica Mun. (Elias Pina Prov.); Dajabon, Partido Mun. (Dajabon Prov.); Pepillo Salcedo Mun. (Monte Cristo Prov.). In general, areas bordering Haiti.

— *Other tropical disease:* Schistosomiasis risk present in restricted areas; most of the country is free of infection. Risk of infection is limited to the area of Hato Major and the surrounding villages in the interior of the eastern part of the country. Dengue fever risk present.

### Water and Food Safety
All local water should be considered contaminated, and all water used for drinking, brushing teeth, and making ice cubes should be boiled for ten minutes. Bottled water is recommended.

Dairy products should not be considered safe. All meat, seafood, poultry, and vegetables must be well cooked and served hot. Salads and cold buffets should be avoided.

## Ecuador
### Vaccinations
No vaccination requirements for any international traveler.

— *Yellow fever:* A yellow fever vaccination certificate is required from travelers visiting rural areas off of the usual tourist itinerary.

— *Hepatitis and typhoid:* Immune globulin and typhoid vaccination are recommended for travelers' protection when visiting rural regions off the usual tourist itinerary.

### Malaria and Tropical Disease Risk
Malaria risk exists throughout the year below 1,500 meters in Esmeraldes, Guayas, Manabí, and El Oro Prov. and in rural areas of Loja, Morona Santiago, Napo, Pastaza, Portoviejo, Puyo, and Zamora Chinchipe Prov. Resistance to chloroquine reported in provinces in interior of country bordering Colombia.

— *Other tropical disease:* No known risk.

### Water and Food Safety
All local water should be considered contaminated, and all water used for drinking, brushing teeth, and making ice cubes should be boiled for ten minutes. Bottled water is recommended.

Dairy products should not be considered safe. All meat, seafood, poultry, and vegetables must be well cooked and served hot. Salads and cold buffets should be avoided.

On the Galápagos Islands, drinking water is chlorinated and generally safe to drink, but variations in local bacterial flora may cause diarrhea in some travelers. Bottled water is recommended for the first few weeks.

## Egypt

### Vaccinations

— *Yellow fever:* A yellow fever vaccination certificate is required from travelers over one year of age coming from infected areas. The following countries and areas are regarded as infected areas.

— *Africa:* Angola, Benin, Botswana, Burundi, Central African Republic, Chad, Congo, Equatorial Guinea, Ethiopia, Gabon, Gambia, Ghana, Guinea, Guinea-Bissau, Ivory Coast, Kenya, Liberia, Malawi, Mali, Mauritania, Niger, Nigeria, Sao Tome and Principe, Rwanda, Senegal, Sierra Leone, Somalia, Sudan (south of 15°N), Togo, Uganda, United Republic of Tanzania, Upper Volta, Zaire, Zambia.

— *America:* Belize, Bolivia, Brazil, Colombia, Costa Rica, Ecuador, French Guiana, Guatemala, Guyana, Honduras, Nicaragua, Panama, Peru, Surinam, Trinidad and Tobago, Venezuela.

— *Hepatitis and typhoid:* Immune globulin and typhoid vaccination are recommended for travelers' protection when visiting rural regions off the usual tourist itinerary.

### Malaria and Tropical Disease Risk

Malaria risk exists from June through October in rural areas of the Nile Delta, El Faiyûm area, the oases, and part of Upper Egypt.

— *Other tropical disease:* Schistosomiasis risk present in entire country, including urban areas. Infection with s. *haematobia* is endemic throughout Egypt. S. *mansoni* is present in the Nile Delta and does not extend further south than El Giza.

### Water and Food Safety

All local water should be considered contaminated, and all water used for drinking, brushing teeth, and making ice cubes should be boiled for ten minutes. Bottled water is recommended.

Dairy products should not be considered safe. All meat, seafood, poultry, and vegetables must be well cooked and served hot. Salads and cold buffets should be avoided.

In Alexandria, Cairo, and Luxor, drinking water is chlorinated and generally safe. However, variations in local bacterial flora may cause diarrhea in travelers, and bottled water is recommended for the first few weeks. Precautions must be maintained regarding dairy products, meat, seafood, poultry, and vegetables.

# El Salvador

## Vaccinations

— *Yellow fever:* A yellow fever vaccination certificate is required from travelers over six months of age coming from infected areas.
— *Hepatitis and typhoid:* Immune globulin and typhoid vaccination are recommended for travelers' protection when visiting rural regions off the usual tourist itinerary.

## Malaria and Tropical Disease Risk

Malaria risk exists throughout the year in the whole country, but is greater below 600 meters in the rainy season.
— *Other tropical disease:* Chagas' disease risk present.

## Water and Food Safety

All local water should be considered contaminated, and all water used for drinking, brushing teeth, and making ice cubes should be boiled for ten minutes. Bottled water is recommended.

Dairy products should not be considered safe. All meat, seafood, poultry, and vegetables must be well cooked and served hot. Salads and cold buffets should be avoided.

# Equatorial Guinea

## Vaccinations

— *Yellow fever:* A yellow fever vaccination certificate is required from travelers coming from infected areas. In addition, it is recommended for all travelers' protection.
— *Hepatitis and typhoid:* Immune globulin and typhoid vaccination are recommended for travelers' protection when visiting rural regions off the usual tourist itinerary.

## Malaria and Tropical Disease Risk

Malaria risk exists throughout the year in the whole country.
— *Other tropical disease:* Schistosomiasis risk is unknown.

## Water and Food Safety

All local water should be considered contaminated, and all water used for drinking, brushing teeth, and making ice cubes should be boiled for ten minutes. Bottled water is recommended.

Dairy products should not be considered safe. All meat, seafood, poultry, and vegetables must be well cooked and served hot. Salads and cold buffets should be avoided.

# Ethiopia

## Vaccinations

— *Yellow fever:* A yellow fever vaccination certificate is required from travelers over one year of age coming from infected areas.
— *Hepatitis and typhoid:* Immune globulin and typhoid vaccination

are recommended for travelers' protection when visiting rural regions off the usual tourist itinerary.

**Malaria and Tropical Disease Risk**

Malaria risk exists throughout the year in the whole country below 2,000 meters.

— *Other tropical disease:* Schistosomiasis risk present in the country; extent of infection not determined.

**Water and Food Safety**

All local water should be considered contaminated, and all water used for drinking, brushing teeth, and making ice cubes should be boiled for ten minutes. Bottled water is recommended.

Dairy products should not be considered safe. All meat, seafood, poultry, and vegetables must be well cooked and served hot. Salads and cold buffets should be avoided.

## Falkland Islands (Malvinas)

**Vaccinations**

No vaccination requirements for any international traveler.

**Malaria and Tropical Disease Risk**

No known malaria risk.

— *Other tropical disease:* No known risk.

**Water and Food Safety**

Local water is safe to drink. Dairy products, meat, poultry, seafood, vegetables, and fruits to are safe to eat.

## Faroe Islands

**Vaccinations**

No vaccination requirements for any international traveler.

**Malaria and Tropical Disease Risk**

No known malaria risk.

— *Other tropical disease:* No known risk.

**Water and Food Safety**

Drinking water is chlorinated and generally safe to drink, but variations in local bacterial flora may cause diarrhea in some travelers. Bottled water is recommended for the first few weeks. Dairy products, meat, poultry, seafood, vegetables, and fruits are safe to eat.

## Fiji

**Vaccinations**

— *Yellow fever:* A yellow fever vaccination certificate is required from travelers over one year of age coming from infected areas.

**Malaria and Tropical Disease Risk**

No known malaria risk.

— *Other tropical disease:* No known risk.

**Water and Food Safety**

Drinking water is chlorinated and generally safe to drink, but

variations in local bacterial flora may cause diarrhea in some travelers. Bottled water is recommended for the first few weeks. Dairy products, meat, poultry, seafood, vegetables, and fruits are safe to eat.

## Finland

### Vaccinations

No vaccination requirements for any international traveler.

### Malaria and Tropical Disease Risk

No known malaria risk.

— *Other tropical disease:* No known risk.

### Water and Food Safety

Local water is safe to drink. Dairy products, meat, poultry, seafood, vegetables, and fruits are safe to eat.

## France

### Vaccinations

No vaccination requirements for any international traveler.

### Malaria and Tropical Disease Risk

No known malaria risk.

— *Other tropical disease:* No known risk.

### Water and Food Safety

Drinking water is chlorinated and generally safe to drink, but variations in local bacterial flora may cause diarrhea in some travelers. Bottled water is recommended for the first few weeks. Dairy products, meat, poultry, seafood, vegetables, and fruits are safe to eat.

In Paris, the drinking water is safe to drink.

## French Guiana

### Vaccinations

— *Yellow fever:* A yellow fever vaccination certificate is required from travelers over one year of age coming from all countries, except those arriving from a noninfected area and staying less than two weeks in French Guiana.

— *Hepatitis and typhoid:* Immune globulin and typhoid vaccination are recommended for travelers' protection when visiting rural regions off the usual tourist itinerary.

### Malaria and Tropical Disease Risk

Malaria risk exists throughout the year in the whole country excluding the town of Cayenne. Resistance to chloroquine reported.

— *Other tropical disease:* Dengue fever risk present. Chagas' disease risk present.

### Water and Food Safety

Drinking water is chlorinated and generally safe to drink, but variations in local bacterial flora may cause diarrhea in some travelers. Bottled drinking water is recommended. Milk and dairy products are not considered safe. Local meat, poultry, seafood, and vegetables are safe to eat.

## French Polynesia (Tahiti)
### Vaccinations
— *Yellow fever:* A yellow fever vaccination certificate is required from travelers over one year of age coming from infected areas.

### Malaria and Tropical Disease Risk
No known malaria risk.
— *Other tropical disease:* Dengue fever risk present.

### Water and Food Safety
Drinking water is chlorinated and generally safe to drink, but variations in local bacterial flora may cause diarrhea in some travelers. Bottled water is recommended for the first few weeks. Dairy products, meat, poultry, seafood, vegetables, and fruits are safe to eat.

## Gabon
### Vaccinations
— *Yellow fever:* A yellow fever vaccination certificate is required from travelers over one year of age coming from infected areas. In addition, it is recommended for all travelers' protection.
— *Hepatitis and typhoid:* Immune globulin and typhoid vaccination are recommended for travelers' protection when visiting rural regions off the usual tourist itinerary.

### Malaria and Tropical Disease Risk
Malaria risk exists throughout the year in the whole country.
— *Other tropical disease:* Schistosomiasis risk present in the country; extent of infection not determined.

### Water and Food Safety
All local water should be considered contaminated, and all water used for drinking, brushing teeth, and making ice cubes should be boiled for ten minutes. Bottled water is recommended.

Dairy products should not be considered safe. All meat, seafood, poultry, and vegetables must be well cooked and served hot. Salads and cold buffets should be avoided.

## Gambia
### Vaccinations
— *Yellow fever:* A yellow fever vaccination certificate is required from travelers over one year of age coming from infected areas.
— *Hepatitis and typhoid:* Immune globulin and typhoid vaccination are recommended for travelers' protection when visiting rural regions off the usual tourist itinerary.

### Malaria and Tropical Disease Risk
Malaria risk exists throughout the year in the whole country.

— *Other tropical disease:* Schistosomiasis risk present in entire country, including urban areas.

**Water and Food Safety**

Due to the presence of *Giardia lamblia,* all local drinking water should be considered contaminated.

Dairy products should not be considered safe. All meat, seafood, poultry, and vegetables must be well cooked and served hot. Salads and cold buffets should be avoided.

## German Democratic Republic (East Germany)

**Vaccinations**

No vaccination requirements for any international traveler.

**Malaria and Tropical Disease Risk**

No known malaria risk.

— *Other tropical disease:* No known risk.

**Water and Food Supply**

Local water is safe to drink. Dairy products, meat, poultry, seafood, vegetables, and fruits are safe to eat.

## Germany, Federal Republic of (West Germany)

**Vaccinations**

No vaccination requirements for any international traveler.

**Malaria and Tropical Disease Risk**

No known malaria risk.

— *Other tropical disease:* No known risk.

**Water and Food Safety**

Local water is safe to drink. Dairy products, meat, poultry, seafood, vegetables, and fruits are safe to eat.

## Ghana

**Vaccinations**

— *Yellow fever:* A yellow fever vaccination certificate is required from travelers over one year of age coming from infected areas. A certificate is required from travelers who have visited an endemic area (appendix C) within the preceding seven days, and it is recommended for travelers arriving from noninfected areas.

— *Hepatitis and typhoid:* Immune globulin and typhoid vaccination are recommended for travelers' protection when visiting rural regions off the usual tourist itinerary.

**Malaria and Tropical Disease Risk**

Malaria risk exists throughout the year in the whole country.

— *Other tropical disease:* Schistosomiasis risk present in entire country, including urban areas.

**Water and Food Safety**

All local water should be considered contaminated, and all water used for drinking, brushing teeth, and making ice cubes should be boiled for ten minutes. Bottled water is recommended.

Dairy products should not be considered safe. All meat, seafood, poultry, and vegetables must be well cooked and served hot. Salads and cold buffets should be avoided.

## Gibraltar

**Vaccinations**

No vaccination requirements for any international traveler.

**Malaria and Tropical Disease Risk**

No known malaria risk.

— *Other tropical disease:* No known risk.

**Water and Food Safety**

Drinking water is chlorinated and generally safe to drink, but variations in local bacterial flora may cause diarrhea in some travelers. Bottled water is recommended for the first few weeks. Dairy products, meat, poultry, seafood, vegetables, and fruits are safe to eat.

## Greece

**Vaccinations**

— *Yellow fever:* A yellow fever vaccination certificate is required from travelers over six months of age coming from infected areas.

**Malaria and Tropical Disease Risk**

No known malaria risk.

— *Other tropical disease:* No known risk.

**Water and Food Safety**

Drinking water is chlorinated and generally safe to drink, but variations in local bacterial flora may cause diarrhea in some travelers. Bottled water is recommended for the first few weeks. Dairy products, meat, poultry, seafood, vegetables, and fruits are safe to eat.

## Greenland

**Vaccinations**

No vaccination requirements for any international traveler.

**Malaria and Tropical Disease Risk**

No known malaria risk.

— *Other tropical disease:* No known risk.

**Water and Food Safety**

Local water is safe to drink. Dairy products, meat, poultry, seafood, vegetables, and fruits are safe to eat.

## Grenada

**Vaccinations**

— *Yellow fever:* A yellow fever vaccination certificate is required from travelers coming from infected areas.

**Malaria and Tropical Disease Risk**

No known malaria risk.

— *Other tropical disease:* Dengue fever risk present.

**Water and Food Safety**

Drinking water is chlorinated and generally safe to drink, but variations in local bacterial flora may cause diarrhea in some travelers. Bottled water is recommended for the first few weeks. Dairy products, meat, poultry, seafood, vegetables, and fruits are safe to eat.

## Guadeloupe

**Vaccinations**

— *Yellow fever:* A yellow fever vaccination certificate is required from travelers over one year of age coming from infected areas.

**Malaria and Tropical Disease Risk**

No known malaria risk.

— *Other tropical disease:* Schistosomiasis risk present in entire country, including urban areas. The islands of Grande-Terre, Basse-Terre, Marie Galante and La Désirade are infected. Dengue fever risk present.

**Water and Food Safety**

Drinking water is chlorinated and generally safe to drink, but variations in local bacterial flora may cause diarrhea in some travelers. Bottled water is recommended for the first few weeks. Dairy products, meat, poultry, seafood, vegetables, and fruits are safe to eat.

## Guatemala

**Vaccinations**

— *Yellow fever:* A yellow fever vaccination certificate is required from travelers over one year of age coming from infected areas.

— *Hepatitis and typhoid:* Immune globulin and typhoid vaccination are recommended for travelers' protection when visiting rural regions off the usual tourist itinerary.

**Malaria and Tropical Disease Risk**

Malaria risk exists throughout the year below 1,500 meters in Dep. of: (a) (excluding urban areas) Baja Verapaz, Chiquimula, Escuintla, Jalapa, El Peten, El Progreso, El Quiche, Santa Rosa, Suchitpequez, Zacapa; (b) Alta Verapaz, Huehuetenango, Izabal, Jutiapa, Retalhuleu; and (c) in the Municipios of Coatepeque (Quetzaltenango Dep.) and Ocós (San Marcos Dep.).

— *Other tropical disease:* Chagas' disease risk present.

**Water and Food Safety**

All local water should be considered contaminated, and all water used for drinking, brushing teeth, and making ice cubes should be boiled for ten minutes. Bottled water is recommended.

Dairy products should not be considered safe. All meat, seafood, poultry, and vegetables must be well cooked and served hot. Salads and cold buffets should be avoided.

**Guiana, French (see French Guiana)**

## Guinea

### Vaccinations

— *Yellow fever:* A yellow fever vaccination certificate is required from travelers over one year of age coming from all countries, except travelers coming from a noninfected area.

— *Hepatitis and typhoid:* Immune globulin and typhoid vaccination are recommended for travelers' protection when visiting rural regions off the usual tourist itinerary.

### Malaria and Tropical Disease Risk

Malaria risk exists throughout the year in the whole country.

— *Other tropical disease:* Schistosomiasis risk present in most of country, except for the following districts in lower Guinea: Boffa, Conakry, Fria, and Telimele.

### Water and Food Supply

All local water should be considered contaminated, and all water used for drinking, brushing teeth, and making ice cubes should be boiled for ten minutes. Bottled water is recommended.

Dairy products should not be considered safe. All meat, seafood, poultry, and vegetables must be well cooked and served hot. Salads and cold buffets should be avoided.

## Guinea-Bissau

### Vaccinations

— *Yellow fever:* A yellow fever vaccination certificate is required from travelers over one year of age coming from infected countries and from the following areas:

— *Africa:* Angola, Benin, Burundi, Central African Republic, Chad, Congo, Djibouti, Equatorial Guinea, Ivory Coast, Kenya, Liberia, Madagascar, Mali, Mauritania, Mozambique, Niger, Nigeria, Sierra Leone, Somalia, Togo, Uganda, United Republic of Tanzania, Upper Volta, Zaire, Zambia.

— *America:* Bolivia, Brazil, Colombia, Ecuador, French Guiana, Guyana, Panama, Peru, Surinam, Venezuela.

*Hepatitis and typhoid:* Immune globulin and typhoid vaccination are recommended for travelers' protection when visiting rural regions off the usual tourist itinerary.

### Malaria and Tropical Disease Risk

Malaria risk exists throughout the year in the whole country.

— *Other tropical disease:* Schistosomiasis risk present in entire country. Major risk area is the northern part of the country only, in the area extending from the coastal region of Cacheu to the border with Guinea, including the valleys of the rivers Cacheu and Geba.

**Water and Food Safety**

All local water should be considered contaminated, and all water used for drinking, brushing teeth, and making ice cubes should be boiled for ten minutes. Bottled water is recommended.

Dairy products should not be considered safe. All meat, seafood, poultry, and vegetables must be well cooked and served hot. Salads and cold buffets should be avoided.

# Guyana

## Vaccinations

— *Yellow fever:* A yellow fever vaccination certificate is required from travelers coming from infected areas, and from the following countries.

— *Africa:* Angola, Benin, Burundi, Central African Republic, Chad, Congo, Ethiopia, Gabon, Gambia, Ghana, Guinea, Guinea-Bissau, Ivory Coast, Kenya, Liberia, Mali, Niger, Nigeria, Rwanda, Sao Tome and Principe, Senegal, Sierra Leone, Somalia, Togo, Uganda, United Republic of Cameroon, United Republic of Tanzania, Upper Volta, Zaire.

— *America:* Belize, Bolivia, Brazil, Colombia, Costa Rica, Ecuador, French Guiana, Guatemala, Honduras, Nicaragua, Panama, Peru, Surinam, Venezuela.

— *Hepatitis and typhoid:* Immune globulin and typhoid vaccination are recommended for travelers' protection when visiting rural regions off the usual tourist itinerary.

## Malaria and Tropical Disease Risk

Malaria risk exists throughout the year in the North West Region and in the Rupununi Region. Resistance to chloroquine reported in areas in interior of country.

— *Other tropical disease:* Dengue fever risk present. Chagas' disease risk present.

## Water and Food Safety

Drinking water is chlorinated and generally safe to drink, but variations in local bacterial flora may cause diarrhea in some travelers. Bottled drinking water is recommended. Milk and dairy products are not considered safe. Local meat, poultry, seafood, and vegetables are safe to eat.

# Haiti

## Vaccinations

— *Yellow fever:* A yellow fever vaccination certificate is required from travelers coming from infected countries.

— *Hepatitis and typhoid:* Immune globulin and typhoid vaccination are recommended for travelers' protection when visiting rural regions off the usual tourist itinerary.

**Malaria and Tropical Disease Risk**
Malaria risk exists throughout the year below 300 meters in suburban and rural areas.
— *Other tropical disease:* Dengue fever risk present.

**Water and Food Safety**
All local water should be considered contaminated, and all water used for drinking, brushing teeth, and making ice cubes should be boiled for ten minutes. Bottled water is recommended.

Dairy products should not be considered safe. All meat, seafood, poultry, and vegetables must be well cooked and served hot. Salads and cold buffets should be avoided.

## Honduras

**Vaccinations**
— *Yellow fever:* A yellow fever vaccination certificate is required from travelers coming from infected countries.
— *Hepatitis and typhoid:* Immune globulin and typhoid vaccination are recommended for travelers' protection when visiting rural regions off the usual tourist itinerary.

**Malaria and Tropical Disease Risk**
Malaria risk exists throughout the year (from May through December in Dep. of Atlantida, Choluteca, Colon, El Paraiso, Gracias a Dios, Olancho, Valle, and Yoro), especially in rural areas.
— *Other tropical disease:* Chagas' disease risk present.

**Water and Food Safety**
All local water should be considered contaminated, and all water used for drinking, brushing teeth, and making ice cubes should be boiled for ten minutes. Bottled water is recommended.

Dairy products should not be considered safe. All meat, seafood, poultry, and vegetables must be well cooked and served hot. Salads and cold buffets should be avoided.

## Hong Kong

**Vaccinations**
No vaccination requirements for any international traveler.

**Malaria and Tropical Disease Risk**
No known malaria risk.
— *Other tropical disease:* No known risk.

**Water and Food Safety**
All local water should be considered contaminated, and all water used for drinking, brushing teeth, and making ice cubes should be boiled for ten minutes. Bottled water is recommended.

Dairy products should not be considered safe. All meat, seafood, poultry, and vegetables must be well cooked and served hot. Salads and cold buffets should be avoided.

## Hungary
### Vaccinations
No vaccination requirements for any international traveler.
### Malaria and Tropical Disease Risk
No known malaria risk.
— *Other tropical disease:* No known risk.
### Water and Food Safety
Drinking water is chlorinated and generally safe to drink, but variations in local bacterial flora may cause diarrhea in some travelers. Bottled water is recommended for the first few weeks. Dairy products, meat, poultry, seafood, vegetables, and fruits are safe to eat.

## Iceland
### Vaccinations
No vaccination requirements for any international traveler.
### Malaria and Tropical Disease Risk
No known malaria risk.
— *Other tropical disease:* No known risk.
### Water and Food Safety
Local water is safe to drink. Dairy products, meat, poultry, sea-food, vegetables, and fruits are safe to eat.

## India
### Vaccinations
— *Cholera:* Travelers proceeding to countries that impose restrictions for arrivals from India or from an infected area in India on account of cholera are required to possess a certificate.
— *Yellow fever:* A yellow fever vaccination certificate is required from travelers (including infants) when arriving within six days of departure from an infected area or who have been in such an area in transit. The following areas and countries are regarded by India as infected:
   — *Africa:* Angola, Benin, Botswana, Burundi, Central African Republic, Chad, Congo, Equatorial Guinea, Ethiopia, Gabon, Gambia, Ghana, Guinea, Guinea-Bissau, Ivory Coast, Kenya, Liberia, Malawi, Mali, Mauritania, Niger, Nigeria, Rwanda, Sao Tome and Principe, Senegal, Sierra Leone, Somalia, Sudan (south of 15°N), Togo, Uganda, United Republic of Cameroon, United Republic of Tanzania, Upper Volta, Zaire, Zambia.
   — *America:* Belize, Bolivia, Brazil, Colombia, Costa Rica, Ecuador, French Guiana, Guatemala, Guyana, Honduras, Nicaragua, Panama, Peru, Surinam, Trinidad and Tobago, Venezuela.
   — *Note.* When a case of yellow fever is reported from any coun-

try, that country is regarded by the government of India as infected with yellow fever and is added to the above list.

— *Hepatitis and typhoid:* Immune globulin and typhoid vaccination are recommended for all travelers.

## Malaria and Tropical Disease Risk

Malaria risk exists throughout the year in the whole country excluding parts of the states of Himachal Pradesh, Jammu and Kashmir, and Sikkim. Resistance to chloroquine reported.

— *Other tropical disease:* Schistosomiasis risk present in a small circumscribed area along the Vashishti River in the District of Ratnagiri, State of Maharashtra (about 250 kilometers south of Bombay). Dengue fever risk present.

## Water and Food Safety

All local water should be considered contaminated, and all water used for drinking, brushing teeth, and making ice cubes should be boiled for ten minutes. Bottled water is recommended.

Dairy products should not be considered safe. All meat, seafood, poultry, and vegetables must be well cooked and served hot. Salads and cold buffets should be avoided.

# Indonesia

## Vaccinations

— *Yellow fever:* A yellow fever vaccination certificate is required from travelers coming from infected areas. The countries and areas included in the yellow fever endemic zone (appendix C) are considered by Indonesia as infected areas.

— *Hepatitis and typhoid:* Immune globulin and typhoid vaccination are recommended for travelers visiting rural regions off the usual tourist itinerary.

## Malaria and Tropical Disease Risk

Malaria risk exists throughout the year in the whole country excluding Jakarta municipality and large cities. Resistance to chloroquine reported.

— *Other tropical disease:* Schistosomiasis risk present in restricted areas; most of the country is free of infection. Two areas of infection are present on the island of Sulawesi (Celebes). In the Lindu valley, in central Sulawesi, the infection is localized around Lake Lindu in the villages of Anca, Tomado, Langko, and Puroo. A recently discovered area of infection is present in Napu valley, about fifty kilometers southeast of Lindu valley, affecting the villages of Wuasa, Maholo, Winowangsa, Altitupu and Watumaeta.

Dengue fever risk present.

## Water and Food Safety

All local water should be considered contaminated, and all water

used for drinking, brushing teeth, and making ice cubes should be boiled for ten minutes. Bottled water is recommended.

Dairy products should not be considered safe. All meat, seafood, poultry, and vegetables must be well cooked and served hot. Salads and cold buffets should be avoided.

## Iran

### Vaccinations

— *Yellow fever:* A yellow fever vaccination certificate is required from travelers coming from infected areas. The countries and areas included in the yellow fever endemic zone (appendix C) are regarded by Iran as infected.

— *Hepatitis and typhoid:* Immune globulin and typhoid vaccination are recommended for all travelers.

### Malaria and Tropical Disease Risk

Malaria risk exists from March through November in the provinces of Sistan-Baluchestan and Hormozgan, the southern parts of the provinces or governorates of Fars, Kohgiluyeh-Boyar, Lorestan, and Chahar Mahal-Bakhtiari, and the north of Khuzestan.

— *Other tropical disease:* Schistosomiasis risk present in restricted areas; most of the country is free of infection. Risk exists only in the plain in the southwestern part of the country bordering Iraq. The area extends from the regions of Dezful and Sar Dasht to Khorramshar and is limited in the east by the Zagros Mountains (Khuzistan Province).

### Water and Food Safety

All local water should be considered contaminated, and all water used for drinking, brushing teeth, and making ice cubes should be boiled for ten minutes. Bottled water is recommended.

Dairy products should not be considered safe. All meat, seafood, poultry, and vegetables must be well cooked and served hot. Salads and cold buffets should be avoided.

## Iraq

### Vaccinations

— *Yellow fever:* A yellow fever vaccination certificate is required from travelers over one year of age coming from infected areas.

— *Hepatitis and typhoid:* Immune globulin and typhoid vaccination are recommended for all travelers.

### Malaria and Tropical Disease Risk

Malaria risk exists from May through November in the Northern Region below 1,500 meters: Duhok, Erbil, Kirkuk, Ninawa, and Sulaimaniya Provinces.

— *Other tropical disease:* Schistosomiasis risk present in most of country, except for the mountainous regions of the northeastern part of the country bordering Iran. Endemic areas are the river systems of Tigris and Euphrates, their tributaries and irrigation canals.

### Water and Food Safety

All local water should be considered contaminated, and all water used for drinking, brushing teeth, and making ice cubes should be boiled for ten minutes. Bottled water is recommended.

Dairy products should not be considered safe. All meat, seafood, poultry, and vegetables must be well cooked and served hot. Salads and cold buffets should be avoided.

## Ireland

### Vaccinations

No vaccination requirements for any international traveler.

### Malaria and Tropical Disease Risk

No known malaria risk.

— *Other tropical disease:* No known risk.

### Water and Food Safety

Local water is safe to drink. Dairy products, meat, poultry, seafood, vegetables, and fruits are safe to eat.

## Israel

### Vaccinations

No vaccination requirements for any international traveler.

### Malaria and Tropical Disease Risk

No known malaria risk.

— *Other tropical disease:* No known risk.

### Water and Food Safety

Drinking water is chlorinated and generally safe to drink, but variations in local bacterial flora may cause diarrhea in some travelers. Bottled water is recommended for the first few weeks. Dairy products, meat, poultry, seafood, vegetables, and fruits are safe to eat.

## Italy

### Vaccinations

No vaccination requirements for any international traveler.

### Malaria and Tropical Disease Risk

No known malaria risk.

— *Other tropical disease:* No known risk.

### Water and Food Safety

Drinking water is chlorinated and generally safe to drink, but variations in local bacterial flora may cause diarrhea in some travelers. Bottled water is recommended for the first few weeks. Dairy products, meat, poultry, seafood, vegetables, and fruits are safe to eat.

## Ivory Coast
### Vaccinations
— *Yellow fever:* A yellow fever vaccination certificate is required from travelers over one year of age coming from infected areas.

— *Hepatitis and typhoid:* Immune globulin and typhoid vaccination are recommended for travelers visiting rural regions off the usual tourist itinerary.

### Malaria and Tropical Disease Risk
Malaria risk exists throughout the year in the whole country.

— *Other tropical disease:* Schistosomiasis risk present in the country; extent of infection not determined.

### Water and Food Safety
All local water should be considered contaminated, and all water used for drinking, brushing teeth, and making ice cubes should be boiled for ten minutes. Bottled water is recommended.

Dairy products should not be considered safe. All meat, seafood, poultry, and vegetables must be well cooked and served hot. Salads and cold buffets should be avoided.

## Jamaica
### Vaccinations
— *Yellow fever:* A yellow fever vaccination certificate is required from travelers over one year of age coming from all countries of which any parts are infected (appendix C).

### Malaria and Tropical Disease Risk
No known malaria risk.

— *Other tropical disease:* Dengue fever risk present.

### Water and Food Safety
Drinking water is chlorinated and generally safe to drink, but variations in local bacterial flora may cause diarrhea in some travelers. Bottled water is recommended for the first few weeks. Dairy products, meat, poultry, seafood, vegetables, and fruits are safe to eat.

## Japan
### Vaccinations
No vaccination requirements for any international traveler.

### Malaria and Tropical Disease Risk
No known malaria risk.

— *Other tropical disease:* Schistosomiasis risk present in restricted areas; most of the country is free of infection. Five areas of infection, four on the main island of Honshu and one on the island of Kyushu, are present: Tone and Edo rivers with tributaries extending through the Prefectures of Chiba, Ibaraki, Saitama and Tokyo; the area of Numazu City (Kise River delta) and Fuji River delta in the Prefecture of Shizuoka; Yamanashi Prefecture with

Kofu as the major focus. The District of Katayama (on the border of the Prefectures of Hiroshima and Okayama, north of the Fukuyama), once a major area of infection, has practically been cleared. On Kyushu the risk is limited to the Chikugo River basin on the border of the Prefectures of Kukuoka and Saga.

**Water and Food Safety**

Local water is safe to drink. Dairy products, meat, poultry, seafood, vegetables, and fruits are safe to eat.

## Jordan

**Vaccinations**

No vaccination requirements for any international traveler.

**Malaria and Tropical Disease Risk**

No known malaria risk.

— *Other tropical disease:* No known risk.

**Water and Food Safety**

All local water should be considered contaminated, and all water used for drinking, brushing teeth, and making ice cubes should be boiled for ten minutes. Bottled water is recommended.

Dairy products should not be considered safe. All meat, seafood, poultry, and vegetables must be well cooked and served hot. Salads and cold buffets should be avoided.

## Kenya

**Vaccinations**

— *Yellow fever:* A yellow fever vaccination certificate is required from travelers over one year of age coming from infected areas. The countries and areas included in the yellow fever endemic zone (appendix C) are considered by Kenya as infected areas.

— *Hepatitis and typhoid:* Immune globulin and typhoid vaccination are recommended for travelers' protection when visiting rural regions off the usual tourist itinerary.

**Malaria and Tropical Disease Risk**

Malaria risk exists throughout the year in the whole country. There is normally little risk in the city of Nairobi and in the highlands (above 2,500 meters) of Central, Rift Valley, Eastern, Nyanza and Western Provinces. Resistance to chloroquine reported.

— *Other tropical disease:* Schistosomiasis risk present in entire country; major risk areas are along the shore of Lake Victoria, in the area of Kisumu; the Kano Plain, in the area of Machakos southeast of Nairobi; and along the Tana River in the northeastern part of the country.

**Water and Food Safety**

All local water should be considered contaminated, and all water used for drinking, brushing teeth, and making ice cubes should be boiled for ten minutes. Bottled water is recommended.

Dairy products should not be considered safe. All meat, seafood, poultry, and vegetables must be well cooked and served hot. Salads and cold buffets should be avoided.

In Nairobi and Mombassa, drinking water is chlorinated and generally safe to drink, but variations in local bacterial flora may cause diarrhea in some travelers. Bottled water is recommended for the first few weeks.

## Kiribati
### Vaccinations
— *Yellow fever:* A yellow fever vaccination certificate is required from travelers over one year of age coming from infected areas.
— *Hepatitis and typhoid:* Immune globulin and typhoid vaccination are recommended for travelers when visiting rural regions off the usual tourist itinerary.
### Malaria and Tropical Disease Risk
No known malaria risk.
— *Other tropical disease:* No known risk.
### Water and Food Safety
All local water should be considered contaminated, and all water used for drinking, brushing teeth, and making ice cubes should be boiled for ten minutes. Bottled water is recommended.

Dairy products should not be considered safe. All meat, seafood, poultry, and vegetables must be well cooked and served hot. Salads and cold buffets should be avoided.

## Korea, Democratic People's Republic of
### Vaccinations
No requirements for any international traveler.
— *Hepatitis and typhoid:* Immune globulin and typhoid vaccination are recommended for travelers' protection when visiting rural regions off the usual tourist itinerary.
### Malaria and Tropical Disease Risk
No known malaria risk.
— *Other tropical disease:* No known risk.
### Water and Food Safety
All local water should be considered contaminated, and all water used for drinking, brushing teeth, and making ice cubes should be boiled for ten minutes. Bottled water is recommended.

Dairy products should not be considered safe. All meat, seafood, poultry, and vegetables must be well cooked and served hot. Salads and cold buffets should be avoided.

## Korea, Republic of
### Vaccinations
— *Cholera:* A cholera vaccination certificate is required from travelers over one year of age arriving from infected areas.

— *Hepatitis and typhoid:* Immune globulin and typhoid vaccination are recommended for travelers' protection when visiting rural regions off the usual tourist itinerary.

**Malaria and Tropical Disease Risk**

No known malaria risk.

— *Other tropical disease:* No known risk.

**Water and Food Safety**

All local water should be considered contaminated, and all water used for drinking, brushing teeth, and making ice cubes should be boiled for ten minutes. Bottled water is recommended.

Dairy products should not be considered safe. All meat, seafood, poultry, and vegetables must be well cooked and served hot. Salads and cold buffets should be avoided.

In Seoul, drinking water is chlorinated and generally safe to drink, but variations in local bacterial flora may cause diarrhea in some travelers. Bottled water is recommended for the first few weeks.

**Kuwait**

**Vaccinations**

No vaccination requirements for any international traveler.

**Malaria and Tropical Disease Risk**

No known malaria risk.

— *Other tropical disease:* No known risk.

**Water and Food Safety**

Drinking water is chlorinated and generally safe to drink, but variations in local bacterial flora may cause diarrhea in some travelers. Bottled water is recommended for the first few weeks. Dairy products, meat, poultry, seafood, vegetables, and fruits are safe to eat.

**Lao People's Democratic Republic**

**Vaccinations**

— *Yellow fever:* A yellow fever vaccination certificate is required from travelers coming from infected areas.

— *Hepatitis and typhoid:* Immune globulin and typhoid vaccination are recommended for travelers' protection when visiting rural regions off the usual tourist itinerary.

**Malaria and Tropical Disease Risk**

Malaria risk exists throughout the year in the whole country, excluding Vientiane. Resistance to chloroquine reported.

— *Other tropical disease:* Schistosomiasis risk present in restricted areas; most of the country is free of infection. The only known endemic area of infection is the Không Island in the Mekong River, in the southwest on the border with Kampuchea. Dengue fever risk present.

**Water and Food Safety**

All local water should be considered contaminated, and all water used for drinking, brushing teeth, and making ice cubes should be boiled for ten minutes. Bottled water is recommended.

Dairy products should not be considered safe. All meat, seafood, poultry, and vegetables must be well cooked and served hot. Salads and cold buffets should be avoided.

## Lebanon

**Vaccinations**

— *Yellow fever:* A yellow fever vaccination certificate is required from travelers coming from infected areas.

**Malaria and Tropical Disease Risk**

No known malaria risk.

— *Other tropical disease:* Schistosomiasis risk present in restricted areas; most of the country is free of infection. Infection is limited to a small area in the southern part of the country. The risk is present in the coastal area of As Sarafand and the Litani River delta, between Sur (Tyre) and Sayda (Sidon).

**Water and Food Safety**

Drinking water is chlorinated and generally safe to drink, but variations in local bacterial flora may cause diarrhea in some travelers. Bottled water is recommended for the first few weeks. Dairy products, meat, poultry, seafood, vegetables, and fruits are safe to eat.

## Lesotho

**Vaccinations**

— *Cholera:* A cholera vaccination certificate is required from travelers coming from infected areas.

— *Yellow fever:* A yellow fever vaccination certificate is required from travelers coming from infected areas.

— *Hepatitis and typhoid:* Immune globulin and typhoid vaccination are recommended for travelers' protection when visiting rural regions off the usual tourist itinerary.

**Malaria and Tropical Disease Risk**

No known malaria risk.

— *Other tropical disease:* No known risk.

**Water and Food Safety**

In Maseru, local water is safe to drink. Dairy products, meat, poultry, seafood, vegetables, and fruits are safe to eat.

## Liberia

**Vaccinations**

— *Yellow fever:* A yellow fever vaccination certificate is required from travelers over one year of age comng from infected areas and from countries in the yellow fever endemic zone (appendix C). Yellow fever vaccination is recommended for all travelers to Liberia.

— *Hepatitis and typhoid:* Immune globulin and typhoid vaccination are recommended for travelers visiting rural regions off the usual tourist itinerary.

### Malaria and Tropical Disease Risk
Malaria risk exists throughout the year in the whole country.

— *Other tropical disease:* Schistosomiasis risk present in most of country, except for the coastal regions.

### Water and Food Safety
All local water should be considered contaminated, and all water used for drinking, brushing teeth, and making ice cubes should be boiled for ten minutes. Bottled water is recommended.

Dairy products should not be considered safe. All meat, seafood, poultry, and vegetables must be well cooked and served hot. Salads and cold buffets should be avoided.

## Libya
### Vaccinations
— *Cholera:* A cholera vaccination certificate is required from travelers coming from infected areas.

— *Yellow fever:* A yellow fever vaccination certificate is required from travelers over one year of age coming from infected areas.

— *Hepatitis and typhoid:* Immune globulin and typhoid vaccination are recommended for travelers' protection when visiting rural regions off the usual tourist itinerary.

### Malaria and Tropical Disease Risk
Malaria risk exists in two small foci in the southwest of the country, from February through August.

— *Other tropical disease:* Schistosomiasis risk present in restricted areas; most of the country is free of infection. Infection exists in the coastal areas of Dabusia and Lathrum (S.h.) west of Darnah (Derna), and in a restricted focus in Taurorga (S.m.) west of Misratah. Risk is also present in the southwestern part of the country in the valleys of Fezzan, including the area of Al Birkah on the Algerian border (S.h.)

### Water and Food Safety
All local water should be considered contaminated, and all water used for drinking, brushing teeth, and making ice cubes should be boiled for ten minutes. Bottled water is recommended.

Dairy products should not be considered safe. All meat, seafood, poultry, and vegetables must be well cooked and served hot. Salads and cold buffets should be avoided.

## Liechtenstein
### Vaccinations
No vaccination requirements for any international traveler.

**Malaria and Tropical Disease Risk**
No known malaria risk.
— *Other tropical disease:* No known risk.
**Water and Food Safety**
Local water is safe to drink. Dairy products, meat, poultry, seafood, vegetables, and fruits are safe to eat.

## Luxembourg
**Vaccinations**
No vaccination requirements for any international traveler.
**Malaria and Tropical Disease Risk**
No known malaria risk.
— *Other tropical disease:* No known risk.
**Water and Food Safety**
Local water is safe to drink. Dairy products, meat, poultry, seafood, vegetables, and fruits are safe to eat.

## Macao
**Vaccinations**
No vaccination requirements for any international traveler.
**Malaria and Tropical Disease Risk**
No known malaria risk.
— *Other tropical disease:* No known risk.
**Water and Food Safety**
All local water should be considered contaminated, and all water used for drinking, brushing teeth, and making ice cubes should be boiled for ten minutes. Bottled water is recommended.
Dairy products should not be considered safe. All meat, seafood, poultry, and vegetables must be well cooked and served hot. Salads and cold buffets should be avoided.

## Madagascar
**Vaccinations**
— *Cholera:* A cholera vaccination certificate is required from travelers over six months of age arriving from infected areas.
— *Yellow fever:* A yellow fever vaccination certificate is required from travelers coming from, or having been in transit in, an area considered to be infected.
— *Hepatitis and typhoid:* Immune globulin and typhoid vaccination are recommended for travelers visiting rural regions off the usual tourist itinerary.
**Malaria and Tropical Disease Risk**
Malaria risk exists throughout the year in all coastal areas. There is normally little risk in the outskirts of Antananarivo and in the towns of Antsirabe, Manjakandriana, Andramasina, and almost no risk in the town of Antananarivo. Resistance to chloroquine reported.

— *Other tropical disease:* Schistosomiasis risk present in most of country, except for the aea of Diego Suarez on the extreme north tip of the island; the area of Antananarivo in the central part of the island; the peninsula Presquile, including the areas of Maroantsetra and Antalaha. *S. haematobium* is prevalent on the western part of the island, while *S. mansoni* is predominant in the eastern part.

**Water and Food Safety**

All local water should be considered contaminated, and all water used for drinking, brushing teeth, and making ice cubes should be boiled for ten minutes. Bottled water is recommended.

Dairy products should not be considered safe. All meat, seafood, poultry, and vegetables must be well cooked and served hot. Salads and cold buffets should be avoided.

## Malawi

**Vaccinations**

— *Yellow fever:* A yellow fever vaccination certificate is required from travelers arriving from infected areas.

— *Hepatitis and typhoid:* Immune globulin and typhoid vaccination are recommended for travelers visiting rural regions off the usual tourist itinerary.

**Malaria and Tropical Disease Risk**

Malaria risk exists throughout the year in the whole country.

— *Other tropical disease:* Schistosomiasis risk present in entire country, including urban areas.

**Water and Food Safety**

All local water should be considered contaminated, and all water used for drinking, brushing teeth, and making ice cubes should be boiled for ten minutes. Bottled water is recommended.

Dairy products should not be considered safe. All meat, seafood, poultry, and vegetables must be well cooked and served hot. Salads and cold buffets should be avoided.

## Malaysia

**Vaccinations**

— *Yellow fever:* A yellow fever vaccination certificate is required from travelers over one year of age coming from infected countries. The countries and areas included in the yellow fever endemic zone (appendix C) are considered by Malaysia to be infected.

— *Hepatitis and typhoid:* Immune globulin and typhoid vaccination are recommended for travelers' protection when visiting rural regions off the usual tourist itinerary.

**Malaria and Tropical Disease Risk**

Malaria risk exists throughout the year in rural areas below 1,700 meters (but excluding most of the coastal areas), particularly in the deep hinterland. Resistance to chloroquine reported.

— *Other tropical disease:* Dengue fever present.

**Water and Food Safety**

All local water should be considered contaminated, and all water used for drinking, brushing teeth, and making ice cubes should be boiled for ten minutes. Bottled water is recommended.

Dairy products should not be considered safe. All meat, seafood, poultry, and vegetables must be well cooked and served hot. Salads and cold buffets should be avoided.

## Maldives

### Vaccinations

— *Cholera:* A cholera vaccination certificate is required from travelers arriving from countries any part of which is infected.

— *Yellow fever:* A yellow fever vaccination certificate is required from travelers arriving from infected areas.

— *Hepatitis and typhoid:* Immune globulin and typhoid vaccination are recommended for travelers visiting rural regions off the usual tourist itinerary.

### Malaria and Tropical Disease Risk

Malaria risk exists throughout the year in the whole country excluding the capital (Male), Kaafu Atoll, and the tourist resorts.

— *Other tropical disease:* Dengue fever risk present.

### Water and Safety

All local water should be considered contaminated, and all water used for drinking, brushing teeth, and making ice cubes should be boiled for ten minutes. Bottled water is recommended.

Dairy products should not be considered safe. All meat, seafood, poultry, and vegetables must be well cooked and served hot. Salads and cold buffets should be avoided.

## Mali

### Vaccinations

— *Cholera:* A cholera vaccination certificate is required from travelers arriving from infected areas.

— *Yellow fever:* A yellow fever vaccination certificate is required from travelers arriving from all countries, except travelers arriving from noninfected areas and staying less than two weeks in the country.

— *Hepatitis and typhoid:* Immune globulin and typhoid vaccination are recommended for travelers visiting rural regions off the usual tourist itinerary.

### Malaria and Tropical Disease Risk

Malaria risk exists throughout the year in the whole country.

— *Other tropical disease:* Schistosomiasis risk present in the country;

extent of infection not determined. Known endemic areas are the river basins of Niger and Senegal and their tributaries.

**Water and Food Safety**

All local water should be considered contaminated, and all water used for drinking, brushing teeth, and making ice cubes should be boiled for ten minutes. Bottled water is recommended.

Dairy products should not be considered safe. All meat, seafood, poultry, and vegetables must be well cooked and served hot. Salads and cold buffets should be avoided.

## Malta

**Vaccinations**

— *Cholera:* A cholera vaccination certificate is required from travelers arriving from infected areas.

— *Yellow fever:* A yellow fever vaccination certificate is required from travelers over six months of age arriving from infected areas.

**Malaria and Tropical Disease Risk**

No known malaria risk.

— *Other tropical disease:* No known risk.

**Water and Food Safety**

Drinking water is chlorinated and generally safe to drink, but variations in local bacterial flora may cause diarrhea in some travelers. Bottled water is recommended for the first few weeks. Dairy products, meats, poultry, seafood, vegetables, and fruits are safe to eat.

## Martinique

**Vaccinations**

— *Yellow fever:* A yellow fever vaccination certificate is required from travelers over one year of age coming from infected areas.

**Malaria and Tropical Disease Risk**

No known malaria risk.

— *Other tropical disease:* Dengue fever risk present.

**Water and Food Safety**

Drinking water is chlorinated and generally safe to drink, but variations in local bacterial flora may cause diarrhea in some travelers. Bottled water is recommended for the first few weeks. Dairy products, meats, poultry, seafood, vegetables, and fruits are safe to eat.

## Mauritania

**Vaccinations**

— *Yellow fever:* A yellow fever vaccination certificate is required from travelers over one year of age coming from all countries except travelers arriving from noninfected countries and staying less than two weeks.

— *Hepatitis and typhoid:* Immune globulin and typhoid vaccination are recommended for travelers visiting rural areas off the usual tourist itinerary.

## Malaria and Tropical Disease Risk

Malaria risk exists throughout the year in the whole country, except in the following areas: Dakhlet-Nouadhibou, Inchiri, Adrar, Tiris-Zemour.

— *Other tropical disease:* Schistosomiasis risk present in the country; extent of infection not determined.

## Water and Food Safety

All local water should be considered contaminated, and all water used for drinking, brushing teeth, and making ice cubes should be boiled for ten minutes. Bottled water is recommended.

Dairy products should not be considered safe. All meat, seafood, poultry, and vegetables must be well cooked and served hot. Salads and cold buffets should be avoided.

# Mauritius

## Vaccinations

— *Yellow fever:* A yellow fever vaccination certificate is required from travelers over one year of age coming from infected areas. The countries and areas in the yellow fever endemic zone (appendix C) are considered by Mauritius to be infected.

## Malaria and Tropical Disease Risk

Malaria risk in the vivax form exists throughout the year in the whole country, apart from Rodriquez Island.

— *Other tropical disease:* Schistosomiasis risk present in entire country, including urban areas.

## Water and Food Safety

All local water should be considered contaminated, and all water used for drinking, brushing teeth, and making ice cubes should be boiled for ten minutes. Bottled water is recommended.

Dairy products should not be considered safe. All meat, seafood, poultry, and vegetables must be well cooked and served hot. Salads and cold buffets should be avoided.

# Mexico

## Vaccinations

— *Yellow fever:* A yellow fever vaccination certificate is required from travelers over six months of age coming from infected areas.

— *Hepatitis and typhoid:* Immune globulin and typhoid vaccination are recommended for travelers visiting rural areas off the usual tourist itinerary.

## Malaria and Tropical Disease Risk

Malaria risk exists in some rural areas that are not often visited by travelers: all year in Chiapas, Guerrero, Michoacan, Nayarit, Oaxaca, and parts of Campeche, Quintana Roo, Tabasco, and Veracruz States; from June through October in Morelos, Puebla (part) States and Alamos Mun. (Sonora State); from May through October in Sinaloa and parts of Chihuahua, Durango, Jalisco States; from May through December in part of Yucatán State.

— *Other tropical disease:* Chagas' disease risk present.

### Water and Food Safety

All local water should be considered contaminated, and all water used for drinking, brushing teeth, and making ice cubes should be boiled for ten minutes. Bottled water is recommended.

Dairy products should not be considered safe. All meat, seafood, poultry, and vegetables must be well cooked and served hot. Salads and cold buffets should be avoided.

## Monaco

### Vaccinations

No vaccination requirements for any international traveler.

### Malaria and Tropical Disease Risk

No known malaria risk.

— *Other tropical disease:* No known risk.

### Water and Food Safety

Drinking water is chlorinated and generally safe to drink, but variations in local bacterial flora may cause diarrhea in some travelers. Bottled water is recommended for the first few weeks. Dairy products, meat, poultry, seafood, vegetables, and fruits are safe to eat.

## Mongolia

### Vaccinations

No vaccination requirements for any international traveler.

### Malaria and Tropical Disease Risk

No known malaria risk.

— *Other tropical disease:* No known risk.

### Water and Food Safety

All local water should be considered contaminated, and all water used for drinking, brushing teeth, and making ice cubes should be boiled for ten minutes. Bottled water is recommended.

Dairy products should not be considered safe. All meat, seafood, poultry, and vegetables must be well cooked and served hot. Salads and cold buffets should be avoided.

## Montserrat

### Vaccinations

— *Yellow fever:* A yellow fever vaccination certificate is required from travelers over one year of age coming from infected areas.

### Malaria and Tropical Disease Risk

No known malaria risk.

— *Other tropical disease:* Schistosomiasis risk present in entire country, including urban areas. Dengue fever risk present.

### Water and Food Safety

Drinking water is chlorinated and generally safe to drink, but variations in local bacterial flora may cause diarrhea in some travelers. Bottled water is recommended for the first few weeks. Dairy products, meat, poultry, seafood, vegetables, and fruits are safe to eat.

## Morocco

### Vaccinations

No vaccination requirements for any international traveler.

— *Hepatitis and typhoid:* Immune globulin and typhoid vaccination are recommended for travelers visiting rural areas off the usual tourist itinerary.

### Malaria and Tropical Disease Risk

Minimal risk exists from May to October in the rural areas of Khémisset and Tata Provinces.

— *Other tropical disease:* Schistosomiasis risk present in entire country; major risk areas are:

- north of Rabat, in the region of the Gharb; and northeast of Larache, in the area of Tieta Rissana.

- in the District of Marrakech: in all towns and villages of the Tensift River valley.

- in the District of Meknes: the valleys of the rivers Guir and Rheris and their tributaries, south of the Atlas Range.

- in the areas of Ouarzazate, Agdz, M'Hamid, Tamgrout, Zagora, and the surrounding villages along the Drâa River.

- south of Agadir, in the region between the river Sous and the western part of the Antiatlas Range, affecting Aït Baha and Anezi.

- in the region south of the Antiatlas Range, affecting Assa, Akka, Tata, and the surrounding villages.

### Water and Food Safety

All local water should be considered contaminated, and all water used for drinking, brushing teeth, and making ice cubes should be boiled for ten minutes. Bottled water is recommended.

Dairy products should not be considered safe. All meat, seafood, poultry, and vegetables must be well cooked and served hot. Salads and cold buffets should be avoided.

## Mozambique
### Vaccinations
— *Cholera:* A cholera vaccination certificate is required from travelers arriving from all countries.
— *Yellow fever:* A yellow fever vaccination certificate is required from travelers over one year of age coming from infected areas.
— *Hepatitis and typhoid:* Immune globulin and typhoid vaccination are recommended for travelers visiting rural areas off the usual tourist itinerary.
### Malaria and Tropical Disease Risk
Malaria risk exists throughout the year in the whole country.
— *Other tropical disease:* Schistosomiasis risk present in entire country, including urban areas.
### Water and Food Safety
All local water should be considered contaminated, and all water used for drinking, brushing teeth, and making ice cubes should be boiled for ten minutes. Bottled water is recommended.

Dairy products should not be considered safe. All meat, seafood, poultry, and vegetables must be well cooked and served hot. Salads and cold buffets should be avoided.

## Namibia
### Vaccinations
— *Yellow fever:* A yellow fever vaccination certificate is required from travelers coming from infected areas. The countries and areas included in the yellow fever endemic zone (appendix C) are regarded by Namibia as infected.
— *Hepatitis and typhoid:* Immune globulin and typhoid vaccination are recommended for travelers visiting rural areas off the usual tourist itinerary.
### Malaria and Tropical Disease Risk
Malaria risk exists in Ovamboland and the Caprivi Strip from November through May.
— *Other tropical disease:* Schistosomiasis risk present in country; major risk areas: only in the north of the country, in a thin strip along the border with Angola extending into the Caprivi Strip between Zambia and Botswana.
### Water and Food Safety
All local water should be considered contaminated, and all water used for drinking, brushing teeth, and making ice cubes should be boiled for ten minutes. Bottled water is recommended.

Dairy products should not be considered safe. All meat, seafood, poultry, and vegetables must be well cooked and served hot. Salads and cold buffets should be avoided.

In Walois Bay and Windhoek, drinking water is chlorinated

and generally safe to drink, but variations in local bacterial flora may cause diarrhea in some travelers. Bottled water is recommended for the first few weeks.

## Nauru

### Vaccinations

— *Yellow fever:* A yellow fever vaccination certificate is required from travelers over one year of age coming from infected areas.

### Malaria and Tropical Disease Risk

No known malaria risk.

— *Other tropical disease:* No known risk.

### Water and Food Safety

Drinking water is chlorinated and generally safe to drink, but variations in local bacterial flora may cause diarrhea in some travelers. Bottled water is recommended for the first few weeks. Dairy products, meat, poultry, seafood, vegetables, and fruits are safe to eat.

## Nepal

### Vaccinations

— *Yellow fever:* A yellow fever vaccination certificate is required from travelers arriving from infected areas.

— *Hepatitis and typhoid:* Immune globulin and typhoid vaccination are recommended for travelers visiting rural areas off the usual tourist itinerary.

### Malaria and Tropical Disease Risk

Malaria risk exists throughout the year in rural areas of the Terai districts (incl. forested hills and forest areas) of Dhanukha, Mahotari, Sarlahi, Rautahat, Bara, Parsa, Rupendehi, Kapilvastu, and especially along the Indian border. Resistance to chloroquine reported.

— *Other tropical disease:* No known risk.

### Water and Food Safety

All local water should be considered contaminated, and all water used for drinking, brushing teeth, and making ice cubes should be boiled for ten minutes. Bottled water is recommended.

Dairy products should not be considered safe. All meat, seafood, poultry, and vegetables must be well cooked and served hot. Salads and cold buffets should be avoided.

## Netherlands

### Vaccinations

No vaccination requirements for any international traveler.

### Malaria and Tropical Disease Risk

No known malaria risk.

— *Other tropical disease:* No known risk.

### Water and Food Safety

Local water is safe to drink. Dairy products, meat, poultry, seafood, vegetables, and fruits are safe to eat.

## Netherlands Antilles

### Vaccinations

— *Yellow fever:* A yellow fever vaccination certificate is required from travelers over six months of age arriving from infected areas.

### Malaria and Tropical Disease Risk

No known malaria risk.

— *Other tropical disease:* Dengue fever risk present.

### Water and Food Safety

Drinking water is chlorinated and generally safe to drink, but variations in local bacterial flora may cause diarrhea in some travelers. Bottled water is recommended for the first few weeks. Dairy products, meat, poultry, seafood, vegetables, and fruits are safe to eat.

## New Caledonia

### Vaccinations

— *Yellow fever:* A yellow fever vaccination certificate is required from travelers over one year of age coming from infected areas. The countries and areas included in the yellow fever endemic zone (appendix C) are regarded by New Caledonia as infected.

— *Hepatitis and typhoid:* Immune globulin and typhoid vaccination are recommended for travelers visiting rural regions off the usual tourist itinerary.

### Malaria and Tropical Disease Risk

No known malaria risk.

— *Other tropical disease:* Dengue fever risk present.

### Water and Food Safety

Drinking water is chlorinated and generally safe to drink, but variations in local bacterial flora may cause diarrhea in some travelers. Bottled water is recommended for the first few weeks. Dairy products, meat, poultry, seafood, vegetables, and fruits are safe to eat.

## New Zealand

### Vaccinations

No vaccination requirements for any international traveler.

### Malaria and Tropical Disease Risk

No known malaria risk.

— *Other tropical disease:* No known risk.

### Water and Food Safety

Local water is safe to drink. Dairy products, meat, poultry, seafood, vegetables, and fruits are safe to eat.

## Nicaragua

### Vaccinations

No vaccination requirements for any international traveler.

— *Hepatitis and typhoid:* Immune globulin and typhoid vaccination are recommended for travelers visiting rural areas off the usual tourist itinerary.

### Malaria and Tropical Disease Risk

Malaria risk exists from May through December in rural areas as well as in the outskirts of Chinandega, León, Granada, Managua, Nandaime, and Tipitapa towns.

— *Other tropical disease:* Schistosomiasis risk present in entire country, including urban areas.

### Water and Food Safety

All local water should be considered contaminated, and all water used for drinking, brushing teeth, and making ice cubes should be boiled for ten minutes. Bottled water is recommended.

Dairy products should not be considered safe. All meat, seafood, poultry, and vegetables must be well cooked and served hot. Salads and cold buffets should be avoided.

## Niger

### Vaccinations

— *Cholera:* A cholera vaccination certificate is required from travelers arriving from infected countries.

— *Yellow fever:* A yellow fever vaccination certificate is required from travelers over one year of age coming from all countries and is recommended for travelers leaving Niger.

— *Hepatitis and typhoid:* Immune globulin and typhoid vaccination are recommended for travelers visiting rural areas off the usual tourist itinerary.

### Malaria and Tropical Disease Risk

Malaria risk exists throughout the year in the whole country.

— *Other tropical disease:* Schistosomiasis risk present in the country; extent of infection not determined. Known endemic areas exist along the Niger River, including the capital, Niamey, the regions of Zinder, Maradi, and Tanout.

### Water and Food Safety

All local water should be considered contaminated, and all water used for drinking, brushing teeth, and making ice cubes should be boiled for ten minutes. Bottled water is recommended.

Dairy products should not be considered safe. All meat, seafood, poultry, and vegetables must be well cooked and served hot. Salads and cold buffets should be avoided.

## Nigeria
### Vaccinations
— *Cholera:* Travelers leaving Nigeria for a country where a cholera vaccination certificate is required will need a vaccination certificate.

— *Yellow fever:* A yellow fever vaccination certificate is required from travelers over one year of age coming from all countries.

— *Hepatitis and typhoid:* Immune globulin and typhoid vaccination are recommended for travelers visiting rural areas off the usual tourist itinerary.

### Malaria and Tropical Disease Risk
Malaria risk exists throughout the year in the whole country.

— *Other tropical disease:* Schistosomiasis risk present in entire country, including urban areas.

### Water and Food Safety
All local water should be considered contaminated, and all water used for drinking, brushing teeth, and making ice cubes should be boiled for ten minutes. Bottled water is recommended.

Dairy products should not be considered safe. All meat, seafood, poultry, and vegetables must be well cooked and served hot. Salads and cold buffets should be avoided.

## Niue
### Vaccinations
— *Yellow fever:* A yellow fever vaccination certificate is required from travelers over one year of age coming from infected areas.

### Malaria and Tropical Disease Risk
No known malaria risk.

— *Other tropical disease:* No known risk.

### Water and Food Safety
Exact water and food safety unknown, but all local water should be considered contaminated, and all water used for drinking, brushing teeth, and making ice cubes should be boiled for ten minutes. Bottled water is recommended.

Dairy products should not be considered safe. All meat, seafood, poultry, and vegetables must be well cooked and served hot. Salads and cold buffets should be avoided.

## Norway
### Vaccinations
No vaccination requirements for any international traveler.

### Malaria and Tropical Disease Risk
No known malaria risk.

— *Other tropical disease:* No known risk.

### Water and Food Safety

Local water is safe to drink. Dairy products, meat, poultry, seafood, vegetables, and fruits are safe to eat.

## Oman

### Vaccinations

— *Yellow fever:* A yellow fever vaccination certificate is required from travelers arriving from infected areas.

— *Hepatitis and typhoid:* Immune globulin and typhoid vaccination are recommended for travelers visiting rural areas off the usual tourist itinerary.

### Malaria and Tropical Disease Risk

Malaria risk exists throughout the year in the whole country.

— *Other tropical disease:* No known risk.

### Water and Food Safety

All local water should be considered contaminated, and all water used for drinking, brushing teeth, and making ice cubes should be boiled for ten minutes. Bottled water is recommended.

Dairy products should not be considered safe. All meat, seafood, poultry, and vegetables must be well cooked and served hot. Salads and cold buffets should be avoided.

## Pacific Islands, Trust Territory of the U.S.A.

### Vaccinations

No vaccination requirements for any international traveler.

### Malaria and Tropical Disease Risk

No known malaria risk.

— *Other tropical disease:* No known risk.

### Water and Food Safety

Drinking water is chlorinated and generally safe to drink, but variations in local bacterial flora may cause diarrhea in some travelers. Bottled water is recommended for the first few weeks. Dairy products, meat, poultry, seafood, vegetables, and fruits are safe to eat.

## Pakistan

### Vaccinations

— *Cholera:* A cholera vaccination certificate is required from travelers arriving from infected areas.

— *Yellow fever:* A yellow fever vaccination certificate is required from travelers arriving from any part of a country in which yellow fever is endemic (appendix C).

— *Hepatitis and typhoid:* Immune globulin and typhoid vaccination are recommended for travelers visiting rural areas off the usual tourist itinerary.

### Malaria and Tropical Disease Risk

Malaria risk exists throughout the year in the whole country below 2,000 meters.

— *Other tropical disease:* No known risk.

### Water and Food Safety

All local water should be considered contaminated, and all water used for drinking, brushing teeth, and making ice cubes should be boiled for ten minutes. Bottled water is recommended.

Dairy products should not be considered safe. All meat, seafood, poultry, and vegetables must be well cooked and served hot. Salads and cold buffets should be avoided.

## Panama

### Vaccinations

No vaccination requirements for any international traveler.

— *Hepatitis and typhoid:* Immune globulin and typhoid vaccination are recommended for travelers visiting rural areas off the usual tourist itinerary.

### Malaria and Tropical Disease Risk

Malaria risk exists throughout the year in rural areas in: Darien, Bocas del Toro, and Colón (excluding Ciudad Colón) Prov.; Santa Fe (Veraguas Prov.), Chepo, Chiman (Panama Prov.) Distr., and Comarca de San Blas. Resistance to chloroquine reported.

— *Other tropical disease:* Chagas' disease risk present.

### Water and Food Safety

All local water should be considered contaminated, and all water used for drinking, brushing teeth, and making ice cubes should be boiled for ten minutes. Bottled water is recommended.

Dairy products should not be considered safe. All meat, seafood, poultry, and vegetables must be well cooked and served hot. Salads and cold buffets should be avoided.

## Papua New Guinea

### Vaccinations

— *Yellow fever:* A yellow fever vaccination certificate is required from travelers over one year of age coming from infected areas.

— *Hepatitis and typhoid:* Immune globulin and typhoid vaccination are recommended for travelers visiting rural areas off the usual tourist itinerary.

### Malaria and Tropical Disease Risk

Malaria risk exists throughout the year in the whole country. Resistance to chloroquine reported.

— *Other tropical disease:* Dengue fever risk present.

### Water and Food Safety

All local water should be considered contaminated, and all water used for drinking, brushing teeth, and making ice cubes should

be boiled for ten minutes. Bottled water is recommended.

Dairy products should not be considered safe. All meat, seafood, poultry, and vegetables must be well cooked and served hot. Salads and cold buffets should be avoided.

## Paraguay

### Vaccinations

— *Yellow fever:* A yellow fever vaccination certificate is required from travelers over six months of age coming from infected areas.
— *Hepatitis and typhoid:* Immune globulin and typhoid vaccination are recommended for travelers visiting rural areas off the usual tourist itinerary.

### Malaria and Tropical Disease Risk

Malaria risk exists from October through May in some rural parts of Alto Parana, Amambay and Canendiyu Departments.

— *Other tropical disease:* Chagas' disease risk present.

### Water and Food Safety

All local water should be considered contaminated, and all water used for drinking, brushing teeth, and making ice cubes should be boiled for ten minutes. Bottled water is recommended.

Dairy products should not be considered safe. All meat, seafood, poultry, and vegetables must be well cooked and served hot. Salads and cold buffets should be avoided.

In Asunción, drinking water is chlorinated and generally safe to drink, but variations in local bacterial flora may cause diarrhea in some travelers. Bottled water is recommended for the first few weeks.

## Peru

### Vaccinations

— *Yellow fever:* A yellow fever vaccination certificate is required from travelers over six months of age coming from infected areas.
— *Hepatitis and typhoid:* Immune globulin and typhoid vaccination are recommended for travelers visiting rural areas off the usual tourist itinerary.

### Malaria and Tropical Disease Risk

Malaria risk exists throughout the year in rural areas below 1,500 meters of Dep. of Amazonas, Cajamarca (excluding Hualgayoc Prov.), La Libertad (excluding Otuzco, Santiago de Chuco Prov.), Lambayeque, Loreto, Piura (excluding Talara Prov.), San Martin, and Tumbes; Prov. of Santa (Ancash Dep.); and parts of Prov. of La Convención (Cuzco Dep.), Tayacaja (Huancavelica Dep.), and Satipo (Junin Dep.). Resistance to chloroquine reported.

— *Other tropical disease:* Chagas' disease risk present.

### Water and Food Safety

All local water should be considered contaminated, and all water

used for drinking, brushing teeth, and making ice cubes should be boiled for ten minutes. Bottled water is recommended.

Dairy products should not be considered safe. All meat, seafood, poultry, and vegetables must be well cooked and served hot. Salads and cold buffets should be avoided.

## Philippines

### Vaccinations

— *Yellow fever:* A yellow fever vaccination certificate is required from travelers who, within the preceding six days, have been in a yellow fever infected area except children under one year of age, who are, however, subject to isolation or surveillance when indicated.

— *Hepatitis and typhoid:* Immune globulin and typhoid vaccination are recommended for travelers visiting rural areas off the usual tourist itinerary.

### Malaria and Tropical Disease Risk

Malaria risk exists throughout the year in areas below 600 meters, except in the provinces of Bohol, Catanduanes, Cebu, Leyte, and Misamis Occidental. No risk is considered to exist in urban and flat areas. Resistance to chloroquine reported.

— *Other tropical disease:* Schistosomiasis risk present in country; known endemic areas are present in:
  — *Luzon:* the area of Sorsogon in the Irosin-Juban valley on the southeastern tip of the island.
  — *Mindoro:* the area surrounding Lake Naujan, including the villages of Pola, Victoria, and Naujan.
  — *Samar:* the main island of Samar Province is infected.
  — *Leyte:* the northeastern plain of the island is infected.
  — *Bohol:* the whole island, located southeast of Leyte, is infected.
  — *Mindanao:* the infection is present throughout the island with the exception of the District of East Misamis.
  Dengue fever risk present.

### Water and Food Safety

All local water should be considered contaminated, and all water used for drinking, brushing teeth, and making ice cubes should be boiled for ten minutes. Bottled water is recommended.

Dairy products should not be considered safe. All meat, seafood, poultry, and vegetables must be well cooked and served hot. Salads and cold buffets should be avoided.

## Pitcairn

### Vaccinations

— *Cholera:* A cholera vaccination certificate is required from travelers coming from infected areas.

— *Yellow fever:* A yellow fever vaccination certificate is required from travelers over one year of age coming from infected areas.

**Malaria and Tropical Disease Risk**

No known malaria risk.

— *Other tropical disease:* No known risk.

**Water and Food Safety**

Drinking water is chlorinated and generally safe to drink, but variations in local bacterial flora may cause diarrhea in some travelers. Bottled water is recommended for the first few weeks. Dairy products, meat, poultry, seafood, vegetables, and fruits are safe to eat.

## Poland

**Vaccinations**

No vaccination requirements for any international traveler.

**Malaria and Tropical Disease Risk**

No known malaria risk.

— *Other tropical disease:* No known risk.

**Water and Food Safety**

Drinking water is chlorinated and generally safe to drink, but variations in local bacterial flora may cause diarrhea in some travelers. Bottled water is recommended for the first few weeks. Dairy products, meat, poultry, seafood, vegetables, and fruits are safe to eat.

## Portugal

**Vaccinations**

— *Yellow fever:* A yellow fever vaccination certificate is required from travelers over one year of age coming from infected areas. The requirement applies only to travelers arriving in or destined for the Azores and Madeira. No certificate is, however, required from transit passengers at Funchal, Porto Santo, and Santa Maria.

**Malaria and Tropical Disease Risk**

No known malaria risk.

— *Other tropical disease:* No known risk.

**Water and Food Safety**

Drinking water is chlorinated and generally safe to drink, but variations in local bacterial flora may cause diarrhea in some travelers. Bottled water is recommended for the first few weeks. Dairy products, meat, poultry, seafood, vegetables, and fruits are safe to eat.

## Puerto Rico

**Vaccinations**

No vaccination requirements for any international traveler.

**Malaria and Tropical Disease Risk**

No known malaria risk.

— *Other tropical disease:* Schistosomiasis risk present in entire country, including urban areas. Low infection rates are reported from all parts of the island. Infection occurs also on the islands of Vieques and Culebra, both located off the eastern coast of Puerto Rico.

Dengue fever risk present.

**Water and Food Safety**

Local water is safe to drink. Dairy products, meat, poultry, seafood, vegetables, and fruits are safe to eat.

## Qatar

**Vaccinations**

— *Yellow fever:* A yellow fever vaccination certificate is required from travelers over one year of age coming from infected areas.

— *Hepatitis and typhoid:* Immune globulin and typhoid vaccination are recommended for travelers visiting rural areas off the usual tourist itinerary.

**Malaria and Tropical Disease Risk**

No known malaria risk.

— *Other tropical disease:* No known risk.

**Water and Food Safety**

All local water should be considered contaminated, and all water used for drinking, brushing teeth, and making ice cubes should be boiled for ten minutes. Bottled water is recommended.

Dairy products should not be considered safe. All meat, seafood, poultry, and vegetables must be well cooked and served hot. Salads and cold buffets should be avoided.

## Reunion

**Vaccinations**

— *Yellow fever:* A yellow fever vaccination certificate is required from travelers over one year of age coming from infected areas.

**Malaria and Tropical Disease Risk**

No known malaria risk.

— *Other tropical disease:* No known risk.

**Water and Food Safety**

All local water should be considered contaminated, and all water used for drinking, brushing teeth, and making ice cubes should be boiled for ten minutes. Bottled water is recommended.

Dairy products should not be considered safe. All meat, seafood, poultry, and vegetables must be well cooked and served hot. Salads and cold buffets should be avoided.

## Romania

**Vaccinations**

No vaccination requirements for any international traveler.

### Malaria and Tropical Disease Risk
No known malaria risk.
— *Other tropical disease:* No known risk.

### Water and Food Safety
Drinking water is chlorinated and generally safe to drink, but variations in local bacterial flora may cause diarrhea in some travelers. Bottled water is recommended for the first few weeks. Dairy products, meat, poultry, seafood, vegetables, and fruits are safe to eat.

## Rwanda
### Vaccinations
— *Yellow fever:* A yellow fever vaccination certificate is required from travelers coming from infected areas.
— *Hepatitis and typhoid:* Immune globulin and typhoid vaccination are recommended for travelers visiting rural areas off the usual tourist itinerary.

### Malaria and Tropical Disease Risk
Malaria risk exists throughout the year in the whole country.
— *Other tropical disease:* Schistosomiasis risk present in the country; extent of infection not determined. Known areas of infection are present along the shores of Lake Kivu.

### Water and Food Safety
All local water should be considered contaminated, and all water used for drinking, brushing teeth, and making ice cubes should be boiled for ten minutes. Bottled water is recommended.

Dairy products should not be considered safe. All meat, seafood, poultry, and vegetables must be well cooked and served hot. Salads and cold buffets should be avoided.

## Saint Helena
### Vaccinations
No vaccination requirements for any international traveler.

### Malaria and Tropical Disease Risk
No known malaria risk.
— *Other tropical disease:* No known risk.

### Water and Food Safety
Drinking water is chlorinated and generally safe to drink, but variations in local bacterial flora may cause diarrhea in some travelers. Bottled water is recommended for the first few weeks. Dairy products, meat, poultry, seafood, vegetables, and fruits are safe to eat.

## Saint Kitts-Nevis
### Vaccinations
— *Yellow fever:* A yellow fever vaccination certificate is required from travelers over one year of age coming from infected areas.

**Malaria and Tropical Disease Risk**

No known malaria risk.

— *Other tropical disease:* Dengue fever risk present.

**Water and Food Safety**

Drinking water is chlorinated and generally safe to drink, but variations in local bacterial flora may cause diarrhea in some travelers. Bottled water is recommended for the first few weeks. Dairy products, meat, poultry, seafood, vegetables, and fruits are safe to eat.

## Saint Lucia

**Vaccinations**

— *Yellow fever:* A yellow fever vacccination certificate is required from travelers over one year of age coming from infected areas. The countries and areas included in appendix C are considered as infected areas.

**Malaria and Tropical Disease Risk**

No known malaria risk.

— *Other tropical disease:* Schistosomiasis risk present in country; major risk areas: Cul de Sav River valley south of Castries; the Roseau valley; and the areas of Soufriere and Riche Fond.

Dengue fever risk present.

**Water and Food Safety**

Drinking water is chlorinated and generally safe to drink, but variations in local bacterial flora may cause diarrhea in some travelers. Bottled water is recommended for the first few weeks. Dairy products, meat, poultry, seafood, vegetables, and fruits are safe to eat.

## Saint-Pierre and Miquelon

**Vaccinations**

No vaccination requirements for any international traveler.

**Malaria and Tropical Disease Risk**

No known malaria risk.

— *Other tropical disease:* No known risk.

**Water and Food Safety**

Unknown. Precautions are recommended.

## Saint Vincent and the Grenadines

**Vaccinations**

— *Yellow fever:* A yellow fever vaccination certificate is required from travelers over one year of age coming from infected areas.

**Malaria and Tropical Disease Risk**

No known malaria risk.

— *Other tropical disease:* Dengue fever risk present.

**Water and Food Safety**

Drinking water is chlorinated and generally safe to drink, but variations in local bacterial flora may cause diarrhea in some travelers. Bottled water is recommended for the first few weeks. Dairy products, meat, poultry, seafood, vegetables, and fruits are safe to eat.

## Samoa
### Vaccinations
— *Yellow fever:* A yellow fever vaccination certificate is required from travelers over one year of age coming from infected areas.
### Malaria and Tropical Disease Risk
No known malaria risk.
— *Other tropical disease:* No known risk.
### Water and Food Safety
Drinking water is chlorinated and generally safe to drink, but variations in local bacterial flora may cause diarrhea in some travelers. Bottled water is recommended for the first few weeks. Dairy products, meat, poultry, seafood, vegetables, and fruits are safe to eat.

## Sao Tome and Principe
### Vaccinations
— *Yellow fever:* A yellow fever vaccination certificate is required from travelers over one year of age coming from all countries, except travelers arriving from a noninfected area and staying less than two weeks in the country.
— *Hepatitis and typhoid:* Immune globulin and typhoid vaccination are recommended for travelers visiting rural areas off the usual tourist itinerary.
### Malaria and Tropical Disease Risk
Malaria risk exists throughout the year.
— *Other tropical disease:* No known risk.
### Water and Food Safety
All local water should be considered contaminated, and all water used for drinking, brushing teeth, and making ice cubes should be boiled for ten minutes. Bottled water is recommended.

Dairy products should not be considered safe. All meat, seafood, poultry, and vegetables must be well cooked and served hot. Salads and cold buffets should be avoided.

## Saudi Arabia
### Vaccinations
— *Yellow fever:* A yellow fever vaccination certificate is required from all travelers coming from countries any parts of which are infected.
— *Hepatitis and typhoid:* Immune globulin and typhoid vaccination are recommended for travelers visiting rural areas off the usual tourist itinerary.

**Malaria and Tropical Disease Risk**
Malaria risk exists throughout the year in areas other than Al-hasa, Arar, Jauf, Quraiya (Gurayyat), Riyad, Tabuk, Taif, and the urban areas of Jeddah, Mecca, Medina, and Qatif.
— *Other tropical disease:* Schistosomiasis risk present in entire country, excluding urban areas. The city centers of Jeddah, Mecca, Medina, Riyadh, Tabruk, Taif, and the coastal areas on the Persian Gulf are risk free. Foci of infection are scattered throughout the country including the areas surrounding the above cities.

**Water and Food Safety**
All local water should be considered contaminated, and all water used for drinking, brushing teeth, and making ice cubes should be boiled for ten minutes. Bottled water is recommended.

Dairy products should not be considered safe. All meat, seafood, poultry, and vegetables must be well cooked and served hot. Salads and cold buffets should be avoided.

## Senegal
**Vaccinations**
— *Yellow fever:* A yellow fever vaccination certificate is required from travelers over one year of age coming from all countries.
— *Hepatitis and typhoid:* Immune globulin and typhoid vaccination are recommended for travelers visiting rural areas off the usual tourist itinerary.

**Malaria and Tropical Disease Risk**
Malaria risk exists throughout the year in the whole country. There is less risk from January through June in the Cap-Vext region.
— *Other tropical disease:* Schistosomiasis risk present in entire country, including urban areas.

**Water and Food Safety**
All local water should be considered contaminated, and all water used for drinking, brushing teeth, and making ice cubes should be boiled for ten minutes. Bottled water is recommended.

Dairy products should not be considered safe. All meat, seafood, poultry, and vegetables must be well cooked and served hot. Salads and cold buffets should be avoided.

## Seychelles
**Vaccinations**
No vaccination requirements for any international traveler.

**Malaria and Tropical Disease Risk**
No known malaria risk.
— *Other tropical disease:* No known risk.

**Water and Food Safety**
Drinking water is chlorinated and generally safe to drink, but

variations in local bacterial flora may cause diarrhea in some travelers. Bottled water is recommended for the first few weeks. Dairy products, meat, poultry, seafood, vegetables, and fruits are safe to eat.

## Sierra Leone
### Vaccinations
— *Yellow fever:* A certificate is required from travelers coming from infected areas.

— *Hepatitis and typhoid:* Immune globulin and typhoid vaccination are recommended for travelers visiting rural areas off the usual tourist itinerary.

### Malaria and Tropical Disease Risk
Malaria risk exists throughout the year in the whole country.

— *Other tropical disease:* Schistosomiasis risk present in most of country, except for coastal regions.

### Water and Food Safety
All local water should be considered contaminated, and all water used for drinking, brushing teeth, and making ice cubes should be boiled for ten minutes. Bottled water is recommended.

Dairy products should not be considered safe. All meat, seafood, poultry, and vegetables must be well cooked and served hot. Salads and cold buffets should be avoided.

## Singapore
### Vaccinations
— *Yellow fever:* A yellow fever vaccination certificate is required from travelers over one year of age coming from infected areas. Certificates of vaccination are required from travelers over one year of age who, within the preceding six days, have been in or have passed through any country partly or wholly endemic for yellow fever. The countries and areas included in appendix C are considered infected areas.

### Malaria and Tropical Disease Risk
No known malaria risk.

— *Other tropical disease:* Dengue fever risk present.

### Water and Food Safety
Drinking water is chlorinated and generally safe to drink, but variations in local bacterial flora may cause diarrhea in some travelers. Bottled water is recommended for the first few weeks. Dairy products, meat, poultry, seafood, vegetables, and fruits are safe to eat.

## Solomon Islands
### Vaccinations
— *Yellow fever:* A yellow fever vaccination certificate is required from travelers coming from infected areas.

**Malaria and Tropical Disease Risk**

Malaria risk exists throughout the year excluding some eastern and southern outlying islets. Resistance to chloroquine reported.

—*Other tropical disease:* Dengue fever risk present.

**Water and Food Safety**

Unknown. Precautions are advised.

## Somalia

**Vaccinations**

— *Cholera:* A cholera vaccination certificate is required from travelers coming from infected areas.

— *Yellow fever:* A yellow fever vaccination certificate is required from travelers coming from infected areas.

— *Hepatitis and typhoid:* Immune globulin and typhoid vaccination are recommended for travelers visiting rural areas off the usual tourist itinerary.

**Malaria and Tropical Disease Risk**

Malaria risk exists throughout the year in the whole country.

— *Other tropical disease:* Schistosomiasis risk present in country; major risk areas: southern part of the country, in the river basins of Scebeli, Juba, and Madagoi.

**Water and Food Safety**

All local water should be considered contaminated, and all water used for drinking, brushing teeth, and making ice cubes should be boiled for ten minutes. Bottled water is recommended.

Dairy products should not be considered safe. All meat, seafood, poultry, and vegetables must be well cooked and served hot. Salads and cold buffets should be avoided.

## South Africa

**Vaccinations**

— *Yellow fever:* A yellow fever vaccination certificate is required from travelers coming from infected areas. The countries or areas included as endemic zones in Africa in appendix C are regarded as infected.

— *Hepatitis and typhoid:* Immune globulin and typhoid vaccination are recommended for travelers visiting rural areas off the usual tourist itinerary.

**Malaria and Tropical Disease Risk**

Malaria risk exists throughout the year in the north, east, and western low altitude areas of Transvaal and in Natal coastal areas north of 28° S (Richards Bay).

— *Other tropical disease:* Schistosomiasis risk present in country. Major risk areas are northeastern and eastern parts of the country. In Transvaal, endemic areas of *S. haematobium* and *S. mansoni* extend from the Limpopo River basin (on the border with Bot-

swana, Zimbabwe, and Mozambique) southward to the northern part of the Witwatersrand mountain chain, including the
Kruger National Park in the east.

A small area of infection by *S. mattheei* is present in Komati-
poort and the Komati River basin, south of the Kruger National
Park.

In the east the area of infection extends over Natal and southward along the coastal areas (east of Drakensberg) of Cape
Province as far south as Humansdorp, about eighty kilometers
west of Port Elizabeth. Infection by *S. haematobium* extends over
the whole above described area, while infection with *S. mansoni*
extends as far south as Durban only.

**Water and Food Safety**

Local water is safe to drink. Dairy products, meat, poultry, seafood, vegetables, and fruits are safe to eat.

## Spain

**Vaccinations**

No vaccination requirements for any international traveler.

**Malaria and Tropical Disease Risk**

No known malaria risk.

— *Other tropical disease:* No known risk.

**Water and Food Safety**

Drinking water is chlorinated and generally safe to drink, but
variations in local bacterial flora may cause diarrhea in some
travelers. Bottled water is recommended for the first few weeks.
Dairy products, meat, poultry, seafood, vegetables, and fruits are
safe to eat.

## Sri Lanka

**Vaccinations**

— *Yellow fever:* A yellow fever vaccination certificate is required from
travelers over one year of age coming from infected areas.

— *Hepatitis and typhoid:* Immune globulin and typhoid vaccination
are recommended for travelers visiting rural areas off the usual
tourist itinerary.

**Malaria and Tropical Disease Risk**

Malaria risk exists throughout the year in the Districts of Am-
parai, Anuradhapura, Badulla (part), Batticaloa, Hambantota,
Jaffna, Kandy, Kegalle, Kurunegala, Mannar, Matale, Matara,
Moneragala, Polonnaruwa, Puttalam, Ratnapura, Trincomalee, and
Vavuniya.

— *Other tropical disease:* Dengue fever risk present.

**Water and Food Safety**

All local water should be considered contaminated, and all water
used for drinking, brushing teeth, and making ice cubes should

be boiled for ten minutes. Bottled water is recommended. Dairy products should not be considered safe. All meat, seafood, poultry, and vegetables must be well cooked and served hot. Salads and cold buffets should be avoided.

## Sudan
### Vaccinations
— *Cholera:* A cholera vaccination certificate is required from travelers coming from infected areas.

— *Yellow fever:* A yellow fever vaccination certificate is required from travelers over one year of age coming from infected areas. The countries and areas included in appendix C are considered by Sudan as infected areas. A certificate may be required from travelers leaving Sudan.

— *Hepatitis and typhoid:* Immune globulin and typhoid vaccination are recommended for travelers visiting rural areas off the usual tourist itinerary.

### Malaria and Tropical Disease Risk
Malaria risk exists throughout the year in the whole country. Resistance to chloroquine reported.

— *Other tropical disease:* Schistosomiasis risk present in the country; extent of infection not determined.

### Water and Food Safety
All local water should be considered contaminated, and all water used for drinking, brushing teeth, and making ice cubes should be boiled for ten minutes. Bottled water is recommended.

Dairy products should not be considered safe. All meat, seafood, poultry, and vegetables must be well cooked and served hot. Salads and cold buffets should be avoided.

## Surinam
### Vaccinations
— *Yellow fever:* A yellow fever vaccination certificate is required from travelers coming from infected areas.

— *Hepatitis and typhoid:* Immune globulin and typhoid vaccination are recommended for travelers visiting rural areas off the usual tourist itinerary.

### Malaria and Tropical Disease Risk
Malaria risk exists throughout the year in the whole country, excluding Paramaribo District and the coastal areas north of 5°N. Resistance to chloroquine reported.

— *Other tropical disease:* Schistosomiasis risk present in restricted areas; most of the country is free of infection. Risks exists in the central part of the coastal region, in the area surrounding the capital Paramaribo. Dengue fever risk present. Chagas' disease risk present.

### Water and Food Safety

Drinking water is chlorinated and generally safe to drink, but variations in local bacterial flora may cause diarrhea in some travelers. Bottled drinking water is recommended. Milk and dairy products are not considered safe. Local meat, poultry, seafood, and vegetables are safe to eat.

## Swaziland

### Vaccinations

— *Yellow fever:* A yellow fever vaccination certificate is required from travelers coming from infected areas.

— *Hepatitis and typhoid:* Immune globulin and typhoid vaccination are recommended for travelers visiting rural areas off the usual tourist itinerary.

### Malaria and Tropical Disease Risk

Malaria risk exists from December through March in the northern border areas: Bordergate, Lomahasha, Mhlume, Tshaneni.

— *Other tropical disease:* Schistosomiasis risk present in entire country, including urban areas.

### Water and Food Safety

In Mbabane, local water is safe to drink. Dairy products, meat, poultry, seafood, vegetables, and fruits are safe to eat.

## Sweden

### Vaccinations

No vaccination requirements for any international traveler.

### Malaria and Tropical Disease Risk

No known malaria risk.

— *Other tropical disease:* No known risk.

### Water and Food Safety

Local water is safe to drink. Dairy products, meat, poultry, seafood, vegetables, and fruits are safe to eat.

## Switzerland

### Vaccinations

No vaccination requirements for any international traveler.

### Malaria and Tropical Disease Risk

No known malaria risk.

— *Other tropical disease:* No known risk.

### Water and Food Safety

Local water is safe to drink. Dairy products, meat, poultry, seafood, vegetables, and fruits are safe to eat.

## Syrian Arab Republic

### Vaccinations

— *Yellow fever:* A yellow fever vaccination certificate is required from travelers coming from infected areas.

— *Hepatitis and typhoid:* Immune globulin and typhoid vaccination

are recommended for travelers visiting rural areas off the usual tourist itinerary.

**Malaria and Tropical Disease Risk**

Malaria risk exists from May through October in the whole country, excluding urban areas and the District of Damascus, Deir-es-Zor, Homs, Sweida, and Tartus.

— *Other tropical disease:* Schistosomiasis risk present in country. Major risk areas are in northeastern part of the country:

- Balikh River basin from the town of Tall al Abyd to Ar Raqqah in the Governorate of Raqqah.

- Jaghjaghah, Jarah, Sublak, and Ramila river systems, their tributaries and canals in the Governorate of Hasakah.

- The river Euphrates from the area of Ar Raqqah to the Syrian border including its tributaries Khabur and Balikh.

**Water and Food Safety**

All local water should be considered contaminated, and all water used for drinking, brushing teeth, and making ice cubes should be boiled for ten minutes. Bottled water is recommended.

Dairy products should not be considered safe. All meat, seafood, poultry, and vegetables must be well cooked and served hot. Salads and cold buffets should be avoided.

In Damascus, drinking water is chlorinated and generally safe to drink, but variations in local bacterial flora may cause diarrhea in some travelers. Bottled water is recommended for the first few weeks.

## Thailand

**Vaccinations**

— *Yellow fever:* A yellow fever vaccination certificate is required from travelers over one year of age coming from infected areas.

— *Hepatitis and typhoid:* Immune globulin and typhoid vaccination are recommended for travelers visiting rural areas off the usual tourist itinerary.

**Malaria and Tropical Disease Risk**

Malaria risk exists throughout the year in rural, especially forested and hilly, areas of the whole country. Resistance to chloroquine reported.

— *Other tropical disease:* Dengue fever risk present.

**Water and Food Safety**

All local water should be considered contaminated, and all water used for drinking, brushing teeth, and making ice cubes should be boiled for ten minutes. Bottled water is recommended.

Dairy products should not be considered safe. All meat, seafood, poultry, and vegetables must be well cooked and served hot. Salads and cold buffets should be avoided.

## Togo

### Vaccinations

— *Yellow fever:* A yellow fever vaccination certificate is required from travelers over one year of age coming from all infected countries.
— *Hepatitis and typhoid:* Immune globulin and typhoid vaccination are recommended for travelers visiting rural areas off the usual tourist itinerary.

### Malaria and Tropical Disease Risk

Malaria risk exists throughout the year in the whole country.

— *Other tropical disease:* Schistosomiasis risk present in entire country, including urban areas.

### Water and Food Safety

All local water should be considered contaminated, and all water used for drinking, brushing teeth, and making ice cubes should be boiled for ten minutes. Bottled water is recommended.

Dairy products should not be considered safe. All meat, seafood, poultry, and vegetables must be well cooked and served hot. Salads and cold buffets should be avoided.

## Tonga

### Vaccinations

— *Yellow fever:* A yellow fever vaccination certificate is required from travelers over one year of age coming from infected areas.

### Malaria and Tropical Disease Risk

No known malaria risk.

— *Other tropical disease:* No known risk.

### Water and Food Safety

Drinking water is chlorinated and generally safe to drink, but variations in local bacterial flora may cause diarrhea in some travelers. Bottled water is recommended for the first few weeks. Dairy products, meat, poultry, seafood, vegetables, and fruits are safe to eat.

## Trinidad and Tobago

### Vaccinations

— *Yellow fever:* A yellow fever vaccination certificate is required from travelers over one year of age coming from infected areas, and from all countries any parts of which are infected.
— *Hepatitis and typhoid:* Immune globulin and typhoid vaccination are recommended for travelers visiting rural areas off the usual tourist itinerary.

### Malaria and Tropical Disease Risk

No known malaria risk.

— *Other tropical disease:* Dengue fever risk present.

### Water and Food Safety

Drinking water is chlorinated and generally safe to drink, but variations in local bacterial flora may cause diarrhea in some travelers. Bottled water is recommended for the first few weeks. Dairy products, meat, poultry, seafood, vegetables, and fruits are safe to eat.

## Tunisia

### Vaccinations

— *Yellow fever:* A yellow fever vaccination certificate is required from travelers over one year of age coming from infected areas.

— *Hepatitis and typhoid:* Immune globulin and typhoid vaccination are recommended for travelers visiting rural areas off the usual tourist itinerary.

### Malaria and Tropical Disease Risk

No known malaria risk.

— *Other tropical disease:* Schistosomiasis risk present in country. Major risk areas are central and southern Tunisia. Risk exists in the areas of Gafsa, Sidi Mansour, Tozeur, the villages surrounding the Shott el Jerid, and the areas of Gabes and Foum Tatouine. The oases of southern Tunisia should be considered infected.

### Water and Food Safety

All local water should be considered contaminated, and all water used for drinking, brushing teeth, and making ice cubes should be boiled for ten minutes. Bottled water is recommended.

Dairy products should not be considered safe. All meat, seafood, poultry, and vegetables must be well cooked and served hot. Salads and cold buffets should be avoided.

## Turkey

### Vaccinations

No vaccination requirements for any international traveler.

— *Hepatitis and typhoid:* Immune globulin and typhoid vaccination are recommended for travelers visiting rural areas off the usual tourist itinerary.

### Malaria and Tropical Disease Risk

Potential malaria risk exists from March to the end of November in the Cukuroka/Amikova areas and from mid-May to mid-October in southeast Anatolia.

— *Other tropical disease:* Schistosomiasis risk present in restricted areas; most of the country is free of infection. A small area of infection is present in the southeastern corner of the country close to the border with Syria: in the villages of Gundek, Grebia, and Kinnik on the Sublak River, Nusseibin Province.

### Water and Food Safety

All local water should be considered contaminated, and all water

used for drinking, brushing teeth, and making ice cubes should be boiled for ten minutes. Bottled water is recommended.

Dairy products should not be considered safe. All meat, seafood, poultry, and vegetables must be well cooked and served hot. Salads and cold buffets should be avoided.

## Tuvalu

### Vaccinations

— *Yellow fever:* A yellow fever vaccination certificate is required from travelers over one year of age coming from infected areas.

### Malaria and Tropical Disease Risk

No known malaria risk.

— *Other tropical disease:* No known risk.

### Water and Food Safety

All local water should be considered contaminated, and all water used for drinking, brushing teeth, and making ice cubes should be boiled for ten minutes. Bottled water is recommended.

Dairy products should not be considered safe. All meat, seafood, poultry, and vegetables must be well cooked and served hot. Salads and cold buffets should be avoided.

## Uganda

### Vaccinations

— *Yellow fever:* A yellow fever vaccination certificate is required from travelers over one year of age coming from all countries.

— *Hepatitis and typhoid:* Immune globulin and typhoid vaccination are recommended for travelers visiting rural areas off the usual tourist itinerary.

### Malaria and Tropical Disease Risk

Malaria risk exists throughout the year in the whole country including the main towns of Fort Portal, Jinja, Kampala, Mbale, and parts of Kigezi.

— *Other tropical disease:* Schistosomiasis risk present in the country; extent of infection not determined. Known areas of infection by *S. haematobium* exist in the Lango area north of Lake Kyoga in the central part of the country. Foci of infection by *S. mansoni* are present in the northern part of the country, and in the areas of Mbale and Tesa in the east, and also along the northern shore of Lake Victoria in the south in Uganda.

### Water and Food Safety

All local water should be considered contaminated, and all water used for drinking, brushing teeth, and making ice cubes should be boiled for ten minutes. Bottled water is recommended.

Dairy products should not be considered safe. All meat, seafood, poultry, and vegetables must be well cooked and served hot. Salads and cold buffets should be avoided.

## Union of Soviet Socialist Republics
### Vaccinations
No vaccination requirements for any international traveler.
— *Hepatitis and typhoid:* Immune globulin and typhoid vaccination are recommended for travelers visiting rural areas off the usual tourist itinerary.
### Malaria and Tropical Disease Risk
No known malaria risk.
— *Other tropical disease:* No known risk.
### Water and Food Safety
Due to the presence of *Giardia lamblia*, all local drinking water should be considered contaminated. Dairy products are considered safe. All meat, poultry, seafood, and vegetables should be well cooked and served while hot. Salads and cold buffets should be avoided.

## United Arab Emirates
### Vaccinations
— *Yellow fever:* A yellow fever vaccination certificate is required from travelers coming from infected areas.
— *Hepatitis and typhoid:* Immune globulin and typhoid vaccination are recommended for travelers visiting rural areas off the usual tourist itinerary.
### Malaria and Tropical Disease Risk
Malaria is not considered to be a risk in the Emirate of Abu Dhabi and the cities of Dubai, Sharjah, Ajman, and Umm El-Quwain. There is malaria risk in the foothill areas and valleys in the mountainous regions of the northern Emirates.
— *Other tropical disease:* No known risk.
### Water and Food Safety
All local water should be considered contaminated, and all water used for drinking, brushing teeth, and making ice cubes should be boiled for ten minutes. Bottled water is recommended.

Dairy products should not be considered safe. All meat, seafood, poultry, and vegetables must be well cooked and served hot. Salads and cold buffets should be avoided.

## United Kingdom (with Channel Islands and Isle of Man)
### Vaccinations
No vaccination requirements for any international traveler.
### Malaria and Tropical Disease Risk
No known malaria risk.
— *Other tropical disease:* No known risk.
### Water and Food Safety
Local water is safe to drink. Dairy products, meat, poultry, seafood, vegetables, and fruits are safe to eat.

# United Republic of Tanzania
## Vaccinations
— *Yellow fever:* A yellow fever vaccination certificate is required from travelers over one year of age coming from infected areas. The countries and areas that are included in appendix C are considered by United Republic of Tanzania as infected areas.
— *Hepatitis and typhoid:* Immune globulin and typhoid vaccination are recommended for travelers visiting rural areas off the usual tourist itinerary.

## Malaria and Tropical Disease Risk
Malaria risk exists throughout the year in the whole country below 1,800 meters. Resistance to chloroquine reported.
— *Other tropical disease:* Schistosomiasis risk present in the country; extent of infection not determined. Known areas of infection by *S. haematobium* and *S. mansoni* are present in the northern part of the country, along the eastern and southern shore of Lake Victoria, including the islands; and in the Tanga District in the northeastern corner of the country. Infection has also been reported from the area of Kasulu, Kigoma District near the northern shore of Lake Tanganyika; the area of Lake Rukwa and the area of Songea in southwestern Tanzania; foci are present in Kidodi, Kitatu, and Ruaha, northeast of Iringa. The islands of Zandibar and Pemba are infected with *S. haematobium.*

## Water and Food Safety
All local water should be considered contaminated, and all water used for drinking, brushing teeth, and making ice cubes should be boiled for ten minutes. Bottled water is recommended.

Dairy products should not be considered safe. All meat, seafood, poultry, and vegetables must be well cooked and served hot. Salads and cold buffets should be avoided.

# United States of America
## Vaccinations
No vaccination requirements for any international traveler.

## Malaria and Tropical Disease Risk
No known malaria risk.
— *Other tropical disease:* No known risk.

## Water and Food Safety
Local water is safe to drink. Dairy products, meat, poultry, seafood, vegetables, and fruits are safe to eat.

# Upper Volta (now called Burkina Faso)
## Vaccinations
— *Yellow fever:* A yellow fever vaccination certificate is required from travelers over one year of age coming from all countries.
— *Hepatitis and typhoid:* Immune globulin and typhoid vaccination

are recommended for travelers visiting rural areas off the usual tourist itinerary.

**Malaria and Tropical Disease Risk**

Malaria risk exists throughout the year in the whole country.

— *Other tropical disease:* Schistosomiasis risk present in entire country, including urban areas.

**Water and Food Safety**

All local water should be considered contaminated, and all water used for drinking, brushing teeth, and making ice cubes should be boiled for ten minutes. Bottled water is recommended.

Dairy products should not be considered safe. All meat, seafood, poultry, and vegetables must be well cooked and served hot. Salads and cold buffets should be avoided.

## Uruguay

**Vaccinations**

No vaccination requirements for any international traveler.

**Malaria and Tropical Disease Risk**

No known malaria risk.

— *Other tropical disease:* Chagas' disease risk present.

**Water and Food Safety**

Drinking water is chlorinated and generally safe to drink, but variations in local bacterial flora may cause diarrhea in some travelers. Bottled water is recommended for the first few weeks. Dairy products, meat, poultry, seafood, vegetables, and fruits are safe to eat.

## Vanuatu

**Vaccinations**

No vaccination requirements for any international traveler.

— *Hepatitis and typhoid:* Immune globulin and typhoid vaccination are recommended for travelers visiting rural areas off the usual tourist itinerary.

**Malaria and Tropical Disease Risk**

Malaria risk exists throughout the year in the whole country excluding Futuna Island. Resistance to chloroquine reported.

— *Other tropical disease:* Dengue fever risk present.

**Water and Food Safety**

Drinking water is chlorinated and generally safe to drink, but variations in local bacterial flora may cause diarrhea in some travelers. Bottled water is recommended for the first few weeks. Dairy products, meat, poultry, seafood, vegetables, and fruits are safe to eat.

## Venezuela

**Vaccinations**

No vaccination requirements for any international traveler.

— *Hepatitis and typhoid:* Immune globulin and typhoid vaccination are recommended for travelers visiting rural areas off the usual tourist itinerary.

## Malaria and Tropical Disease Risk

Malaria risk exists throughout the year in rural areas in part of Terr. Fed. Amazonas, Apure, Bolivar, Barinas, Merida, Tachira, and Zulia States. Resistance to chloroquine reported.

— *Other tropical disease:* Schistosomiasis risk present in country; major risk areas are confined to the central part of northern Venezuela, the area covered by the Federal District (Caracas) and the surrounding states: Aragua, Carabobo, Guarico, Maracay, and Miranda. Chagas' disease risk present.

## Water and Food Safety

Drinking water is chlorinated and generally safe to drink, but variations in local bacterial flora may cause diarrhea in some travelers. Bottled water is recommended for the first few weeks. Dairy products, meat, poultry, seafood, vegetables, and fruits are safe to eat.

# Vietnam

## Vaccinations

— *Yellow fever:* A yellow fever vaccination certificate is required from travelers over one year of age coming from infected areas.

— *Hepatitis and typhoid:* Immune globulin and typhoid vaccination are recommended for travelers visiting rural areas off the usual tourist itinerary.

## Malaria and Tropical Disease Risk

Malaria risk exists in the country excluding urban centers and the deltas. Resistance to chloroquine reported.

— *Other tropical disease:* Dengue fever risk present.

## Water and Food Safety

All local water should be considered contaminated, and all water used for drinking, brushing teeth, and making ice cubes should be boiled for ten minutes. Bottled water is recommended.

Dairy products should not be considered safe. All meat, seafood, poultry, and vegetables must be well cooked and served hot. Salads and cold buffets should be avoided.

# Virgin Islands (U.S.A.)

## Vaccinations

No vaccination requirements for any international traveler.

## Malaria and Tropical Disease Risk

No known malaria risk.

— *Other tropical disease:* Dengue fever risk present.

## Water and Food Safety

Drinking water is chlorinated and generally safe to drink, but

variations in local bacterial flora may cause diarrhea in some travelers. Bottled water is recommended for the first few weeks. Dairy products, meat, poultry, seafood, vegetables, and fruits are safe to eat.

**Virgin Islands, British (See British Virgin Islands)**

**Wake Island**

**Vaccinations**

No vaccination requirements for any international traveler.

**Malaria and Tropical Disease Risk**

No known malaria risk.

— *Other tropical disease:* No known risk.

**Water and Food Safety**

Drinking water is chlorinated and generally safe to drink, but variations in local bacterial flora may cause diarrhea in some travelers. Bottled water is recommended for the first few weeks. Dairy products, meat, poultry, seafood, vegetables, and fruits are safe to eat.

**Yemen**

**Vaccinations**

— *Yellow fever:* A yellow fever vaccination certificate is required from travelers over one year of age coming from infected areas.

— *Hepatitis and typhoid:* Immune globulin and typhoid vaccination are recommended for travelers visiting rural areas off the usual tourist itinerary.

**Malaria and Tropical Disease Risk**

Malaria risk exists from September through February in the whole country excluding the Provinces of Hajja and Sada.

— *Other tropical disease:* Schistosomiasis risk present in the country; extent of infection not determined.

**Water and Food Safety**

All local water should be considered contaminated, and all water used for drinking, brushing teeth, and making ice cubes should be boiled for ten minutes. Bottled water is recommended.

Dairy products should not be considered safe. All meat, seafood, poultry, and vegetables must be well cooked and served hot. Salads and cold buffets should be avoided.

**Yugoslavia**

**Vaccinations**

No vaccination requirements for any international traveler.

**Malaria and Tropical Disease Risk**

No known malaria risk.

— *Other tropical disease:* No known risk.

**Water and Food Safety**

Drinking water is chlorinated and generally safe to drink, but

variations in local bacterial flora may cause diarrhea in some travelers. Bottled water is recommended for the first few weeks. Dairy products, meat, poultry, seafood, vegetables, and fruits are safe to eat.

## Zaire

### Vaccinations

— *Yellow fever:* A yellow fever vaccination certificate is required from travelers over one year of age coming from infected areas.

— *Typhoid:* Vaccination against typhoid is recommended.

### Malaria and Tropical Disease Risk

Malaria risk exists throughout the year in the whole country.

— *Other tropical disease:* Schistosomiasis risk present in country. Risk of infection by *S. mansoni* is present in

- the northern and northeastern regions along the Kibali-Uele rivers and their tributaries, Lake Mobutu, Ituri River, and tributaries.

- the eastern part of the country, the areas of Lake Edward, Lake Kivu, and Lake Tanganyika.

- the south of the country: the southeastern parts of Shaba (Katanga) and East Kasai.

- a small area in Lower Zaire, in the area of Kimpesi.

Risk of infection by *S. haematobium* is present in the southeastern parts of the country, in the river basins of Lualaba (Congo) and Luapula, Province of Shaba.

Risk of infection by *S. intercalatum* is present along the Lualaba River (Congo) from the area of Kongolo downstream to the confluence of the Lomami River north of Kisangani (Stanleyville).

### Water and Food Safety

All local water should be considered contaminated, and all water used for drinking, brushing teeth, and making ice cubes should be boiled for ten minutes. Bottled water is recommended.

Dairy products should not be considered safe. All meat, seafood, poultry, and vegetables must be well cooked and served hot. Salads and cold buffets should be avoided.

## Zambia

### Vaccinations

— *Yellow fever:* A yellow fever vaccination certificate is required from travelers over one year of age coming from infected areas.

— *Hepatitis and typhoid:* Immune globulin and typhoid vaccination are recommended for travelers visiting rural areas off the usual tourist itinerary.

## Malaria and Tropical Disease Risk

Malaria risk exists from November through May in the whole country.

— *Other tropical disease:* Schistosomiasis risk present in entire country, including urban areas.

## Water and Food Safety

All local water should be considered contaminated, and all water used for drinking, brushing teeth, and making ice cubes should be boiled for ten minutes. Bottled water is recommended.

Dairy products should not be considered safe. All meat, seafood, poultry, and vegetables must be well cooked and served hot. Salads and cold buffets should be avoided.

In Livingstone (Maramba) and Lusaka, drinking water is chlorinated and generally safe to drink, but variations in local bacterial flora may cause diarrhea in some travelers. Bottled water is recommended for the first few weeks.

# Zimbabwe

## Vaccinations

— *Yellow fever:* A yellow fever vaccination certificate is required from travelers coming from infected areas.

— *Hepatitis and typhoid:* Immune globulin and typhoid vaccination are recommended for travelers visiting rural areas off the usual tourist itinerary.

## Malaria and Tropical Disease Risk

Malaria risk exists in the Zambesi valley and other areas below 1,500 meters.

— *Other tropical disease:* Schistosomiasis risk present in entire country, including urban areas.

## Water and Food Safety

Drinking water is chlorinated and generally safe to drink in the major towns and cities, but variations in local bacterial flora may cause diarrhea in some travelers. Bottled water is recommended for the first few weeks. Dairy products, meat, poultry, seafood, vegetables, and fruits are safe to eat.

# APPENDIX B

# State Departments of Health in the United States

State Departments of Health in the United States provide a valuable source of information for travelers. Your local office has up-to-date information on international vaccination requirements, countries reported to be infected with yellow fever or cholera, and countries infected with malaria. In addition, your local health department can direct you to the nearest Yellow Fever Vaccination Center if this vaccination is required for your itinerary.

**ALABAMA**
Alabama Department of Public
  Health
206 State Office Building
Montgomery, AL 36130
205-832-3194

**ALASKA**
Division of Public Health
Pouch H-06H
Juneau, AK 99811
907-465-3141

**ARIZONA**
Arizona Department of Health
  Services

1740 West Adams Street
Phoenix, AZ 85007
602-255-1008

**ARKANSAS**
Arkansas Department of Health
4815 W. Markham
Little Rock, AR 72201
501-661-2352

**CALIFORNIA**
Department of Health Services
714/744 ''P'' Street
Sacramento, CA 95814
916-322-4787

**COLORADO**
Colorado Department of Health
4210 East 11th Avenue
Denver, CO 80220
303-320-6137

**CONNECTICUT**
State of Connecticut Department
of Health Services
79 Elm Street
Hartford, CT 06106
203-566-4800

**DELAWARE**
Division of Public Health
Capitol Square
Dover, DE 19901
302-736-4724

**DISTRICT OF COLUMBIA**
D.C. Department of Human Services
1875 Connecticut Avenue, N.W.
Washington, D.C. 20009
202-673-6738

**FLORIDA**
Department of Health
1317 Winewood Boulevard
Building 6, Room 276
Tallahassee, FL 32301
904-488-2901

**GEORGIA**
Department of Human Resources
2 Martin Luther King Jr. Drive
12th Floor
Atlanta, GA 30334
404-656-7038

**GUAM**
Department of Public Health &
Social Services
P.O. Box 2816
Government of Guam

Agana, Guam 96910
671-734-2951

**HAWAII**
State Department of Health
P.O. Box 3378
Honolulu, HI 96801
808-548-5886

**IDAHO**
Department of Health and Welfare
Statehouse Mail
Boise, ID 83720
208-334-4386

**ILLINOIS**
Illinois Department of Public
Health
535 West Jefferson
Springfield, IL 62761
217-785-2060

**INDIANA**
Indiana State Board of Health
1330 West Michigan Street
P.O. Box 1964
Indianapolis, IN 46206
317-633-0267

**IOWA**
State Department of Health
Lucas State Office Building
3rd Floor
Des Moines, IA 50319
515-281-3583

**KANSAS**
Kansas Department of Health
and Environment
Forbes Field, Building 321
Topeka, KS 66620
913-862-9360

**KENTUCKY**
Department of Human Resources

275 E. Main Street
Frankfort, KY 40621
502-564-6620

**LOUISIANA**
Office of Health Services and
Environmental Quality
325 Loyola Avenue, Room 304
New Orleans, LA 70112
504-568-5413

**MAINE**
Department of Human Services
Bureau of Health
State House, Station #11
Augusta, ME 04333
207-289-3201

**MARIANA ISLANDS**
Department of Health Services
Trust Territory of the Pacific Is-
lands
Office of the High Commissioner
Saipan, Mariana Islands 96950

**MARYLAND**
Maryland Department of Health
and Mental Hygiene
300 West Preston Street
Baltimore, MD 21201
301-383-2636

**MASSACHUSETTS**
Massachusetts Department of
Public Health
600 Washington Street
Boston, MA 02111
617-727-7170

**MICHIGAN**
Michigan Department of Public
Health
3500 North Logan
P.O. Box 30035
Lansing, MI 48909
517-373-9437

**MINNESOTA**
Minnesota Department of Health
717 Delaware Street, S.E.
Minneapolis, MN 55440
612-623-5100

**MISSISSIPPI**
Mississippi State Board of Health
P.O. Box 1700
Jackson, MS 39205
601-354-6680

**MISSOURI**
Missouri Division of Health
P.O. Box 570
Jefferson City, MO 65102
314-751-2017

**MONTANA**
Montana Department of Health
& Environmental Sciences
Cogswell Building
Helena, MT 59620
406-449-4740

**NEBRASKA**
State of Nebraska
Department of Health
301 Centennial Mall South
P.O. Box 95007
Lincoln, NE 68509
402-471-2101

**NEVADA**
Department of Human Re-
sources
Room 200 Kinhead Building
505 E. King Street
Carson City, NV 89710
702-885-4740

**NEW HAMPSHIRE**
New Hampshire Division of
Public Health
Health and Welfare Building
Hazen Drive

Concord, NH 03301
603-271-4551

**NEW JERSEY**
New Jersey Department of
Health
John Fitch Plaza, CN 364
Trenton, NJ 08625
609-292-4076

**NEW MEXICO**
Health & Environmental Depart-
ment
P.O. Box 968
Santa Fe, New Mexico 87504
505-984-0030

**NEW YORK**
New York State Health Depart-
ment
Tower Building, Room 1084
Empire State Plaza
Albany, NY 12237
518-474-5370

**NORTH CAROLINA**
North Carolina Department of
Human Resources
P.O. Box 2091
Raleigh, NC 27602
919-733-7081

**NORTH DAKOTA**
State Health Department
Capitol Building
Bismarck, ND 58505
701-224-2367

**OHIO**
Ohio Department of Health
246 North High Street
P.O. Box 118
Columbus, OH 43216
614-466-4626

**OKLAHOMA**
Oklahoma Department of Health
N.E. 10th and Stonewall
Oklahoma City, OK 73152
405-271-5601

**OREGON**
Department of Human Re-
sources
508 State Office Building
1400 S.E. 5th
P.O. Box 231
Portland, OR 97207
503-299-6760

**PENNSYLVANIA**
Pennsylvania Department of
Health
P.O. Box 90
Harrisburg, PA 17108
717-787-5900

**PUERTO RICO**
Puerto Rico Department of
Health
San Juan, PR 00908
809-765-4175

**RHODE ISLAND**
Rhode Island Department of
Health
103 Cannon Building
75 Davis Street
Providence, RI 02908
401-277-2853

**SOUTH CAROLINA**
South Carolina Department of
Health and Environmental
Control
2600 Bull Street
Columbia, SC 29201
803-758-5555

**SOUTH DAKOTA**
State of South Dakota Health
Department
523 E. Capitol
Pierre, SD 57501
605-773-3737

**TENNESSEE**
State Department of Health
State Office Building
Ben Alles Road
Nashville, TN 37216
615-741-7366

**TEXAS**
Texas Department of Health
1100 West 49th Street
Austin, TX 78756
512-458-7405

**UTAH**
Utah Department of Health
P.O. Box 2500
Salt Lake City, UT 84110
801-533-6120

**VERMONT**
State Health Department
60 Main Street
Burlington, VT 05401
802-862-5701, Ext. 207

**VIRGINIA**
Virginia State Health Depart-
ment
Room 100, 109 Governor Street

Richmond, VA 23219
804-786-3551

**VIRGIN ISLANDS**
Virgin Islands Department of
Health
P.O. Box 520, Christiansted
St. Croix, U.S.V.I. 00820
809-773-1311

**WASHINGTON**
Department of Social and Health
Services
Mail Stop LB12C
Olympia, WA 98504
206-753-5909

**WEST VIRGINIA**
West Virginia Department of
Health
1800 Washington Street, Room
535
Charleston, WV 25305
304-348-0644

**WISCONSIN**
State Health Department
P.O. Box 309
Madison, WI 53701
608-266-0923

**WYOMING**
Department of Health and Social
Services
Hathaway Building, 4th Floor
Cheyenne, WY 82002
307-777-6011

# APPENDIX C

# Yellow Fever Endemic Zones

# MAP 1.  YELLOW FEVER ENDEMIC ZONE IN AFRICA

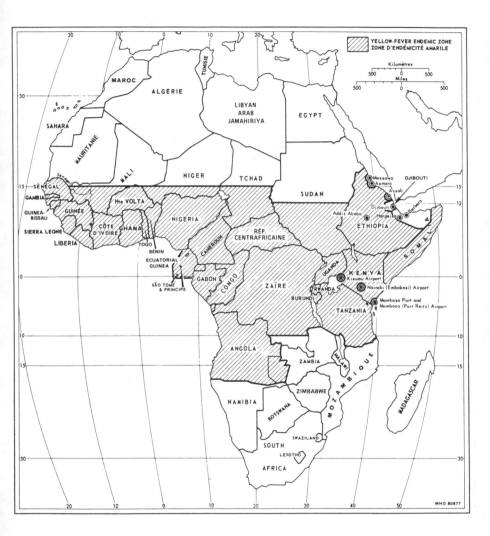

*NOTE:* Although the yellow fever endemic zones are no longer included in the International Health Regulations, a number of countries (most of them being not bound by the Regulations or bound with reservations) consider these zones as infected areas and require an international certificate of vaccination against yellow fever from travelers arriving from those areas. The above map has therefore been included in this book for practical reasons.

# MAP 2.   YELLOW FEVER ENDEMIC ZONE IN  THE AMERICAS

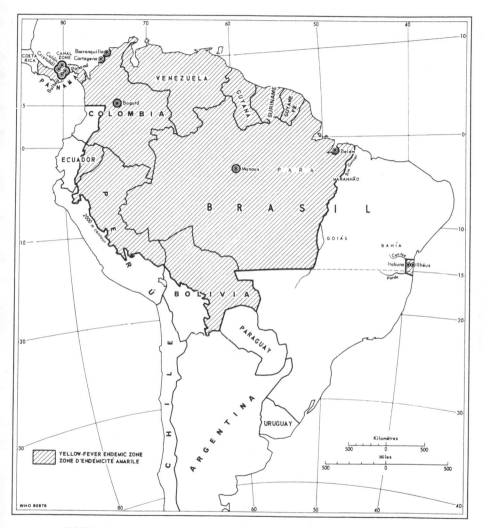

*NOTE:* Although the yellow fever endemic zones are no longer included in the International Health Regulations, a number of countries (most of them being not bound by the Regulations or bound with reservations) consider these zones as infected areas and require an international certificate of vaccination against yellow fever from travelers arriving from those areas. The above map has therefore been included in this book for practical reasons.

# APPENDIX D

# U. S. Embassies and Consulates

| Country | City | Local Telephone Number |
|---------|------|------------------------|
| AFGHANISTAN | Kabul | 24230-9 |
| ALGERIA | Algiers | 601425/255/186 716/828 |
| | Oran | 355502 |
| ARGENTINA | Buenos Aires | 774-7611/8811 9911 |
| ANTIGUA | Saint Johns | 462-3506 |
| AUSTRALIA | Canberra | 73-3711 |
| | Melbourne | 699-2244 |
| | Sydney | 264-7044 |
| | Perth | 322-4466 |
| AUSTRIA | Vienna | (222) 31-55-11 |
| BAHAMAS | Nassau | 322-4753/6 |
| BAHRAIN | Manama | 713323 |
| BANGLADESH | Dacca | 244220 thru 29 |
| BARBADOS | Bridgetown | 6357-7 |
| BELGIUM | Brussels | (02) 513-3830 |
| | Antwerp | (031) 321800 |

| Country | City | Local Telephone Number |
|---------|------|------------------------|
| BELIZE | Belize City | 3261/2/3 |
| BENIN | Cotonou | 31-26-92/50 |
| BERMUDA | Hamilton | 295-1342 |
| BOLIVIA | La Paz | 350251 |
| BOTSWANA | Gaborone | 53982/3/4 |
| BRAZIL | Brasilia | (061) 223-0120 |
| | Rio de Janeiro | (021) 292-7117 |
| | Sao Paulo | (011) 881-6511 |
| | Porto Alegre | (051) 31-1888 |
| | Recife | (081) 221-14-12 |
| | Salvador | (071) 245-6691/92 |
| BULGARIA | Sofia | 88-48-01 thru 05 |
| BURMA | Rangoon | 82055 |
| BURUNDI | Bujumbura | 34-54 |
| CAMEROON | Yaounde | 221633 |
| | Douala | 423434 |
| CANADA | Ottawa, Ontario | 238-5335 |
| | Calgary, Alberta | 266-8962 |
| | Halifax, Nova Scotia | 429-2480 |
| | Montreal, Quebec | 281-1886 |
| | Quebec, Quebec | 692-2095 |
| | Toronto, Ontario | 595-1700 |
| | Vancouver, British Columbia | 685-4311 |
| | Winnipeg, Manitoba | 284-3039 |
| REPUBLIC OF CAPE VERDE | Praia | 553 and 761 |
| CENTRAL AFRI-CAN REP. | Bangui | 61-02-00, 05, 10 |
| CHAD | N'Djamena | 30-91/2/3/4 |
| CHILE | Santiago | 710 133/90 |
| CHINA | Beijing | 52-2033 |
| | Guangzhou | 69-900 |
| | Shanghai | not available |

| Country | City | Local Telephone Number |
|---------|------|------------------------|
| COLOMBIA | Bogotá | 285-1300 |
| | Cali | 88-11-36/7 |
| | Barranquilla | 56599 |
| CONGO, PEOPLE'S REP. OF THE | Brazzaville | 81-20-70 |
| COSTA RICA | San Jose | 22-55-66 |
| CUBA | Havana (USINT) | 320551, 329700 |
| CYPRUS | Nicosia | 65151/5 |
| CZECHOSLOVA-KIA | Prague | 53 66 41/8 |
| DENMARK | Copenhagen | (01) 423144 |
| DJIBOUTI, REP. OF | Djibouti | 35-38-49 |
| DOMINICAN RE-PUBLIC | Santo Domingo | 682-2171 |
| ECUADOR | Quito | 548-000 |
| | Guayaquil | 511 570 |
| EGYPT | Cairo | 28219/11 |
| | Alexandria | 801911, 25607, 22861 |
| EL SALVADOR | San Salvador | 26-7100, 25-9984 |
| ETHIOPIA | Addis Ababa | 110666/117/129 |
| FIJI | Suva | 23031 |
| FINLAND | Helsinki | 171931 |
| FRANCE | Paris | 296-1202 |
| | Bordeaux | 56/52-65-95 |
| | Lyon | 24-68-49 |
| | Marseille | 54-92-00 |
| | Strasbourg | (88) 35-31-04/5/6 |
| FRENCH CARIB-BEAN | Martinique | 71.93.01/03 |
| GABON | Libreville | 72-20-03/04 |
| GAMBIA, THE | Banjul | 526-7 |

| Country | City | Local Telephone Number |
|---------|------|------------------------|
| GERMAN DEM. REP. | Berlin | 2202741 |
| GERMANY, FED. REP. OF | Bonn | (02221) 89, 55 |
| | Berlin | (030) 819-7561 |
| | Dusseldorf | (0211) 49 00 81 |
| | Frankfurt | (0611) 74-50 04 |
| | Hamburg | (040) 44 1061 |
| | Munich | (089) 2 30 11 |
| | Stuttgart | (0711) 21 02 21 |
| GHANA | Accra | 66811 |
| GREECE | Athens | 712951 |
| | Thessaloniki | 266-121 |
| GUATEMALA | Guatemala City | 31-15-41 |
| GUINEA | Conakry | 415-20 thru 24 |
| GUINEA-BISSAU | Bissau | 28-16/7 |
| GUYANA | Georgetown | 02-54900 |
| HAITI | Port-au-Prince | 20200 |
| HONDURAS | Tegucigalpa | 32-3121/2/3/4 |
| HONG KONG | Hong Kong | 239011 |
| HUNGARY | Budapest | 329-375 |
| ICELAND | Reykjavik | 29100 |
| INDIA | New Delhi | 690351 |
| | Bombay | 363611/8 |
| | Calcutta | 44-3611/6 |
| | Madras | 83041 |
| INDONESIA | Djakarta | 340001-9 |
| | Medan | 322200 |
| | Surabay | 69287/8 |
| IRAQ | Baghdad | 96138/9 |
| IRELAND | Dublin | 688777 |
| ISRAEL | Tel Aviv | 6544338 |
| ITALY | Rome | (06) 4674 |
| | Genoa | (010) 282-741 |

| Country | City | Local Telephone Number |
|---------|------|------------------------|
| ITALY | Milan | (02) 652-841 |
| | Naples | (081) 6600966 |
| | Palermo | 291532-35 |
| | Florence | (055) 298-276 |
| | Trieste | 040 68728/29 |
| IVORY COAST | Abidjan | 53-09-79 |
| JAMAICA | Kingston | 92-94850 |
| JAPAN | Tokyo | 583-7141 |
| | Naha, Okinawa | (0988) 77-8142 |
| | Osaka-Kobe | (06) 341-2754 |
| | Fukuoka | (092) 751-9331 |
| | Sapporo | (011) 641-1115/7 |
| JERUSALEM | Jerusalem | 226312 |
| JORDAN | Amman | 44371-6 |
| KENYA | Nairobi | 334141 |
| KOREA | Seoul | 72-2601 thru 19 |
| KUWAIT | Kuwait | 424-1519 |
| LAOS | Vientiane | 3126, 3570 |
| LEBANON | Beirut | 361-800 |
| LESOTHO | Maseru | 22666/7 |
| LIBERIA | Monrovia | 22991 thru 4 |
| LIBYA | Tripoli | 34021/6 |
| LUXEMBOURG | Luxembourg | 40123 thru 7 |
| MADAGASCAR | Antananarivo | 212-57 |
| MALAWI | Lilongwe | 730-166 |
| | Blantyre | 635 721 |
| MALAYSIA | Kuala Lumpur | 26321 |
| MALI | Bamako | 224834/35 |
| MALTA | Valletta | 623653 |
| MAURITANIA | Nouakchott | 52660 |
| MAURITIUS | Port Louis | 2-3218/9 |

| Country | City | Local Telephone Number |
|---|---|---|
| MEXICO | Mexico City | 553-3333 |
| | Guadalajara | 25-29-98 |
| | Hermosillo | 3-89-22 thru 24 |
| | Monterrey | 4306 50/59 |
| | Tijuana | 6-1001 |
| | Ciudad Juarez | 34048 |
| | Matamoros | 2-52-50/1/2 |
| | Mazatlán | 1-29-05 |
| | Merida | 5-54-09, 5-50-11 |
| | Nuevo Laredo | 4-05-12 |
| MOROCCO | Rabat | 62265 |
| | Casablanca | 22-41-49 |
| | Tangier | 359-05 |
| MOZAMBIQUE | Maputo | 26051/2/3 |
| NEPAL | Katmandu | 12718, 11199 |
| NETHERLANDS | The Hague | (070) 62-49-11 |
| | Amsterdam | (020) 790321 |
| | Rotterdam | (010) 117560 |
| NETHERLANDS ANTILLES | Curacao | 613066, 613350 |
| NEW ZEALAND | Wellington | 722-068 |
| | Auckland | 30-991 |
| NICARAGUA | Managua | 23061 |
| NIGER | Niamey | 72-26-61 |
| NIGERIA | Lagos | 610097 |
| | Kaduna | 213043 |
| NORWAY | Oslo | 56-68-80 |
| OMAN | Muscat | 745-231 |
| PAKISTAN | Islamabad | 24071 |
| | Karachi | 515081 |
| | Lahore | 870221 |
| | Peshawar | 73061 |
| PANAMA | Panama | 27-1777 |
| PAPUA NEW GUINEA | Port Moresby | 211455 |

| Country | City | Local Telephone Number |
|---------|------|------------------------|
| PARAGUAY | Asunción | 201-040 |
| PERU | Lima | 286000 |
| PHILIPPINES | Manila | 598-011 |
| | Cebu | 7-95-10 |
| POLAND | Warsaw | 283041 |
| | Krakow | 29764 |
| | Poznan | 595-86/87 |
| PORTUGAL | Lisbon | 570102 |
| | Oporto | 6-3094/5/6 |
| | Ponta Delgada | 22216/17 |
| QATAR | Doha | 870 701/2/3 |
| ROMANIA | Bucharest | 12-40-40 |
| RWANDA | Kigali | 5601 |
| SAUDI ARABIA | Jidda | 6670080 |
| | Dhahran | 8643200 |
| | Riyadh | 464-0012 |
| SENEGAL | Dakar | 21-42-96 |
| SEYCHELLES | Victoria | 23921 |
| SIERRA LEONE | Freetown | 26481 |
| SINGAPORE | Singapore | 30251 |
| SOMALIA | Mogadishu | 28011 |
| SOUTH AFRICA | Pretoria | 48-4266 |
| | Cape Town | 021-471280 |
| | Durban | 324-737 |
| | Johannesburg | (011) 21-1684 |
| SPAIN | Madrid | 276-3400 |
| | Barcelona | 319-9550 |
| | Seville | 23-18-85 |
| | Bilbao | 435-8308 |
| SRI LANKA | Colombo | 21271 |
| SUDAN | Khartoum | 74611 |
| SURINAM | Paramaribo | 76459, 76507, 72900 |

| Country | City | Local Telephone Number |
|---------|------|------------------------|
| SWAZILAND | Mbabane | 2272 |
| SWEDEN | Stockholm | (08) 63-05-20 |
| SWITZERLAND | Bern<br>Zurich<br>Geneva | (031) 437011<br>(01) 552566<br>(022) 327020 |
| SYRIA | Damascus | 332315 |
| TANZANIA | Dar-es-Salaam | 22775 |
| THAILAND | Bangkok<br>Chiang Mai<br>Songkhla<br>Udorn | 252-5040<br>23-5566<br>311-589<br>221548 |
| TOGO | Lome | 29-91 |
| TRINIDAD/<br>TOBAGO | Port-of-Spain | 62-26371 |
| TUNISIA | Tunis | 282 566 |
| TURKEY | Ankara<br>Istanbul<br>Izmir<br>Adana | 265470<br>436200<br>219104/5<br>14702 |
| UGANDA | Kampala | not available |
| UNION OF SO-<br>VIET SOCIALIST-<br>REPUBLICS | Moscow<br>Leningrad | 252-24-51<br>(812) 274-8235 |
| UNITED ARAB<br>EMIRATES | Abu Dhabi<br>Dubai | 61534<br>29003 |
| UNITED KING-<br>DOM | London<br>Belfast (N. Ire.)<br>Edinburgh | (01) 499-9000<br>(0232) 28239<br>031-556-8315 |
| UPPER VOLTA | Ouagadougou | 35442 |
| URUGUAY | Montevideo | 40-90-51 |
| VENEZUELA | Caracas<br>Maracaibo | 284-7111<br>(061) 51-65-06 |
| YEMEN ARAB REP. | Sanaa | 2790 |

| Country | City | Local Telephone Number |
|---------|------|------------------------|
| YUGOSLAVIA | Belgrade | 645655 |
|  | Zagreb | 444-800 |
| ZAIRE | Kinshasa | 25881 |
|  | Bukavu | 2594 |
|  | Lubumbashi | 2324 |
| ZAMBIA | Lusaka | 50222 |
| ZIMBABWE | Salisbury | 791586/7 |

# APPENDIX E

## Foreign Phrase and Phonetic Pronunciation Guide to Quick Medical Help in Seventeen Languages

### *Arabic (Egyptian)*

1. I'm not feeling well.
   *ue ash'or aenni kwaeyyis*
2. Can you get me a doctor?
   *otlob li doktor min far*
3. Get a doctor—quick!
   *otlob doktor, bisoraa*
4. I've got a pain here.
   *indi aelaem honae*
5. I/He/She's got a . . .
   headache/backache
   fever/sore throat
   *indi/indo/indaehae*
   *sodaa/aelaem fil dahr*
   *harara/aelaem fil holok*

### *Chinese (Mandarin)*

1. I'm not feeling well.
   *wǒ jué-de bù shū-fu*
2. Can you get me a doctor?
   *nǐ néng gěi wǒ qǐng yí-wèi dài-fū mā*
3. Get a doctor—quick!
   *kuài qǐng yi-shēng lái*
4. I've got a pain here.
   *wǒ zhè-li tòng*

5. I've got (a) . . .

wŏ . . .

    backache           bèi-tòng
    headache         tóu-tòng
    sore throat        hóu-lóng-tòng
    stomachache     wèi-tòng

## Dutch

| | | |
|---|---|---|
| 1. I'm not feeling well. | Ik voel mij niet goed. | *ik vool maiy neet ghoot* |
| 2. Can you get me a doctor? | Kunt u een dokter roepen? | *kurnt ew ayn dokterr roopern* |
| 3. Get a doctor quickly! | Haal vlug een dokter! | *haal vlurkh ayn dokterr* |
| 4. I've got a pain here. | Ik heb hier pijn. | *ik hehp heer paiyn* |
| 5. I've/He's/She's got a/an . . .  backache  fever  headache  sore throat | Ik heb/Hij heeft/Zij heeft . . .  hoofdpijn  rugpijn  koorts  keelpijn | *ik hehp/haiy hayft/zaiy hayft  hoaftpaiyn  rurghpaiyn  koarts  kaylpaiyn* |

## Finnish

| | | |
|---|---|---|
| 1. I'm not feeling well. | En voi hyvin. | |
| 2. Can you get me a doctor? | Voitteko hankkia minulle lääkärin? | *voaⁱttaykoa hahnkkiah minnoollay lækærin* |
| 3. Get a doctor— quick! | Noutakaa nopeasti lääkäri! | *noaᵒᵒtahkaa noapay-ahsti lækæri* |
| 4. I've got a pain here. | Minulla on tuskia tässä. | *minnoollah oan tooskiah tæssæ* |
| 5. I've/He's/She's got (a) . . .  backache  fever  headache  sore throat | Minulla on/Hänellä on . . .  selkä\|särkya  kuumetta  pään\|särkyä  kurkku\|kipua | *minnoollah oan/hænayllæ oan saylkæsaerkewæ koōmayttah pænsærkewæ ˌooˌ ˌˌookippooah* |

## French

| 1. I'm not feeling well. | Je ne me sens pas bien. | *zher ner mer sahng* |
| 2. Can you get me a doctor? | Pouvez-vous m'appeler un médecin? | *poovay voo mahperlay ang maydssang?* |
| 3. Get a doctor quickly! | Appelez un médecin, vite. | *ahperlay ang maydssang veet.* |
| 4. I've got a pain here. | J'ai mal ici. | *zhay mahl eessee.* |
| 5. I've got a . . . | J'ai . . . | *zhay* |
| headache | mal à la tête | *mahl ah lah teht* |
| backache | mal au dos | *mahl oa doe* |
| fever | de la fièvre | *der lah fyehvr* |
| sore throat | mal à la gorge | *mahl ah lah gorge* |

## German

| 1. I'm not feeling well. | Ich fühle mich nicht wohl. | |
| 2. Can you gèt me a doctor? | Können Sie einen Arzt fur mich finden? | *kurnern zee ighnern ahrts fewr mikh findern* |
| 3. Get a doctor quickly! | Rufen Sie schnell einen Arzt! | *roofern zee shnehl ighnern ahrtst* |
| 4. I've got a pain here. | Ich habe hier Schmerzen. | *ikh harber heer schmehrtsern* |
| 5. I've got (a) . . . | Ich habe . . . | *ikh harber* |
| backache | Ruckenschmerzen | *rewkernshmehrtsern* |
| fever | Fieber | *feeberr* |
| headache | Kopfschmerzen | *kopfshmehrtsern* |
| sore throat | Halsschmerzen | *hahlsshmehrtsern* |

## Hebrew

| 1. I'm not feeling well. | *ani lo margish tov* |
| 2. I need a doctor—quickly. | *ani tzarikh rofe dahuf* |
| 3. Get a doctor—quick! | *rofe maher* |
| 4. I've got a pain here. | *yesh li keevim kan* |

5. I/He/She's got (a/an) . . .      yesh li/lo/la . . .
   headache                    keev rosh
   backache                    keev gav
   fever                       hom
   sore throat                 keev garon


## Hungarian

1. I'm not feeling       Rosszul érzem ma-      rawss-sool ayrzaem
   well.                  gam.                   moggom
2. Can you get me a      Tudna hívni orvast?    toodno hēēvnee
   doctor?                                       awrvawsht
3. Get a doctor          Kérem, azonnal         kayraem ozzawn-nol
   quickly!               hívjon orvost!         heevyawn
                                                 awrvawsht
4. I've got a pain       Itt fáj valami.        eet faa$^y$ vollommee
   here.
5. I've got a . . .      Fáj a . . .            faa$^y$ o . . .
   backache               hátam                  haatom
   headache               fejem                  fae$^y$aem
   sore throat            torkom                 tawrkawm


## Italian

1. I feel sick.          Sto male.              staw MAH-lay
2. Please get a doc-     Chiami un medico,      KYAH-mee ooon
   tor.                   per favore.            MEH-dee-koh,
                                                 payr fah-VOH-
                                                 ray.
3. I have a pain         Ho un dolore qui.      aw oon doh-LOH-ray
   here.                                         kwee.
4. I have . . .          Ho . . .               aw . . .
   a headache             un dolor di testa      oon doh-LOHR dee
                                                 TEHS-tah
   a stomachache          mal di stomaco         mahl dee STAW-
                                                 mah-koh
   fever                  febbre                 FEHB-bray
   a sore throat          mal di gola            mahl dee GOH-lah

## Japanese

1. I'm not feeling well. — *kibun ga suguremasen*
2. Can you get me a doctor? — *isha o yonde kudasaimasu ka*
3. Get a doctor—quick! — *hayaku isha o*
4. I've got a pain here. — *koko ga itamimasu*
5. I/He/She's got (a/an) . . . — *watashi wa/kare wa/kanojo wa . . .*
   - headache — *atama*
   - backache — *senaka*
   - sore throat — *nodo*

## Norwegian

| | | |
|---|---|---|
| 1. I'm not feeling well. | Jeg føler meg ikke bra. | *yay furlerr may ikker braa* |
| 2. Can you get me a doctor? | Kan De skaffe meg en lege? | *kahn dee skalffer may ehn layger* |
| 3. Get a doctor—quick! | Hent en lege, fort! | *hehnt ehn layger foo't* |
| 4. I've got a pain here. | Jeg har vondt her. | *yay haar voont hær* |
| 5. I've/He's/She's got (a) . . . | Jeg/han/hun har . . . | *yay/hahn/hewn haar . . .* |
| backache | vondt i ryggen | *voont ee rewggern* |
| fever | feber | *fayberr* |
| headache | vondt i hodet | *voont ee hooder* |
| sore throat | vondt i halsen | *voont ee hahlssern* |

## Polish

| | | |
|---|---|---|
| 1. I'm not feeling well. | Źle się czuję. | *zyleh syeh chooyeh* |
| 2. Can you get me a doctor? | Proszę wezwać lekarza. | *prosheh vehzvahtsh lehkahzhah* |
| 3. I need a doctor quickly. | Proszę prędko wezwać lekarza. | *prosheh prehntko vehzvahtsh lehkahzhah* |
| 4. I've got a pain here. | Boli mnie tutaj. | *boolee mñeh tootigh* |

5. I've got a . . .       Mam . . .            *mahm* . . .
   headache              ból glowy            *bool gwovi*
   backache             bol w plecach         *bool fplehtsahh*
   fever                gorączkę              *goronchkeh*
   sore throat          ból gardla            *bool gahrdwah*

## Portuguese

1. I'm not feeling       Não me sinto bem.    *nahng^w mer seengtoo*
   well.                                      *bayng*
2. Can you get me a      Pode chamar-me       *podher shermahr mer*
   doctor?               um médico?           *oong mehdhikkoo*
3. Get a doctor          Chame um médico      *shahmer oong mehd-*
   quickly!              depressa!            *hikkoo derprehs-*
                                              *ser*
4. I've got a pain       Tenho uma dor        *tehnyoo oomer doar*
   here.                 aqui.                *erkee*
5. I've/He's/She's       Tenho/Ele tem/Ela    *tehnyoo/ayler*
   got (a/an) . . .      tem . . .               *tayng/ehler tayng*
   headache              dor de cabeça        *doar der kerbhaysser*
   backache             dor nas costas        *doar nersh koshtersh*
   fever                febre                 *fehbrer*
   sore throat          dor de gorganta       *doar der gerrggahn-*
                                              *ter*

## Russian

1. I'm not feeling well.          *yah plokhah syeebyah chyoost-*
                                  *vooyoo*

2. I need a doctor—quickly.       *mnyeh noozhin vrahch skahryehyeh*

3. Get a doctor—quick!            *pahzahveetyee vrahchyah skahrye-*
                                  *hyeh*

4. I've got a pain here.          *toot bahlyeet*

5. I've got a . . .               *oo myeenyah*
   headache                          *gahlahvnahyah bol*
   backache                         *bol v speenyeh*
   fever                           *tyeempyeerahtoorah*
   sore throat                     *bahlyeet goriah*

## Spanish/Latin American

| | | |
|---|---|---|
| 1. I'm not feeling well. | No me encuentro bien. | *noa may aynkwayntroa byayn* |
| 2. Can you get me a doctor? | ¿Puede usted buscarme un médico? | *pwayday oostayd booskahrmay oon maydeekoa* |
| 3. Get a doctor quickly! | ¡Llamen a un médico rápidamente! | *yahmayn a oon maydeekoa rahpeedahmayntay.* |
| 4. I've got a pain here. | Tengo un dolor aquí. | *tayngoa oon doaloar ahkee.* |
| 5. I've got a . . . | Tengo . . . | *tayngoa . . .* |
| backache | dolor de espalda | *doaloar day ayspahldah* |
| headache | dolor de cabeza | *doaloar day kahbayssah* |
| fever | fiebre | *fyaybray* |
| sore throat | garganta irritada | *gahrgahntah eerreetahdah* |

## Swahili

| | |
|---|---|
| 1. I wish to visit a physician. | *Nataka kwenda kwa daktari* |
| 2. Please call a doctor. | *Tafadhali mwite daktari.* |
| 3. I have hurt my . . . | *Nimeumia* |
| arm | *mkono* |
| leg | *mguu* |
| chest | *kifua* |
| head | *kichwa* |
| back | *mgongo* |
| stomach | *tumbo* |

## Swedish

| | | |
|---|---|---|
| 1. I'm not feeling well. | Jagkänner mig inte bra. | *yaa(g) khehnerr may inter bra* |
| 2. Can you get me a doctor? | Skulle ni kunna skaffa mig en doktor? | *skewler nee kewnah skahfay may ehn doktor* |

| 3. | Get a doctor—quick! | Skaffa genast en doktor! | *skahfah yaynahst ehn doktor* |
|---|---|---|---|
| 4. | I've got a pain here. | Jag har ont här. | *yaa(g) haar oont hær* |
| 5. | I've/He's/She's got (a) . . . | Jag/han/hon har . . . | *yaa(g)/hahn/hon haar . . .* |
| | backache | ont i ryggen | *oont ee rewgern* |
| | fever | feber | *fayberr* |
| | headache | huvudvärk | *hewvewdvaerk* |
| | sore throat | ont i halsen | *oont ee hahlssern* |

# APPENDIX F

# Checklist for Traveling Well

## CHECKLIST

Preparation is the key to traveling well. Before you leave home, consider the following:

A. *Health Care Before You Go*
- Do you need a medical checkup?
- Do you need a written medical summary?
- Do you have an adequate supply of medications?
- Do you have copies of your prescriptions?
- Do you need a dental checkup?
- Do you have an extra pair of glasses or contact lenses?
- Do you need to carry a medical kit?

B. *Health Insurance*
- Are you protected while traveling overseas?
- Are emergency medical evacuations covered?
- Do you need extra insurance?

C. *Vaccinations*
- Is your routine series of vaccinations up-to-date?
- Are any vaccinations required by International Health Regulations?
- Do you need an International Vaccination Certificate?
- Are any additional vaccinations recommended for your itinerary?

273

D. *Preventing Motion Sickness*
- Are you concerned about motion sickness?
- Do you have the appropriate antimotion-sickness medicine?

E. *Flying Well*
- Do you know how to reduce the effects of jet lag?
- Or overcome the fear of flying?
- Or avoid barotitis and barosinusitis?

F. *Health Care Abroad*
- Do you know how to locate qualified, English-speaking doctors overseas?
- Do you know who to call in case of an emergency?

G. *Malaria and Tropical Disease*
- Will you be exposed to malaria?
- Are there reports of chloroquine-resistant malaria?
- Do you have the appropriate antimalarial medications?
- Will you be exposed to other tropical diseases?

H. *Water and Food Safety*
- Do you know the safety of food and water at your destination?
- Do you know what sources of food and water are safe and which ones to avoid?
- Do you know how to purify drinking water?
- Do you know how to choose a restaurant?

I. *Travelers' Diarrhea*
- Do you know how to reduce the risk of travelers' diarrhea?
- Do you know how to safely treat diarrhea when it occurs?
- Or when to use antibiotics?

J. *Traveling Well Outdoors*
- Do you know how to protect yourself against sunburn?
- How to avoid overexposure to the heat?
- How to protect yourself in the cold?
- How to avoid altitude sickness?

K. *Other Problems*
- Do you know how to avoid bites and stings?
- How to prevent accidents while traveling?
- How to treat common health problems that occur?

L. *Traveling With Health Problems*
- Do you know what special health preparations are necessary for traveling with health problems?

- What organizations to contact?
- How to ask for help in a foreign language?
- How to order special diets?
- How to travel safely during pregnancy?

# APPENDIX G

# Suggested Reading List

The following books are recommended as additional sources of information for travelers with chronic health problems, disabilities, or requiring a special medical diet.

*Traveling Healthy,* Sheila Hillman and Robert Hillman, M.D., New York: Penguin Books, 1980. This guide provides lists of health facilities in 23 countries and 115 cities and is especially valuable for travelers with chronic health problems planning to travel in Europe, Japan, Mexico, or the Soviet Union.

*Access to the World,* Louise Weiss, New York: Chatham Square Press, 1977. This is an excellent and comprehensive travel guide for travelers with mobility impairments or other disabilities.

*The Special Diet Foreign Phrase Book,* Helen Saltz Jacobson, Emmaus, PA: Rodale Press, 1982. This is a good guide for travelers who need to follow a special medical diet—diabetic, low sodium, etc.—(see p. 151) anywhere Spanish, German, French, or Italian is spoken.

# INDEX